The New York Times

SUNDAY IN THE PARK CROSSWORDS
75 Pleasurable Puzzles

Edited by Will Shortz

ST. MARTIN'S GRIFFIN ⚬ NEW YORK

ACROSS

1 Outputs from El Chichón
6 Bellyached
12 The Scourge of God
18 Cassandra, e.g.
20 Additions at school?
22 Neptune satellite
23 Conductor Georg got high praise from his peers?
26 Like a solar event
27 Panache
28 Come-ons
29 Hides
30 Go-carts
33 Curtain material
35 Chunk
37 Half of a Vegas duo
38 D.C. figures: Abbr.
39 Wiped out
43 "Blueberry Hill" singer is the only portly person in the family?
50 Analogous (to)
51 "Bravo!"
52 King's title, for short
53 Baseball's Caminiti
54 Burden
55 Bonaparte aide
56 Numerical prefix
58 Change for the better
60 Overthrew
64 O.T. book read at Purim
66 Antiquated
69 Japanese violinist is bored by her Calif. performance?
75 Church assembly
76 Small field
77 Computer language
78 Virile
81 __ ghost
83 "7 Faces of Dr. __" (1964 movie)
85 Salon stuff
86 Clay, now
87 Some radios, for short

90 Thin skin
93 Stadium level
94 Rap Queen loves her supporters?
98 Lender's protection
99 Fan sounds
100 Amalgamate
101 __-Cat
102 Three-time N.F.L. M.V.P. Brett
104 Show biz's Peggy and Mama
107 Twilight, old-style
111 Composed
114 "The Wild Duck" playwright
116 Given to burrowing, maybe
118 Pianist Ruth's audience knows exactly when to clap?
122 Armpit, anatomically
123 One surrounded by raised hands
124 Tampa neighbor
125 Sotheby's visitor
126 William Jennings __ "Cross of Gold" speech
127 Mosquito type

DOWN

1 Shakes off
2 Hard as __
3 Singer with a falsetto
4 Playing a part from
5 Is tricked by
6 Venetian boat song
7 Chemical ending
8 Ultimate
9 Reduced in number
10 Board members
11 Big name in paperbacks
12 Take-out counter?
13 Chirrup
14 Most well-kept
15 Pour __
16 "St. Elmo's Fire" actor
17 Raggedy __ (dolls)

19 Newt
21 Drivel
24 Component of "fully loaded"
25 Redresser
31 "Beat the Clock" TV host
32 Glanced at
34 Ferry terminus, maybe
36 Salaam
38 Marginal notation
40 Get off on
41 Composed
42 Make (one's way)
43 Fact or factoid
44 Safari sight
45 Kind of review
46 Mail or fax
47 Injury around a horse's hoof
48 News head
49 Hindu incarnation
57 Birds-feather link
59 Best-selling computer game
61 Nibble
62 Stand in the sun, say
63 German one
65 Wriggly creature
67 Develop
68 Traffic caution
70 Freudian concerns
71 Jaguars and such
72 "Live free __" (New Hampshire motto)
73 Snowfall
74 Lulus
78 Retailer's place
79 Game ending?
80 Give as an example
82 Group of poems
84 Service sites
88 Sportscaster Albert
89 "Funny Girl" co-star
91 Weather stats
92 Maximum limits?
93 English novelist Anthony
95 Where home is
96 Adar's predecessor
97 Food eaten

103 Confuse
104 French equivalent of the Oscar
105 Impatient
106 Prince, e.g.
108 Made smooth, in a way
109 "Go fly __!"
110 Old Persians
111 Hunk
112 Shout in bad weather?
113 Saharan
115 Kind of appeal
117 Some football linemen: Abbr.
119 Scull
120 "Give __ rest!"
121 Blokes

by David J. Kahn

2 PLUS TAX

ACROSS

1 Slow-witted
4 Gum site
8 Norms: Abbr.
12 O. Henry specialty
17 When to call, in some want ads
19 "The Alienist" author Carr
21 Kind of cut
22 Blazing stars
23 Carom
24 "Like me"
25 "A waking dream," according to Aristotle
26 Supports a scheme
27 Very old I.R.S. employee?
31 They're good for the biceps
32 "___ Mio"
33 Delighted condition?
36 On the lam
37 Some western New York legislation?
41 Hallow ending
42 Class
44 Blueprint item
45 Blockage
46 Orch. section
47 Office mail
50 Big inits. in cellular technology
53 Madison and Monroe
57 Cry of economic liberation?
65 Part of Latin I conjugation
66 Just make, with "out"
68 Steamed
69 Anthology
70 Hobbyist purchases
71 I.R.S. target in Calif.?
74 Colosseum cover-up
75 Guarantee
77 Something to lend
78 Clockmaker Terry
79 Follow
80 Assessment of a comedian?
83 Tom and Diane
85 Subj. for immigrants
86 "The Time Machine" race
88 Actress Scala
89 Company recruits, for short
93 Mammilla
97 Let out
99 Sot sound
102 Stones' request of their accountant?
107 "The House of Blue Leaves" playwright
109 Tommy of "Finian's Rainbow"
110 English dramatist George
111 Bulldog, e.g.
113 April 15 greeting?
117 Language from which "mako" comes
119 Side in a debate
120 Jaleel White role on "Family Matters"
121 Cold coating
122 Quite dissimilar
123 "___ happens . . ."
124 Brouhaha
125 Intimate
126 "Saturday Night Live" announcer
127 Jiffs
128 Fast fleet
129 H.M.O. personnel

DOWN

1 Disaster
2 Fictional friend of Isaac of York
3 One may be honorable
4 Diving duck
5 Slips past
6 De-bused, e.g.
7 Mother of Castor and Pollux
8 Trains
9 Slattern
10 Exhaust
11 Popeye's ___ Pea
12 Place for a male trio
13 Emotionless
14 In general
15 Styron's Turner
16 Proposal response
18 D.C. team, for short
20 ___ chocolates
28 Searches
29 Davis was its Pres.
30 "Friends" co-star
34 ___-Coat (floor wax brand)
35 Not necessarily exact: Abbr.
38 Einstein's birthplace
39 Poetic measures
40 Crowning point
43 Like a tundra
46 Plays matchmaker
48 Funny brothers
49 Rust
51 Bearing
52 Follower: Suffix
53 Nicholson film "The Two ___"
54 ___ acid
55 Disputed island in the East China Sea
56 Music with jazzlike riffs
58 Like some arrangements
59 Embarrassed
60 Just beat
61 One of the Jacksons
62 Desert home
63 Rocker Bob
64 Cafeteria supply
67 Handy abbr.
72 Get ___ for effort
73 Loop runners
76 Manhattan ingredient
81 ___ Loma, Calif.
82 Delete
84 Extemporize
87 Tchaikovsky's Symphony No. 5 ___ minor
89 Bygone sports cars
90 Accepted the bait
91 David Brinkley's autobiography
92 Practiced yellow journalism
94 Sweep
95 Germfree
96 Something awful
98 Let in advance
99 Twice as perilous
100 Lou Gehrig or Cal Ripken
101 They're swung in church
103 Winter 1997–98 newsmaker
104 Writer Josephine
105 Nevada town
106 "___ pray"
108 180, so to speak
112 Strikes out
114 Lukas of "Witness"
115 Rainbows
116 Jaguar models
117 It works according to scale
118 King intro

by Randolph Ross

3 WORLD CAPITALISM

ACROSS

1 Lemony, say
7 "Time Cycle" composer Lukas ___
11 One of a secretive trio
19 Utica's county
20 "Yeah, sure"
21 School part
22 Eastern European hill?
24 West African fliers?
25 Subjects for special fx artists
26 Alley prowler
27 Afford without a problem
29 Smudge
30 Driver's invitation
33 Most hectic
35 Coeur d'___
36 Oriental Miss Universe?
39 Pretentious
41 "Domani" singer
42 Boxers' beefs
43 Fax cover-page word
44 "Married to the ___" (1988 film)
47 Six-time N.L. home run champ
48 Bumped into
49 Break out
50 Increase in strength, with "up"
51 Suspected
55 Restored photo, perhaps
59 Means
61 Resting place
63 Central European sensors?
65 Southeast Asian go-getter?
67 Eastern European vestments?
68 Hint
69 Five-time Emmy-winning actress
70 Similarity symbol, in math
71 Lure with music
75 On the quiet side?
76 "To what do I ___ . . ."
78 Hip friend
80 Yet, poetically
81 Contribute
82 Turmoil
83 Shade of brown
86 Fastened, in a way
89 Hung. neighbor
90 Mideast exam administrators?
92 Western law enforcement group
95 Gorilla
97 City on the Allegheny
98 London's ___ of Court
99 Glorify
100 Hackneyed
101 Bygone pol. cause
104 Far Eastern nourishment?
108 South central Asian gems?
112 Deviations
113 Promising words
114 Move stealthily
115 Office supply items
116 Succeeding
117 "Potemkin" setting

DOWN

1 Furnace fuel
2 Letter of approval?: Abbr.
3 Souvenir shop items
4 Mo. or Miss.
5 First name in exiles
6 Saloon
7 Shoot
8 Oriental tie
9 Epicurean
10 Increases
11 Spikes
12 Patriots' grp.
13 Nice view
14 School grp.
15 Hard on the feet
16 Papal vestment
17 Squelch
18 Kind of test
21 1990 Best New Artist Grammy winner
23 Attached houses?: Abbr.
28 Isles
31 Spanish seer?
32 Tecs
33 Sugar source
34 Royal residence of early Ireland
35 It can help if you're short
36 Throw away
37 "I can't ___ thing"
38 Tournament helper
40 The Twelve Tables' contents
43 Hardly hide
44 Bucks
45 ___ probandi
46 Buzzer
48 Noted Charlton Heston role
50 Student, at times
52 Color on the Irish flag
53 Hullabaloo
54 Kewpie doll features
55 Period of time
56 Messed up
57 Out
58 "___ to Pieces" (1965 hit)
60 Style of expression
62 Self-conscious laugh
64 Keep an ___ the ground
65 Stale
66 Islands dish
67 Combine
69 Farm call
72 Witnesses
73 Lecherous look
74 Parts to tie
77 Dating
78 [Sans warning!]
79 Blame
82 Word of lawyerly advice
83 Suffix with motor
84 Rain gear material
85 Campaign
86 Maintains
87 Whiz
88 Penn, e.g.: Abbr.
89 Take on
90 Attendance preventers
91 Go around in circles
92 Galileo, for one
93 Bridge call, for short
94 Condescending type
96 Handheld instruments
100 Bounce
102 Old Oldses
103 Fishing, perhaps
105 Spot for a computer
106 St. Augustine's locale: Abbr.
107 Suffix with fact
109 Swing in a ring
110 Thrice daily, in prescriptions
111 Expose, poetically

by Rich Norris

4 BASES LOADED

ACROSS

1 Men in the hood?
5 Head lock
10 "Damn Yankees" vamp
14 School subj.
18 "La Bohème," updated
19 Back-country
20 Dostoyevsky novel, with "The"
22 Digging, so to speak
23 Sgt. Snorkel's dog
24 Labor organizer's cry
25 Full shopping cart?
27 Coffee filter?
30 Small-time
31 "The Benefactor" novelist
32 Whirlpool whereabouts
33 Captain Kirk's log entry
35 Commemorative pillar
38 They, to Thibaudet
40 Mayflower Compact signer
41 Journalist's question
44 Drama in three acts?
47 Be reasonable
51 Wifey's mate
53 Little or Short
54 Is near bankruptcy
56 Poltergeist manifestation
57 Area east of the Bosporus
58 Mountain goat's perch
59 Matriculate
61 "Superman II" villainess
62 Pat Nixon's real first name
64 Like party punch
66 Farm alarms
68 Kind of division
70 Not sharply defined, as a computer image
72 Drag queen's collection
73 Food fish
77 Like some undercover cops
79 Loafer, e.g.
83 Seat of Allen County, Kansas
84 Port on the English Channel
86 Like a Windsor tie
88 The Blue Devils
89 John known as "The Father of Television"
91 Body that includes SHAPE
92 Mystical saying
93 He caught Larsen's perfect game
94 Plumed headgear
95 Apply cosmetics to wild animals?
98 Stirrup site
99 Wharton's farmer
102 Brownie
103 N.B.A. Rookie of the Year, 1993
105 Goofing, with "up"
108 Org. founded by Samuel Gompers
110 Nagana carrier
114 Talmud Torah teacher
115 Bromo salesman?
119 December 25?
121 Go gaga over
122 One in a receiving line?
123 Bogarde of "Darling"
124 Pick up on
125 Comparatively congenial
126 Shore soarer
127 Nordstrom competitor
128 A little night music
129 Brats
130 Kind of organ

DOWN

1 The second plague, in Exodus
2 From an earlier era
3 Composer Bruckner
4 Strong porters
5 Weary walker
6 They're always made at home
7 The Phantom of the Opera
8 Renders replete
9 Less lively
10 Luce publication
11 Olfactory input
12 "Turandot" slave
13 Of an arterial trunk
14 Plastered at a picnic?
15 Mint bar
16 Cubic meter
17 Divided
21 Car in a Beach Boys tune
26 Like much of Chile
28 Spruce
29 Feeler
34 Jazz pianist Billy
36 Unbelievable one
37 Knock for a loop: Var.
39 Bad-mouth
41 Journalist's question
42 "Not another word!"
43 Tony's cousin
45 8½" × 14"
46 Land alternative
48 Like some consequences
49 Pre-1991 atlas abbr.
50 Subjects of Mendelian experiments
52 Robinson and Thomas?
55 Vulgarian
58 Switch-hit?
59 Out of this world
60 Like some interpretations
63 Bushy hair
65 Ranch hand
67 Baseball's Maglie
69 Mouth widener
71 Clinch
73 They're all in the family
74 Ancient mariner
75 Others, to Ovid
76 Tars
78 Down Under dog
80 Unalloyed
81 Creole vegetable
82 Close in on
85 Student-focused org.
87 One who makes an admission?
90 Bread
92 Brutes
93 Brute
96 Tel Aviv carrier
97 Trades
100 1936 Olympics hero
101 Car-racing class
104 Libertine
105 Olive brown
106 Bob Cratchit, e.g.
107 Understanding
109 Showed the way, in a way
111 "So ___!"
112 Hanging net
113 Flubbed a fly
114 Fashionable dressers
116 Head set
117 Central points
118 Attend Andover, e.g.
120 Watson-Crick model

by Fran and Lou Sabin

ACROSS

1 Discussed thoroughly, with "out"
7 Florentine family name
13 Flattened at the poles
19 Diffuse
20 Medium-sweet sherry
22 Introduction
23 Song from "Holiday Inn"
25 Meteorological menace
26 Holiday in Hue
27 Skyrocket
28 Bamako is its capital
30 Univ. awards
31 Modest bathing suit
34 Lustrous hue
38 Notre Dame name
39 Feature of some modems
40 99-Down, Down Under
41 Oft-scripted Baroness Orczy novel
50 Smash letters
52 Limerick language
53 One of the Reiners
54 Gospel music award
55 Moonshine
58 Cautious stock inv.
60 Spring bloomer
63 Op. __
64 Botanist's workplace
66 74-Down's opposite
68 Constriction worker?
70 6-pointers
71 Theme of this puzzle
75 Small shot
76 Landed a haymaker
77 Sked guesses
78 Quits working
80 Name of 13 popes
81 "Iceland" star
83 Cager Kukoc
85 React to a bad joke, perhaps
86 Gore's grp.
88 Infielder Joey __
90 Warehouse supply: Abbr.
92 Shoe box marking
93 Peaked
100 "Hot Diggity" singer
101 Aurora's counterpart
102 Crack team?: Abbr.
103 Boiled holiday treat
108 Loaf locale
113 Get wind of
114 Mountain lake
115 Slapstick ammo
116 Suffix with duct
117 Theseus' land
120 Counterirritant concoction
125 First Olympic Hall of Fame gymnast
126 Under political attack, maybe
127 Plan
128 Stalk
129 Cartoon cat
130 Oater groups

DOWN

1 Popular book genre
2 Wheyfaced
3 Whack
4 In great demand
5 Journal addendum?
6 Cut
7 Code name
8 Medicine Nobelist Metchnikoff
9 Afro and bob
10 "Just Another Girl on the __" (1993 drama)
11 Cause for pause
12 Soul singer Hayes
13 Stadium cheer
14 __ Paese cheese
15 Fred Mertz, notably
16 Exiter's exclamation
17 Hint
18 Nephew of Cain
21 Where Dick Button won gold
24 Epitaph starter
29 S.D.I. concern
32 "Phooey!"
33 Fury
34 Bud, to Lou
35 Business biggie
36 Ford Sterling played one
37 Exiter's exclamation
39 Chilean president, 1964–70
41 Delicious
42 Holy war
43 Starwort, e.g.
44 Most difficult to believe
45 Buttinsky
46 Feeling lousy
47 Chopin works
48 Exhibits, basically
49 Answer to "Shall we?"
50 "Put a lid on it!"
51 Kind of float
56 Revolutionary name
57 Pawn
59 Speaker's spot
61 Putting up with
62 Dictionary abbr.
65 "Here comes trouble!"
67 Inc. relative
69 Have __ (overreact)
72 Open-mouthed quintet
73 "A votre __!"
74 Chabrier's "Le Roi malgré __"
75 Palace or prison, e.g.: Abbr.
79 "I told you so!"
82 D.S.M. recipient
84 "Singing journalist" Phil
87 Guards, collectively
89 Yemeni port
91 Slalom maneuver
94 Henri or Pierre, e.g.
95 Roadie's load
96 Shutout
97 Dress (up)
98 Shepherd's locale
99 Stripling
103 Nursery rhyme boy
104 Starbucks serving
105 Stops up
106 Solicits, with "up"
107 Map of the Aleutians, usually
108 Fussbudget
109 House mem.
110 What anglers want that campers don't
111 "Mr. Belvedere" actress Graff
112 School clique, maybe
113 Kind of seal
115 Ready for surgery
118 Whisper sweet nothings
119 Cape __
121 Chi preceder
122 Humerus locale
123 Year abroad
124 Most letters in D.C.

by Brendan Emmett Quigley

6 VEE FORMATION

ACROSS

1 "Say You, Say Me" singer, 1985
7 Gets rid of
13 Goalie's area
19 1804 symphony
20 Chiang Kai-shek's capital
21 Lizard
22 Salesman's sprees?
24 Puts forward
25 In addition
26 Gridiron specialist
27 Prepare mushrooms
29 Full deck, to Caesar?
30 Scottish landowner
32 B.&O. stop
33 Seat option
34 Saltimbocca base
35 Tilde wearers
36 Fall wear?
40 Wallop
41 $C_{14}H_9Cl_5$
42 Best Actress of 1987
43 Minimum
44 Took five
45 Little bit
46 Potato chip brand
47 Roper undertaking
48 Peter Pan's loss
52 "Red Red Wine" and "Gitarzan"?
55 Long haul
59 Flush
60 Aurifies
61 Prime time for Nick
62 Hot issue?
63 Like the Kara Kum
64 Groundwork
65 Boy-meets-girl event
66 Construction piece
67 Called up
68 Send out
69 Something to read
70 Insinuating
71 Take off
72 Akin to barrel-chested?
74 "I'll Take __" (Bob Hope film)
75 Not walk straight
77 Suffered a sell-off
78 Little white thing
79 Rock group?
82 Be a cast member of
84 Tops
85 Cookbook abbr.
88 Actor Burton
89 Obnoxious Presidential advisers?
91 Take a loss on, so to speak
92 Child's appliance
93 Dungeons & Dragons set
94 Attorney's deg.
95 Judge Kenneth
97 To be, in Barcelona
98 Kafka hero Gregor
99 Captivate
102 Florentine flower
103 Confuse
105 The Bible?
108 Holiday quenchers
109 One by one?
110 Jazz star
111 Annette, in "Beach Blanket Bingo"
112 Hereditary ruler
113 Like some college programs

DOWN

1 Made merry
2 Greatest source of 1840's immigration
3 Be composed (of)
4 It's quarry
5 Water cooler
6 Clanton foe
7 Loud speaker
8 Magdalene College student
9 Subject of a Car and Driver rating
10 Takeoff artist
11 Part of w.p.m.
12 Pantywaists
13 Societal division
14 Con
15 Poetic preposition
16 Close
17 Fill to the brim
18 Put fodder away
21 __ Ste. Marie
23 Without a cent
28 Helper, in brief
31 No, for one
33 "Halt!" to a salt
34 Queue at the bank?
37 Plug in the mouth
38 Veldt sights
39 Spanish royalty
40 Bud
44 Conundrum
46 Bebe Neuwirth TV role
47 Man of Principle
48 Winter wear
49 Every 60 minutes
50 Dior creation
51 L.A. team vehicle?
52 Short stay
53 One way to stand
54 Put the kibosh on
56 Overzealous
57 Duck
58 An original Mouseketeer
60 Anwar's predecessor
64 Cut at an angle
65 Saudi city
69 Kind of acid
70 Candy, in Canterbury
73 Ethyl acetate, e.g.
74 Fourier series function
76 It's always in verse
78 Tower site
79 Made annotations
80 Whodunit motive, perhaps
81 Garden-variety
82 Prepares for a shoot
83 Given the go-ahead
84 Minor malady
85 Dainty restaurant
86 Without exception
87 Flattered
89 Improvises chords
90 Strident sounds
93 Distance between rails
96 Put off
98 Blackthorn fruit
99 Balanced
100 Gulf of Finland feeder
101 Dudley Do-Right's org.
104 Three min. in the ring
106 TV Tarzan
107 Musician's pride

by Rich Silvestri

GREEN EGGS AND HAMLET

ACROSS

1 Be unwarrantably bold
8 Occultism
14 Modus operandi
20 One seen at trackside
22 Moonstruck
23 Lizard with a serrated crest
24 Start of an imaginary soliloquy
27 Inoffensive
28 Accepted
29 Kind of ticket
30 Enzyme suffix
31 Part 2 of the soliloquy
41 Walker's aid
42 Uris novel "___ 18"
43 Buddhist who has attained Nirvana
44 Sitter's charge
47 Halfwit
48 Tierra-Fuego bridge
49 Spirited meeting?
52 Part 3 of the soliloquy
61 Ref's call
62 Part of many Arab names
63 Favorite
64 International money
65 Part 4 of the soliloquy
72 Prefix with nucleotide
73 French cleric
74 Controversial teachings
75 Promising words
76 Part of a G.I.'s address
79 50's baseball nickname
81 Samantha's daughter on TV
85 1976 album "Olé ___"
86 Declinations
87 1939 Humphrey Bogart role
88 Rattling trains
89 Catch, as flies
90 Type
92 Part 5 of the soliloquy
103 To me, to Mimi
104 Psychoanalyst Fromm
105 Introduction to marketing?
106 Picnic spoiler
107 Part 6 of the soliloquy
114 Popular van Gogh painting
115 She's a deer
116 Kind of tin
117 Brillo rival
118 Entanglement
120 Holds
122 Pickle place
123 Part 7 of the soliloquy
133 Took place
134 Airport feature
135 Nasser's org.
136 Genoan V.I.P., once
137 End of the soliloquy
147 Put on ice
148 Arbitrates
149 Bawl out
150 One of the Munsters
151 It has its ups and downs
152 African menaces

DOWN

1 Smarten up
2 Ham's need
3 Dangerous bacteria
4 Lets fly
5 Actor Tognazzi
6 Zinger
7 Elusive one
8 Word with wheel or engine
9 At all
10 Dog-scolding word
11 "What's in ___?"
12 Put aboard
13 Land around the Brahmaputra Valley
14 Station in space
15 Something to stroke
16 King of song
17 "Very funny!"
18 Quick round of tennis
19 Stunt man, e.g.
21 ___ la Plata
22 Obfuscate
25 "The Birth of a Nation" grp.
26 Journalist Nellie
32 One ___ (ball game)
33 "I'm a Stranger Here Myself" poet
34 Put on the throne
35 Insect nests
36 Narrow valley
37 Reach on foot
38 "The ___ Love"
39 Killer whale
40 Classical music features
44 Noted Yugoslav patriot
45 Mixed dish
46 Fill-in
49 1979 exile
50 Naturalness
51 Churchill contemporary
53 Checkup
54 Second degree?
55 Go ___ for
56 When repeated, an old-fashioned cry
57 Spinner
58 "Here's ___ your eye!"
59 Southwest land
60 Dummies
66 Grated on
67 Fatuous
68 Abate
69 Theological belief
70 Long island community
71 Reef, maybe
76 Oilman Khashoggi
77 Blurb, e.g.
78 Part of a yoke
80 Flashlight carriers
82 Definitive word
83 Cacao exporter
84 Veep before Ford
91 First name in opera
93 More smooth
94 Artist with collectible lithos
95 Equivocator's forte
96 Some I.B.M. products
97 Tail
98 A year in the life of St. Anselm
99 Barked
100 Muzzles
101 Popular snack cracker
102 Explosives
108 Parched
109 Oberhausen one
110 "___ lay me down . . ."
111 Target of a bang-up job?
112 Actress Taylor
113 Sinn ___
118 Bandage
119 Legit
121 Gulf war weapons
122 Father-and-daughter actors
123 Swagger
124 Depot abbr.
125 Narc activities
126 Person with a mike
127 1982 Michener epic
128 "Bali ___"
129 Word on a ticket
130 Teams up with
131 Type size
132 Reminders
138 "Nightmare" street
139 Kitty in "The Killers," 1946
140 Hamilton is on it
141 Flower on a French shield
142 Author LeShan
143 Just-hired
144 Rod
145 Common possessive
146 It has a bite and hops

by David J. Kahn and Hillary B. Kahn

ACROSS

1 Like some Swift writing
7 Gallery event
14 "My Cup Runneth Over" singer, 1967
20 Zane Grey classic
21 Blows the joint
22 Egghead
23 Fence builder's job?
25 Storied raider
26 Writer Ferber
27 Minds, with "to"
28 Green hole
29 Chinese dynasty when Jesus lived
30 Roots may need this
31 El __
32 Bygone music genre
35 Giving the once-over
37 Architect's job?
42 Winner's look
44 Least bit of concern
45 Pre-Columbian Peruvian
46 Strip
47 Singer profiled in "Sweet Dreams"
48 Unit of 97-Across
49 Push to the limit
50 Ends of letters, briefly
51 Steeple musician's job?
57 "What Kind of Fool __"
58 Authority, metaphorically
59 Like an empty ship at sea
60 Judge's cry
64 Ball park licensee
67 Fliers with narrow waists
69 Cinch
70 Singed parts, usually
71 Kind of drum

73 Chaney, the Man of a Thousand Faces
75 "Fancy that!"
76 Sculptor's job?
82 __-Magnon
84 Shoe color
85 Drive
86 Puts to flight
87 Runners' location
88 Rock projection
90 It's fit to be tried
91 Leaves
92 Politician's job?
96 1970 hit "Hitchin' __"
97 Poet's concern
98 It's not free of charge
99 Natl. Popcorn Poppin' Month
102 Time div.
103 Main ingredient in a Monte Carlo
105 Like some pitches
109 Tudor queen
110 Bear
112 Feather packer's job?
115 Sen. Gaylord __, who originated Earth Day
116 Make more precipitous
117 __ Park, N.Y.
118 They're driven in droves
119 Some TV spots
120 One with a light workload?

DOWN

1 Barbara Stanwyck film "Woman __"
2 Word before "go"
3 Just like ewe?
4 Mercury org.
5 Chemical suffix
6 Stealthy
7 Fortas and Lincoln
8 Cessation
9 Poet laureate of 1692

10 Maintain, as attention
11 Warmly welcomes, perhaps
12 "Fairy tale"
13 Alien force, briefly
14 Isaac's eldest
15 Decked out
16 Gardner of "The Snows of Kilimanjaro"
17 Automatons
18 Magnifies
19 Manager of five straight World Series champions
24 Screen
28 Like some lenses
31 Best-selling author Carr
33 Reagan prog.
34 Middle: Prefix
36 Chatterboxes
37 Like some vases
38 "Grab __!"
39 Clinker
40 Photo process
41 Hack
42 Covered with goo
43 Potential space colony activity
47 Want
48 Andy Capp's wife
52 Make muffs
53 VCR button
54 Kind of I.R.A.
55 Hosp. hot spots
56 Bamboozle
61 Bench locale
62 Builds
63 Offends olfactorily
65 Put in plaintext
66 City in Kyrgyzstan
67 Servicewoman, acronymically
68 "Speak!" response
69 Exterior lineman
71 "Puh-lease!"
72 Generic
73 Access the Web
74 Rousing cheer
77 Longing
78 Long in politics

79 Bombeck of "At Wit's End"
80 Oscilloscope inventor Karl
81 Forsaken
82 Mozart solo feature
83 Arouse again
87 Pollen bearers
89 Snagged
90 Disrespects
91 Ballyhoo
93 Guerrilla's campaign
94 Lipton rival
95 Lowdown
99 Spring locales
100 Belief
101 One catching his opponent's ear?
104 Longs
106 Blockhead
107 Classical decorative object
108 Landers and others
109 Start of something big
111 Purpose
112 Clock std.
113 Time for les vacances
114 Something to chew on

ACROSS

1 Heath ___ (flowering perennial)
6 Some are inflatable
11 1980's Geena Davis sitcom
15 During
19 Verdi's Aïda, e.g.
20 Dazzle
21 Lover of Aphrodite
22 Goya's Maja is one
23 Movie kvetch in the woods?
25 Arbitrary decree
26 Old Pontiacs
27 Catchers in tag
28 "There's Something About ___ (That Reminds Me of You)"
29 Newborn's bed
31 Leg scratchers
34 Madras wear
35 Robert ___
37 Kvetch's game show?
40 Charges
42 Basis of the marine food chain
45 Job ad letters
46 Seles rival
48 Pavarotti possessive
49 What kvetches do at grocery stores?
55 Steeping gadget
57 Prefix with light or night
58 Rock's ___ Heep
59 Prefix with sphere or system
61 Surfeited
62 Spot for a nosh
65 ___ apple
67 Mrs. Flagston of the comics
68 Remember a kvetch in one's will?
72 Maj. Houlihan portrayer in "M*A*S*H"
74 Round trip?
75 Contradicts
79 No-waist dresses
81 Visit
82 More than irked
84 Newcomer, briefly
85 Cloaks
87 Angry kvetching?
91 Annihilation
92 They often don't speak to each other
94 "-speak"
95 Tangent, e.g.
96 By ___ (via)
98 Nickname for a kvetch maven?
104 "The Thief of Bagdad" star, 1940
105 Football's Flash Herber
106 Primitive time
110 Small pipe organ
112 Reject
114 Triangle part
115 Susan Lucci's eluder
117 Popular soap
118 Film title kvetch?
121 Kind of club
122 French quarters
123 Heard cases
124 Pronouncement
125 Surround
126 Richard of "Final Analysis"
127 Riding lawnmower maker
128 "The Devil and Daniel Webster" writer

DOWN

1 Comparable to a fiddle
2 A deadly sin
3 Tibiae neighbors
4 Brink
5 Legal matter
6 Rue
7 Transversely
8 Bugs
9 Subdued
10 Big initials at Indy
11 Occasion for a game plan?
12 Stemming
13 Get back, as authority
14 Piedmont province
15 Actress Bassett
16 Kiddie kvetches' game?
17 Oft-broken promise
18 ___ Arc, Ark.
24 Indian percussion rhythm
29 Cousin of "Phooey!"
30 Like some Clement Moore snow
32 Kind of meet
33 Train in a celebrated song
34 ___ Pea (Popeye's kid)
36 Ancient Roman officials
38 Prefix with store
39 Middle English letter
41 Realtor sign add-on
42 "Rigoletto" has three
43 Croquet site
44 Yago Sant'___ (wine brand)
47 N.R.C. predecessor
50 Low note provider
51 Curtain call call
52 Drying frames
53 Overhaul
54 Fink
56 Human apes
60 Some fraternity members
63 Actor Montgomery
64 A lot of tea
65 Lawyer: Abbr.
66 '54 defense pact
69 "___ your pardon?"
70 Bleacher feature
71 Feudal estate
72 Journalist Alexander et al.
73 Zephyr's kvetching?
76 Premed subj.
77 Elusive creature
78 Arty Big Apple area
79 Small merganser
80 What an "F" may indicate
82 ___ jure (by law)
83 Site of a wreck
86 Begin wedding plans
88 "Able was ___ . . ."
89 Birdhouse dweller
90 Undone?
93 Peace Corps director Sargent
97 Minded
99 Sheathe
100 Daughter of Ingrid Bergman
101 Illegal lender
102 Big step
103 Conclusion of many firm names
107 Detective Pinkerton
108 Followers
109 Wading bird
111 Cassini with designs on Jackie
112 Withered
113 ___-dieu (kneeling bench)
115 Prod
116 Year in Leo IX's papacy
118 Bouquet sender's abbr.
119 Brew milieu
120 Strummer's instrument

by Cathy Millhauser

ACROSS

1 ___ salad
6 Attempts
11 Churchill's "few"
14 Cassius's costume
18 Welcome sight
19 The Sorbonne, e.g.
20 Paella pot
22 Comet competitor
23 Q: ___ A: Later
27 Café additive
28 "Beverly Hills 90210" restaurant owner and others
29 Passionate desire
30 Originate
31 Sister of Terpsichore
33 Happy-lark go-between
34 Open, in a way
35 Q: ___ A: Out
44 It's charged
45 Egg manufacturer
46 Hallow ending
47 ___ Bator
48 Indian Prime Minister, 1991–96
49 The others
51 Sch. supporters
52 River of Tours
53 Aeronautical feat
54 Q: ___ A: O.K.
59 Some computer keys
60 Med. drips
61 Comprise
62 Payments for releases
64 Genetic inits.
65 Took off a ship
68 Just beat
69 Play to the camera
70 Five-time Kentucky Derby winner
71 Q: ___ A: Friends
79 "B.C." creator
80 Teased teen-agers
81 Laugh syllable
82 First name in cosmetics
83 Charlottesville-to-Richmond dir.
84 Romanian ruler known as "the Impaler"
85 Rye filler
86 Craggy peak
88 Part of X-X-X
89 Q: ___ A: I don't have any
95 "Jug handles"
96 Bond rating
97 Descriptive words for Ben Jonson
98 Painter El ___
100 "Makin' Whoopee" songwriter
102 Vault
103 Tierra del Fuego, e.g.
107 Q: ___ A: I don't need one
111 Tuner
112 Crewmate of Scotty
113 Instant
114 Words of wisdom
115 Not rash
116 Vegas action
117 Bury
118 Code name

DOWN

1 Hood
2 A few laughs
3 Actor Morales
4 Tailor, at times
5 Retired Atl. speedster
6 Blood component
7 Colorless ketone
8 Farm females
9 Frazier foe
10 Gets into trouble, maybe
11 Popular fast-food chain, informally
12 Very much
13 Winter woe
14 Exotic vacation spot
15 Spanish eyes
16 Willing
17 Fire
21 Button sources
24 Greatly admiring
25 Poi party
26 Joyce's homeland
32 One who believes "practice makes perfect"
33 Per annum
34 Genesis
35 On the same side as
36 Santa sounds
37 Poetically sufficient?
38 "___ pray"
39 Harbor markers
40 He directed Marlon
41 Good routine
42 Like an angel
43 Bushwhacker, e.g.
50 Tried to hit, in dialect
51 Geneva Convention concern
52 Hot rocks
53 Trails
55 Like some shows
56 Israeli day
57 Dog, Down Under
58 Tour operator, at times
62 Go over old territory?
63 Renée of the silents
64 Area covers
65 Press
66 Staff sgt., e.g.
67 Charlie of the 60's Orioles
69 Confuse
70 Weather prefix
71 "That was close!"
72 Neighborhood
73 Cheers
74 Master's ordeal
75 "If ___ nickel . . ."
76 Put ___ (ask hard questions of)
77 Eye drop
78 "Darn it!"
85 China's Yellow Emperor
86 Arsonist
87 N.C.A.A. World Series site
90 Irk
91 Western city or its radio station
92 Diamond Head locale
93 "Well begun is half done" writer
94 Nut
98 Classic Italian car
99 Tom Clancy hero
100 Actor MacLachlan
101 Month of l'été
102 Busy
104 Capone trademark
105 Totes
106 Suit to ___
107 O.E.D. entries
108 Container
109 Directional suffix
110 Cartesian conclusion

by Randolph Ross

ACROSS

1 It finds itself in hot water
7 Comics debut of 1941
13 No longer shrink-wrapped
19 Socks pattern
20 It didn't keep Little Boy Blue awake
21 Jinx
22 Breakfaster's favorite drama?
25 Crime mystery writer Paretsky
26 Fluency
27 Discredit
28 Resort souvenir
29 Breakfaster's query?
35 Associate of Zhou
38 Have breakfast, e.g., in Germany
39 Church part
40 Nasty
44 Waters and Mertz
46 Whispered call
47 ACTH or thyroxine
50 Bright-colored blooms
52 E. coli, for one: Abbr.
53 Heads toward
54 Fielding brother
55 Breakfaster's personal credo?
58 "Jaws" sighting
59 Loose, in a manner of speaking
60 The L of L-dopa
61 Dry as a bone
62 Is in peak singing condition?
64 Marked by drinking
66 First name in jeans
68 Williams and Kennedy
70 "The Conqueror Worm" poet
71 One way to run
74 Peel
76 1997 Peter Fonda title role
78 Isle of Man man
81 Dolt
82 Breakfaster's maids?
85 Just
86 Remove all restrictions on
88 L'eau lands?
89 Mouthed but not spoken
91 "Amadeus" role
92 Cause of a non sequitur
93 Salt of element #53
94 Meg's "Prelude to a Kiss" co-star
95 Wear well
96 Feeding tube?
99 Formerly named
100 How a breakfaster views himself?
106 Cap initials at Busch Stadium
109 Have a loan from
110 Make
111 Part of the eye
115 Waiters' reaction after breakfast was over?
121 ___ Forest (W.W. I battle site)
122 "Bewitched" husband
123 One in the can
124 Holiday driver, in a phrase
125 Place beside
126 Sharp-pointed instrument

DOWN

1 ___ Ski Valley, N.M.
2 Author Bombeck
3 Golden-___
4 Legally
5 It may be involved in a draft
6 Pick up
7 Wear off
8 Bran accompanier
9 Like some chairs
10 ___ et ubique (here and everywhere)
11 Female name suffix
12 Swellhead
13 Roasters
14 Second of a historical trio
15 Cedar ___ (lumber source)
16 "Capital"
17 Plain Jane
18 Astronaut Slayton
21 Actress McClurg
23 "No ___ allowed"
24 Confront
30 Start with pad or port
31 Lash out at
32 Violinist Heifetz
33 Surprise challenger
34 Mashed dish
35 Cross, of a sort
36 Eric Rohmer's "___ of Winter"
37 Breakfaster's sad comment?
41 Breakfaster's U.N. guest?
42 How tuna may be packed
43 Screendom's Laura and Bruce
45 Escape artist
46 Hand, informally
47 "Gotcha!"
48 "Is that all right?"
49 Swab again
51 Illustrator Silverstein
52 Second-rate film
53 Kind of linebacker
56 Opposed
57 Jams
63 Run a charity, e.g.
65 Giggle
67 Black to the max
69 Will be, to Doris Day
71 March music maker
72 Ear part
73 Wrong end?
75 Enlarge
77 Observation
79 Select or elect
80 Paris school
83 It releases a dangerous spray
84 Spirit
87 It may be polished
90 1956 Allen Ginsberg poem
92 Dodger name of fame
95 Lo-cal
96 Flow stoppage
97 Capital city spelled with an umlaut
98 Registered, with "up"
101 Sondheim song "We're ___ Be All Right"
102 Oscar winner Edmund of "Miracle on 34th Street"
103 Golfer Ballesteros
104 Prefix with transmitter
105 Scrumptious
106 Try
107 Like some traffic
108 Runners
112 Kind of chops
113 Renaissance art patron
114 "I'd hate to break up ___"
116 ___ Kippur
117 Easy mark
118 Dadaist Jean
119 It might halt traffic on the Rhine
120 Many a worker

by Manny Nosowsky

ACROSS

1 1997 N.H.L. M.V.P. Dominik
6 Kind of range
11 Not right?
18 Romeo, e.g.
20 Two for the road
21 Ennoble
22 +43
24 Sticks
25 Like jambalaya
26 Once, once
28 Papas in films
29 "___ speak"
32 −32
36 What's-his-face
38 Won over
39 "The Black Cat" writer
42 Mentor's charge
43 Blacken, as steak
45 Acropolis figure
47 Tolkien creature
48 −3
54 Like wedding cakes
55 Rtes.
56 Key rings?
57 Designer Cassini
59 Uniform alternative
60 "Casablanca" role and others
62 Unkind look
63 "Maid of Athens, ___ part": Byron
64 "Wheel of Fortune" request
65 −41
70 "Foucault's Pendulum" author
71 Progress impeders
73 Toward the caboose
74 Writer Fannie
76 Up
77 Dry fuel
78 Eritrean capital
81 "___ vous plait"
84 Rodeo grounds features
86 −31
88 Suffix with corpus
89 Its main street is Last Chance Gulch
90 Santa's spot?
91 Deadly virus
93 Wall Street whiz
94 Homers reach them
99 Sponges
101 −90 or −94, among others
104 Depilatory brand
105 Less tanned
108 Dirt
109 Item on a list
111 One who studies irises
113 −100
119 Like a gridiron
120 Omega competitors
121 Like the heavens
122 Calculator figures
123 Glyceride, e.g.
124 Wake the dead?

DOWN

1 That ship
2 It may be pint-sized
3 Saucehound
4 Lacking vigor
5 See 58-Down
6 Indian princess
7 C.D. offering: Abbr.
8 Safe-products org.
9 Paul Bunyan, e.g.
10 Develop
11 Podium speaker
12 U.N. arm
13 Running late
14 Three-time Wimbledon champ
15 Pink, so to speak
16 Solar deity
17 ___-majesté
19 Coral assemblies
20 Graphic head?
23 60's–70's Italian P.M.
27 Site of many losses
29 Daisy relative
30 Unflawed
31 +29 or +44 or +69, etc.
33 Burning passions
34 Crucifix letters
35 "I earn that ___": "As You Like It"
37 "L'Absinthe" painter
39 −29
40 Ring combination
41 Lady of a 1932 song
43 Quarter-millennium
44 1940's Tigers All-Star New-houser
46 Posting in a French store
49 Ship sunk at Pearl Harbor
50 "Can't do it"
51 Beethoven's birthplace
52 Zeno's home
53 Rustic pipe
58 With 5-Down, a TV gourmet
61 Emissary
62 Elton John, e.g.
64 Pollen container
66 Actress Mary et al.
67 Bring in
68 Stuff
69 Doctor Zhivago
71 Nickname for Alexander
72 Loud
75 Advertising figures
78 Give ___ of one's own medicine
79 Traffic caution
80 Engineer's sch.
82 Words after "Well"
83 Minimal
85 Mordant Mort
87 Book after Neh.
92 Male slave
95 Privileged classes
96 Zeus, to Cronus
97 Pour out freely
98 Squares things
99 Streep's "___ in the Dark"
100 The slightest amount
101 C.S.A. general
102 House & Garden topic
103 Bugs
105 "Passion" star Negri
106 Kind of indigestion
107 Capital of Denmark in the Middle Ages
110 Gonzo
112 Avg.
114 Potted
115 Island guitar
116 "My man!"
117 Go wrong
118 Ham sandwicher

by Jim Page

ACROSS

1 Conduct, in a way
6 Innocent
10 Pasta or potato, to an athlete
14 Saint in Italy
19 Showy flower
20 Daminozide, commercially
21 'Hood
22 Edit, as a soundtrack
23 The exterminator ordered ___
25 The horologist ordered ___
27 Em, for example
28 Song word after "Aba"
30 Cell division process
31 Introduction to physics?
33 Disinfest
36 Blue book filler
37 Razor-billed bird
40 Stampeders
42 Gray wolf
43 Pantry pest
44 The inept furniture mover ordered ___
48 The wild pitcher ordered ___
53 Illegal parker's worry
54 Petitions
56 Liszt's "La Campanella," e.g.
57 Old shoe polish brand
60 Discloses
61 Withdraws, with "out"
63 Beneficiary of nepotism: Abbr.
64 Evening event
66 Rival of Helena
68 Domino, e.g.
69 The real estate agent ordered ___
72 The comedian ordered ___
74 Politico Bayh
75 Cremona craftsman
77 River crosser, perhaps
78 Campaign feature, maybe
79 Hardly a blabbermouth
80 Pump, e.g.
82 1962 Paul Anka hit
86 "The Last Command" locale
88 Giggled
91 Longer in the tooth
92 The used-car dealer ordered ___
94 The mama's boy ordered ___
97 Initials since 1933
98 Whence the Magi, with "the"
100 Port of Egypt
101 "Hoo" preceder
102 More cluttered
105 Fore-and-after
107 Like some questions
110 Showstoppers?
112 One of TV's Mavericks
114 Vacillate
117 The panhandler ordered ___
120 The munitions expert ordered ___
123 Crow's home
124 Ham's punctuation
125 Bit of fast food
126 Land
127 He was a real dummy
128 Channels
129 Pack
130 Like smokestacks

DOWN

1 Office dupes, for short
2 Result of a crack?
3 Diamond family name
4 Actress Massey
5 Whole bunch
6 Like some coifs
7 Climber's challenge
8 Duster
9 Scratch
10 Sporty car
11 "Exodus" role
12 Nickelodeon cartoon character
13 Toto's creator
14 Masks
15 Balloon or dirigible
16 Milton, for one
17 Saint ___ (Florida county)
18 Having made substantial gains?
24 Flexible
26 Two-stage missile
29 Place for bats?
32 Kill ___ killed
34 "SOS" singers
35 Directly opposed
37 "Hamlet" quintet
38 Unsettling comment from a pilot
39 Apteryx australis
41 Slowest on the uptake
45 Scribes
46 Smoking gun
47 "L'___ c'est moi"
49 Slander
50 "Foreign Affairs" author Alison
51 ___ Rogers St. Johns
52 Took out
55 Oahu-to-Maui dir.
58 Major defense contractor
59 Lively
62 Caterpillar constructions
65 Navigation units
67 Diatribes
68 Raise again . . . and again
69 Pertaining to 73-Down
70 Seed structure
71 Word of politeness
73 Hospital supply
76 Professional suffix
77 Ring fighter
79 Reached the vanishing point
81 Bully
83 Wired
84 Utah state flower
85 Give or take
87 Gesturer
89 Cousin of a canvasback
90 Time of decision
93 Goa garment
95 Tries not to attract attention
96 Car bomb?
99 Gets serious, with "up"
102 Vanquishes
103 Let out
104 Halitosis fighter
106 Younger siblings, traditionally
108 Crows' homes
109 Prefix with -pathy
111 Square-ended vessel
113 The "id" in "id est"
115 Sleekly designed
116 Flaw
118 Hollywood autobiography subtitled "My Story"
119 Bit of Florida
121 Nonpolluting
122 El adjoiner

by Fred Piscop

14 "DROP IT!"

ACROSS

1 Spot on a cliff
5 Pound (down)
9 First baseball player to make $1 million a year
13 Big splash
18 "Thérèse Raquin" novelist
19 Girl in a #1 Everly Brothers hit
20 Part of a meter
21 Ruth's mother-in-law
22 Turning points
23 Critic Judith
24 Genius?
26 Beige shirt with khaki pants?
29 "Bulworth" star
30 "Yo!"
31 Grp. in peace accords
32 Person of high position
33 A new twist?
39 Toshiba competitor
42 "The Last Time I Saw Paris" composer
43 Wagner heroine
44 Twist
48 Solely
49 Job for a seamstress
52 Part of a plane
53 Partner of Brahma and Vishnu
54 Rather soft
56 Like many a castle
58 Not just given
59 Farm sound
60 Calmer
62 Kilmer communicates with the deaf?
64 Headline trumpeting a new wedding veil?
68 Hairdo for the office?
70 "Phantom Lady" actress, 1944
71 Far East carrier, for short
73 Black Sea locale
74 Challenging reply
76 Answers
78 "Seven" or "10," e.g.
79 Qatar's capital
81 Took steps
84 "Here __ Again" (1987 #1 hit)
85 Writer Harte
86 St. __, Switzerland
88 Agape
89 Journal unit
90 Ex-hoopster Dave, after he went to Washington?
93 His name's an anagram of "gaoler"
96 Calendar abbr.
97 Supply boat
102 Split
103 Places where graft is most common?
108 Case for Ace Ventura?
110 Having fine threads
111 The Miners of the N.C.A.A.
112 Kind of bit
113 Cutlass, e.g.
114 Great interest
115 Repeated cry in a children's argument
116 Obdurate
117 Word after who or what
118 Gamepieces
119 Certain constellation star

DOWN

1 Bohemian, e.g.
2 "Good Times" star, in 70's TV
3 Calm
4 Needing a pat on the back, say
5 Gang's domain
6 __ were
7 Like a golf ball in the rough
8 Czar of 1682–1725
9 European capital
10 Fabrication
11 Home of the Cyclones
12 TV's "The __ Today"
13 Sportscaster Dick
14 Stone size
15 Hesitant
16 Concord
17 Baby
19 Absolutely clean
25 Hearty entree
27 Goal-oriented activity
28 Rikki-tikki-__
32 Plate ump's call
34 A little work
35 Belief that all natural objects have souls
36 Lord's worker
37 A three or a five, for instance
38 Literary inits.
39 Sound at the door
40 37-Down, e.g.
41 How "Lili Marlene" is played
44 Laughs hysterically
45 Psalms writer
46 Still
47 Rolls
50 "Take two" was his motto
51 Receipts
53 Disrespect
55 Sits, slangily
57 Sad
58 Tigers foe
60 Concert sites
61 Each
62 Of the belly
63 Ancient greeting
65 __ dixit
66 Dapper ones
67 Funny one
68 Starting point
69 Lilac, e.g.
72 Tour grp.
74 Shred
75 Owns, once
76 Kind of sale
77 Sauce ingredient
79 Ready to come out of the oven
80 Ending of many Web site names
82 One who stays up late
83 Make some fast food
86 1993 A.F.C. Rookie of the Year Rick
87 Bite, so to speak
90 Flaubert creation
91 Strengthen
92 Revolt
93 Eskimo-__ (language group)
94 Discharge
95 Ancient Greek physician
98 Leftover
99 Woman of "Today"
100 It happens
101 Aggressive
102 Workers in columns
103 Battery
104 Tips
105 A bell ringer closes it: Abbr.
106 Wallop
107 Wherry equipment
109 Runner Sebastian

by Joe DiPietro

ACROSS

1 Meager
5 Pen name
8 Tried to lose?
15 Mediocre
19 Hawaiian winter wind
20 She danced with John in "Pulp Fiction"
21 Woman in Charles's life
22 Relaxation
23 Start of a quip
26 Mysterious character
27 They let you know you're wanted
28 Solar system mockup
29 Vacillated
31 Abundance
32 Tykes
33 The other team in "Damn Yankees"
34 Homer Simpson's exclamation
36 Ike's command: Abbr.
37 Inheritance?
38 Dickens the sketchwriter
41 Suffix with macro-
44 As soon as
46 C's in shop class?
50 Town SE of Bakersfield, Calif.
52 Scepter adornment
54 Family
55 Zulus, e.g.
56 Political practice, perhaps
58 Quip, part 2
62 Forster's "___ With a View"
63 Gull
65 Asia Minor region
66 Quip, part 3
69 Like a banshee
71 Without
72 Gone by
76 Quip, part 4
78 Tolkien tree-man

79 "The Player" director, 1992
80 Article in El Pais
81 Citric cooler
82 Addams Family member
84 E-9: Abbr.
88 Painter Anthony Van ___
91 Spread out
92 Calendar units: Abbr.
93 Unsurprising
95 Japanese honorific
97 Ilex, for one
99 Noted site of foreign study
102 Kind of train
105 Nearly sacrificed son
110 Expurgated, with "up"
111 "Tobacco Road" father Jeeter ___
112 Actress Dolores
113 Plant-growth retardant
114 End of the quip
117 Bean town?
118 More blackened
119 Animation unit
120 Take out of context?
121 Secretary, for one
122 Lev Bronstein's alias
123 Fire
124 Tried to beat the tag

DOWN

1 Captains, informally
2 O.K. for the diet-conscious
3 Architect Jones
4 "Politically Incorrect" host
5 Chums
6 1965 Yardbirds hit "___ Man"
7 Lakeside sight
8 Build up
9 Enjoyed

10 The Sage of Concord
11 Easter emblem
12 Toymaker, maybe
13 Largo, vis-à-vis presto
14 Adirondack lake
15 Big pistol manufacturer
16 1985 newsmaking ship Achille ___
17 "Roots" Emmy winner
18 Follows
24 Cézanne's "Boy in ___ Vest"
25 Madness?
30 Colorado resort
32 Horse's halter
33 Cordwood measure
35 Publisher Adolph
38 Tolerate
39 "Oops!"
40 Emil ___, 1948–52 Czech track gold medalist
42 Did some scouting
43 Impart erroneously
45 They're on top of things
47 "The Drew Carey Show" woman
48 Entreaty
49 Partake at 30-Down
50 As yet unscheduled: Abbr.
51 Dense clouds
53 Fetched, to a hillbilly
57 Free-for-all
58 Duck
59 Nevertheless
60 Wedding vow infinitive
61 Bennett song start
63 Vladivostok villa
64 Nouvelle Calédonie, e.g.
67 Thrice daily, in pharm.
68 Preface
69 Jets or Sharks

70 Makeup lessons?: Abbr.
73 Gen. Bradley
74 Flees
75 Modern-day evidence
76 Clear the tables
77 Mix up
79 Writer Quindlen
83 Sans pass
85 Mideast leader beginning 1981
86 "Chacun ___ goût"
87 Marilyn Monroe's birthday
89 "The Screwtape Letters" writer
90 Name in Chinese history
94 Multipurpose conjunction
96 One with a lot of paperwork
98 Ukraine's capital
99 Almost boil
100 Stan's pal
101 Lots and lots
103 Bottom line
104 "All My Children" role
106 Coasters
107 Synthetic fiber
108 Garlicky mayonnaise
109 Intimidated
111 Trent of the Senate
112 Lowland
115 CC
116 Spell

by Henry Hook

"LET'S HAVE SOME QUIET HERE!"

ACROSS

1 Pill popper's pop
7 It's supposed to come first
13 Rotating bodies
20 On the decline?
21 Old French colony
22 Turned a deaf ear to
23 Head man on ice?
25 Envoys
26 10th anniversary gift
27 African plains grazer
28 India/Pakistan events
30 Strip off
31 Look of one needing a comeuppance
33 Man to "tell 'em what they won" on many game shows
36 College credits
38 Christie detective
40 Early "S.N.L." star
43 "Out!"
47 Absent-minded barber's request?
51 Light on the moon
52 Lounging
53 Here's one pour vous
54 Woofer output
55 Kind of bar
56 Psis' predecessors
57 Not doing well in a race
60 Peeples of "North Shore," 1987
62 Sandwiches for dessert
63 Comparatively stewed
65 Boat propellers
67 Marabou, for one
69 Make final
70 Chan's silent "You got me"?
73 Stand in
76 They can go to blazes
77 "C'mon, be ___"
78 Saint-___ (Loire's capital)
80 10, in a way

83 N.L. Central team inits.
85 Ham
87 "There!"
88 University of California site
89 La la starter
91 Prefix with duct
92 Sign-on requirement, often
94 Like a 911 call: Abbr.
95 Remnants in Ohio?
99 Nimble
100 Operatic passage
101 Coffeecake
102 Joltless joe
104 "Jerusalem Delivered" poet
106 Stool, in a manner of speaking
110 Paler that pale
112 Fasten with a pop
115 Kabuki alternative
117 Italian note
118 Cubist before Rubik
120 Gift holders?
124 Why plants turn to the sun
125 Unreadable
126 Kind of center
127 Sling mud
128 What to do
129 Most curious

DOWN

1 Autograph holders
2 Don't leave at the doorstep
3 Kind of geometry
4 Parking place
5 Bons mots
6 Neighbor of Mo.
7 Airline to Stockholm
8 Rhine whine
9 Electrical unit
10 Rags have them
11 Sticking point
12 Ties up the phone
13 Light lager
14 "T" size: Abbr.
15 Worry
16 Flood survivor's pet?
17 Art Deco illustrator

18 Got ready to drive, with "up"
19 Old sit-in org.
24 Aquarium staple
29 Sandwich filler
32 ___
34 Vocally
35 Reason to go back to school
37 Forms grp.
39 Pot containers
41 "The light dawns!"
42 Bruce of "Family Plot"
44 Vaudeville dancer's accessory
45 Ray of film
46 Building blocks, e.g.
47 Milk: Prefix
48 Work ___
49 Snow, in Bordeaux
50 Soprano Scotto
55 Welsh dog
58 Old Dodge
59 Purplish-red
61 "___ Grows in Brooklyn"
64 Gimlets and screwdrivers
66 Hit (the brakes)
68 Fast exodus
71 European language of one million
72 Czechs' cousins
73 Bag
74 Opened
75 Worrier's handful
76 Abominable Snowman?
79 Timeless, in olden times
80 Monthly occurrence
81 Dewy
82 "Did you ___?"
84 Off one's rocker
86 Son of Vespasian
90 Part of H.R.H.
93 Guide and protector
95 Dump
96 Trying
97 Never, never, never
98 Little PC pictures
103 Mate's assent
105 Playwright Chekhov

107 Satirical production
108 "Bonanza" deputy and others
109 Sets upon
110 Something to put on?
111 Old English bard
113 Three oceans touch it
114 Hungry feeling
116 "___ be in England"
118 Sch. group
119 Viper's sound
121 Put two and two together
122 Large amount
123 Lassie's mate

by Nancy Salomon

17 DOUBLE HEADERS

ACROSS
1 Kaiser, once
4 Daughter of William the Conqueror
9 Irritate
13 Slow movement
19 Flap
20 Biological group
21 Inner: Prefix
22 Whalesucker
23 Gong worn on the head?
26 Plug for a cask
27 Having the biggest lip?
28 Set-tos
30 In a bit
31 "Oh, I see"
32 Ran riot
33 Beat
35 First note at the Moulin Rouge?
40 Contest for Atalanta
43 Wheelhouse direction
44 Check mates
45 Strauss opera
47 Cambodia's Lon ___
48 Dallas icemen
50 Baja cheer
51 Birling surface
52 Pulitzer Prize category
54 Rug rat
55 Fast Chinese food?
61 Biol. subject
62 Ingle glowers
63 Diamond flaw?
64 What you will
66 Clean
69 Downhill gold medalist of 1994
70 Travelers' gear
71 Rival of Billie Jean
72 Kind of skirt
74 Author Puzo
75 Women, slangily
76 Off-limits craziness?
79 Flight
82 ___ alia
84 Popular card game
85 Start of the fifth century
86 More than see
88 "Rock 'N' Roll Is King" group
89 Prevents
92 Having tears
94 Skim along
95 Crossword grid feature
97 Dog pedigree?
100 "Hernando's Hideaway," e.g.
101 Go formal
102 Auto of long ago
103 It may be thrown into a pot
104 They make connections
106 Nautical hanger-on
111 Lit up
113 Farewell to balloting?
115 Where Mark Twain is buried
116 Director Riefenstahl
117 Backgammon piece
118 Fatima's spouse
119 Optimally
120 Hebrides tongue
121 Bars
122 Vintage

DOWN
1 Notable opening of 10/7/82
2 Fall guy?
3 Alitalia stop
4 Hercule's creator
5 Humbles
6 Chimp in space
7 The hots
8 Olive relative
9 Weasel out
10 Buck features
11 Mount
12 Go (over)
13 ___ Nova (music style)
14 Left
15 Key of Mendelssohn's Symphony No. 3
16 Disco fruit?
17 Press agent?
18 Meal starter
24 U.P.S. inquiry
25 "It's ___ World" ('62 sitcom)
29 Foil on the stage
32 Renaissance fiddle
34 Opposite of heter-
35 Calculate astrologically
36 ___-relievo
37 Straight
38 "Becket" star
39 Cheap magazines
40 Ground meal
41 Partner, redundantly
42 Delights
46 To boot
49 Show disdain for
53 Tangent or secant
56 "Adam's Rib" actress
57 Confine
58 Home of the Black Bears
59 Exhibit vanity
60 Millennium makeup
62 Use a thurible
65 Less upfront
66 Files in the face of
67 With nothing left over
68 Drummer's affliction?
70 Go "poof!"
72 Tick off
73 Continuous-play tape
74 Member of a corps
77 Best in the regatta
78 Garbage haulers
79 Caron role
80 Speller's phrase
81 Allocate, with "out"
83 Corrects the ledger
87 In good financial shape
90 Brit. money
91 Multiplex multitude
92 Sphagnous
93 Gullywasher
96 Henry James title character
98 The Love Bug, of Disney films
99 Señor on the Sullivan show
101 Utility room item
103 Revolver inventor
105 Suffix with collect
106 1976 Kiss hit
107 1966 N.L. batting champ
108 "So long!"
109 Be a couch potato
110 Arthurian lady
111 Where the buoys are
112 Not dis
114 Lombard Street feature

by Richard Silvestri

ACROSS

1 Court conference
8 Cakes of a sort
13 Gotham City do-gooder
19 It began around 1100 B.C. in Europe
20 Fires
21 In a New York minute
22 1960's foursome
23 Monumental foursome
25 1996 Tony winner
26 Tight
27 You wouldn't want to be caught in one
28 Bean __
29 Singer in a field
32 __ Varner, Faulkner woman
33 German electricity-producing city
35 Baseball stats
36 Photographer Goldin
37 Silent
39 Tin Pan Alley org.
44 Noncash deposit
45 Literary foursome
48 __-ran
49 Semiannual occurrence
51 Components of some campaigns
52 Country club figure
53 Pitch
54 Ransom __ Olds
55 Fields of activity
57 Certain turn-on
58 "O For a Thousand Tongues" composer
59 Changes a file listing, e.g.
61 Not staccato
65 French F.B.I.
67 Con: Var.
68 Critical foursome
71 White wine aperitif
72 Native-born Israelis
75 Fenway Park locale

76 Their words are divine
80 Get via roving eyes
81 Outwits
83 Tex-Mex snacks
85 "Eldorado" rock group
86 Bickerer in the "Iliad"
87 __ de Triomphe
88 "We __ the World"
90 Rocky Mountain pass
92 Bankrolls
93 Court foursome
96 Dedicated
97 Symbols of obstinacy
99 A "Doctor Zhivago" setting
100 One of Ophelia's flowers
101 Tennis legend Lacoste
102 Super Bowl XXXII outcome
104 Some Pablo Neruda works
106 Enters cyberspace
108 Duchamp contemporary
111 "The Crying Game" star
112 Home of Ephesus
114 Corn __
115 TV foursome
118 Annual foursome
122 What une plume writes on
123 Scroogelike
124 Rustled
125 Devotes
126 Brahman, e.g.
127 Spanish saint and namesakes

DOWN

1 Rival, perhaps
2 Dander
3 Edmond O'Brien film noir, 1950
4 Consigns

5 Bundles
6 Mulder of "The X-Files," for one
7 Word with cure or room
8 Barbecue
9 Overdid the flattery
10 Jolly Roger feature
11 Like Radio city Music Hall
12 Latvia, once: Abbr.
13 Ellington contemporary
14 Greek Minerva
15 Nursery rhyme boy
16 Alphabetical foursome
17 Prefix with phobia
18 Indigence
20 Total
24 Overcoats
29 Inferior
30 Jim Palmer was one
31 Yuletide foursome
32 Like Baby Bear's porridge
34 Noted alpine tunnel
36 Like Miss Congeniality
38 Cries on seeing a cute baby
40 Like "The Bonfire of the Vanities"
41 Lucky foursome
42 It may be fixed
43 Oater group
45 Bills paid in Italy, once
46 Surgeons' tools
47 Signs of approval
50 Bucs' home
56 Ken-L Ration competitor
60 Lackland, e.g.
62 Rod
63 Does penance
64 The housewife in "Diary of a Mad Housewife"
66 Decree
69 Way out of the public eye

70 "Get outta here!"
72 Either end of Alaska
73 Parts
74 Variety of herring
77 Tramp
78 Weather whipping boy
79 Soaked
82 Awakening
84 Santa __
88 Penultimate word of Warner Brothers cartoons
89 Like the sound of a gong
91 Big tips
94 Castro's predecessor
95 Kind of spoon
98 Went through channels?
103 Squints (at)
105 Sad music
106 "Gigi" composer
107 "Live"
108 Venomous ones
109 Gather
110 "__ down now!"
113 Miss in a 1934 song
114 Sound before "Yeah, you!"
116 Palindromic diarist
117 U.S. Army medal
119 Words of understanding
120 Org. in the Mapplethorpe brouhaha
121 Newsmaking 60's grp.

by Nancy Nicholson Joline

19 VICIOUS CIRCLE

ACROSS

1 Launch of July 1962
8 The "E" in E.L. Doctorow
13 Rattles, for 1-Across
20 Trapped
21 1930's–40's director Zoltan ___
22 Secondary result
23 Hardly used
24 Writer who said "Satire is what closes Saturday night"
26 Pulitzer-winning biographer Leon
27 Sundial letters
29 Junglelike
30 Ere
31 "I wish you a meretricious and a happy New Year" penner
37 Mom-and-pop grp.
40 Kind of condor
41 Dealer's nemesis
42 Smart
46 Patches again
48 One of the Allies of W.W. II
51 0 degrees
53 Anxious
54 Where the smart set sat [answer to be entered in the appropriate manner]
57 Green, maybe
58 1966 movie that won Best Original Score
60 Novel by 47-Down
61 Universités
62 Island in French Polynesia
63 Gov. Landon
65 "___ on $45 a Day"
67 A reduced state
68 Park toy
71 Made for a mortise
73 Binary ___
76 Thoroughly confine
78 Plaza abbr.
79 Handlebar feature
82 Bun, for one
84 Japanese portal
86 Prairielike
89 Sanford of "The Jeffersons"
90 See 54-Across
92 French flier
93 Center or end
95 Snick-or-___
96 Taras Bulba, notably
97 Munich's river
98 Matador's opponent
101 Like some diets
103 Word before "loves me" and "loves me not"
104 "From Bed to Worse" writer
108 Floor
112 Eastern pooh-bah
113 Games grp.
114 ___-American
118 She said "You can lead a horticulture, but you can't make her think"
123 More eccentric
125 Certain sweaters
126 Zaps, in a way
127 Treater's words
128 Nocturnal noisemaker
129 Upriver spawner
130 Reversion

DOWN

1 Scrabble draw
2 Site of Vance Air Force Base
3 Camp locale
4 Rock layer
5 Lot
6 With 87-Down, Wit's End resident called "Old Vitriol and Violets"
7 Goes back to the start
8 Hosp. test
9 Mr. X
10 In the majority?
11 Leaking
12 Loose overcoat
13 Name as a price
14 Grant giver, for short
15 Waters
16 Back talk
17 San ___
18 Brand of daminozide
19 Neck band?
25 Collection of legends
28 Whom "I Like"
32 Summoned, as a butler
33 Island southeast of Borneo
34 Schools for engrs.
35 "What ___ the odds?"
36 "Papillon" star
37 "No ___!" (slangy O.K.)
38 Drift
39 "'Tis ___ bagatelle!"
42 Editor who "looked like a dishonest Abe Lincoln"
43 Handy
44 Buntlines, e.g.
45 Pigtail
47 She replied to Noël Coward's "You look almost like a man!" with "And so do you"
49 Nursery rhyme residence
50 Confute
52 Dean Smith's sch.
54 See 54-Across
55 Buenos ___
56 See 54-Across
59 Leisure
64 One facing life, maybe
66 Smut
69 Loner
70 East wind, in Greek myth
72 Chanel fragrance
73 Hot dog garnish
74 Haven
75 Casualty of 1997
77 Subatomic particle
80 Abstractions
81 Gorgeous Georgian?
83 J.F.K. or F.D.R.
85 Sherlock's lady friend
87 See 6-Down
88 52-Down rival
91 It's a gas
94 Bean
96 ___ Mounds (Illinois historical site)
99 Collect
100 They may be vital
102 Chem. or biol.
104 So out it's in
105 Guitar sound
106 Winner of a noted 1978 Supreme Court case
107 Comedian Smirnoff
108 Wife of Esau
109 Glandular fever, for short
110 Medea rode on it
111 Kind of suit
115 Done, in Verdun
116 Sleep phenomena
117 Utah city
119 Turn left
120 Fashion inits.
121 Snake ___
122 Alphabetic sequence
124 Actress Massen of "Tokyo Rose"

by Christopher Hurt

ACROSS

1 Cough medicine ingredient
7 Time changes?
12 Finishes
18 Rachmaninoff song, with "The"
19 Earth threatener
21 Attitudinize
22 Duck and dodge
24 Not according to Hoyle
25 He played Bob in "La Bamba"
26 Patois
27 Mexican restaurant entree
29 Part of NATO: Abbr.
30 Coagulation protein
32 Forgets one's lines, e.g.
34 Hunted
35 Marathoner's compliant
38 Book end?
39 Danielle Steel's "Message From ___"
40 Note in the B major scale
42 E'en if
43 Warhol subject
46 Diner offering
49 Receivers of children's "telephones"
51 Last word of the year, often
52 Beamed
54 Wahoos of the A.C.C.
55 Logging-on requirement
56 Baseball V.I.P.'s
57 Mexican beans?
58 "Abdul Abulbul ___" (1927 tune)
59 Cry of pain
60 Hard up
62 Fryolator fill
64 Place for padding or paddling

65 Like clothes at the laundromat
68 Exert pressure (on)
69 Béjart of ballet
71 Some are cheap
72 First name in 60's rock
73 Co-___ (appropriates)
74 "Demian" author
77 Fulfilled
78 1924 gold medal swimmer
81 Cager Longley
82 Without
83 "Meet the Press" host Russert
84 Like punkies, vis-à-vis fleas
85 Kind of cuisine
87 Excalibur, e.g.
90 Minnesota twins?
91 Actresses Eleniak and Alexander
93 Maritime inits.
94 Dutch piano center
95 Bone: Prefix
96 Part of WATS
98 Charging need
100 Soprano Swarthout
102 Celtic Neptune
103 Night: Prefix
104 Bounce
106 Kind of radio
109 Unoccupied
111 Animal of American folklore
115 Went wide of
116 Drain blocker
117 Very detailed
118 Lipton competitor
119 "See ya"
120 Spliced, so to speak

DOWN

1 They, in Calais
2 Scafell ___ (highest point in England)
3 "The Whiffenpoof Song" singers
4 Wine order

5 When Macbeth slays Duncan
6 Chicago hrs.
7 Professor ___
8 Vouchsafe
9 "Make ___!" (captain's order)
10 Legal precedent
11 Trifle
12 Controversial premiere of 1879, with "A"
13 1952 Winter Olympics site
14 When Nancy is hot
15 Tchaikovsky dancers
16 Hot
17 Nice girl?
20 Defaulter's worry
21 A lot
23 Women's groups
28 Giraffes' cousins
31 One with light locks
33 WellCare, for one
34 Start to mature
35 One of the Near Islands
36 XXX, in a way
37 General Mills cereal
39 Twaddle
41 Gig gear
43 Asian capital of 2.6 million
44 Best Supporting Actress of 1992
45 Diminutive suffix
47 Lake of Geneva resort
48 Cutting
50 Old yellers
53 Lincoln in-law
56 Econ. concern
57 Some royal tombs
58 "2001" extras
61 W.W. II gen.
63 Skipped
64 Shot
65 Gone out with
66 Agenda listing
67 Exaggerator's suffix

69 Lawn wrecker
70 "Crystal Silence" jazzman
72 Booed
75 Venn diagram representation
76 Georgia was one: Abbr.
79 Time to give up
80 Highlands tongue
82 Year in Sylvester II's papacy
83 Gustatory sensor
84 So far
86 "We Do Our Part" org.
88 Non's opposite
89 Goes back on one's word
92 Curvilinear
95 Royal fern
96 Poe's middle name
97 "Somewhere in Time" star
99 Rights
100 Beginning, in slang
101 Clinton was one
103 Uncovered
105 Luke Skywalker, e.g.
107 Family troubles
108 Flyspeck
110 Canine command
112 ___ mort (melancholy)
113 325i or Z3
114 Crossed (out)

by Brendan Emmett Quigley

ACROSS

1 Crowning
8 Lawrence Welk favorites
14 Slope sight
18 Kind of case
19 Not set
21 Dynamic beginning
22 "You don't have to cook all night"?
24 The Vamp
25 Angle shape
26 Computerphile
27 Celebrity
29 Guard
32 Nonplussed
34 Corker
35 Cobb and others
36 Get hoary
37 Bender
39 Target
41 Nicotine source
43 Idle question to a bakery chef?
48 Polish
50 Pun-prone poet
51 Jog
52 Bridge section
54 Send all over the place
56 Hurricane or tornado
60 Press one's suit
61 "Our Gang" member
62 ___ strip
65 Jester Jay
66 Lots
68 W.W. II field
69 Decision for newlyweds?
74 Tiny taste
75 Highway ___
77 Fashion designer Schiaparelli
78 Some snares
80 Places for studs
81 Designate
84 Dune
86 Actor Baskin of "Air Force One"
87 Party
89 ___-pointe (ballet position)
90 Branches
94 Develop
96 Jed Clampett, in Beverly Hills?
100 Strict
102 Commercial prefix with vision
103 Be short of
104 It might show its face in Vegas
105 Female gametes
107 Stalk in a swamp
109 Lace part
112 Cleave
114 Zealot
117 Starch tree
118 Singer's syllable
119 Over the bounding main
120 Restrict windfall profits?
126 Break
127 Exhibits fear
128 Dregs
129 The Charleses' canine
130 Expunges
131 Forthcoming

DOWN

1 It's game
2 Plains dweller
3 School org.
4 "Politically Incorrect" host
5 Spotted cats
6 Mild-flavored onion
7 A Turner
8 Whence the phrase "pass the buck"
9 Binge, in a way
10 Neighbor of Syr.
11 Strikeout symbols, in baseball
12 "Forever Your Girl" singer
13 Excellent, in British lingo
14 Checks
15 What maligned celebrities would like to do?
16 Collection
17 Laughs loudly
19 Cattle feed
20 Narrow margin
23 Spitz stroke
28 Gordon or Ginsburg
29 Stooge
30 Turkish leader
31 Some parties
33 1984–88 Olympic skating champ
38 "___ be in England . . ."
40 Plaint at a door
42 French film award
44 Spicy cuisine
45 It's not up to par
46 Expiate
47 Pooh pal
49 Oft-toasted Melba
53 Kunta Kinte's slave name
55 Aristophanes play, with "The"
57 Chops up, in a way
58 Feodor, e.g.
59 Drugstore dispensations
61 Crave, with "over"
62 Haggard of C & W
63 "The Stunt Man" star
64 Loving phrase for a British policeman?
67 Years of Caesar's reign
70 Memory unit
71 Swordsman
72 Good ___
73 Game played for the Thomas Cup
76 Swains
79 King Harald's pre-decessor
82 Ex-wife of Mickey and Frank
83 Old Spanish viceroyalty
85 "The ___ Report" (1976 best seller)
87 Ticket stub, e.g.
88 Kind of moth
91 Harass
92 Eshkol's successor
93 Popeye's ___ Pea
95 Perkins who wrote "Blue Suede Shoes"
97 Washington's Birthday event
98 Infidel
99 Deal with
101 Professor's goal
105 "Butterfield 8" author
106 Wedgwood products
108 Inhibit
110 Passages
111 Hindrances to settlements
113 Equestrian's attire
115 Facts and figures
116 Start of a 1961 nonsense song
121 Small ammo
122 Prefix with angle or athlete
123 "Star Trek: D.S.9" character
124 1980's TV drama "___ House"
125 Born

by Nelson Hardy

ACROSS

1 Son of Zeus
5 Caucus selection
13 Online feature
18 Apple seeds' site
19 Poisonous shrub
20 Spheres
22 Make jerky
23 Hypochondriac?
26 Run out
28 Van Morrison's "___ the Mystic"
29 Oscar winner Kedrova
30 Go right
31 None too brainy
32 Former mile record-holder
33 Magical symbol
36 Christmas leapers, in song
38 Bolt down
39 Pub order
41 Overcast
42 Classroom accessory
43 Like denim
45 Showed fright, in a way
47 Soccer team
48 "Vissi d'arte," e.g.
49 Like the Trojan horse
51 Food stat.
52 D.C. setting
53 Quick-starting worker?
56 American naturalist John
57 Bernie's partner in songwriting
58 Checks
59 Cudgel
60 Jet follower
63 Sibyl
64 North Dakota city
65 Upside-down sleeper
66 Stay near the shore
67 TV adjustment: Abbr.
68 Ottoman, e.g.
69 Late puppeteer Lewis
70 Hyperion, for one
71 x and y
72 Grade-C movies?
74 It may be lent or bent
77 Addr. book entry
78 Dramatists' devices
79 Bartlett's abbr.
80 Water cannon target
82 Colorings
83 Take offense
86 Certain suit
87 Secluded
88 Drop off
90 Clansman's wear
91 Meager
92 Commuter's home, perhaps
94 On
95 Slog
97 Interminable time
98 Eastern royal
100 Some bends
102 Less original
103 Ancient Greek puzzle?
108 ___ libre (poetry style)
109 Deceive
110 Pacific Rim capital
111 Year, on monuments
112 Florists' units
113 Sticky-toed critter
114 "Nana" actress

DOWN

1 Consented
2 Roll of coins
3 Wild-eyed orator?
4 Percolates
5 Fuller construction
6 High priest at Shiloh
7 Multitudinous
8 Took in
9 No-see-um
10 "Later!"
11 Common base
12 Prior to
13 The Three Bears, e.g.
14 Grad student's grilling
15 Queen Elizabeth's daggers?
16 Prefix with sex
17 Everglades evergreen
21 Source of growth
24 Story of a siege
25 Take umbrage at
27 Like Monica Seles, by birth
32 Prompt
34 Block house?
35 Waxed
37 ___ Miss
40 Oil of ___
44 Warmth
45 Not legitimate evidence
46 Bygone request
47 Woodrow's second First Lady
49 Carrion feeders
50 Stew ingredient
51 Snuffy Smith, for one
53 Coordinate
54 It may be on a roll
55 Worthless talk
56 Tiki carvers
59 Hold responsible
60 Unfulfilled potential?
61 First of all
62 Co-star of Mia in "Another Woman"
64 Coke, sometimes
65 Shucks
66 They often brown-bag it
68 Matchmaking industry?
69 Huff
70 Like the little finger
72 Long-time Moore co-star
73 Links rental
74 Takes back the lead?
75 Reduce engine heat, in a way
76 Courts
78 Hokkaido people
81 ___-mile (freight unit)
82 Like locoweed
83 Cavern sight
84 One of the Andrews Sisters
85 1964–65 Wimbledon winner Roy
87 ___ Tomb
88 Raring to go
89 Watering hole
93 European capital
96 They go with the flow
99 Jot
101 Brain area
102 Bunch
104 Singer, of a sort
105 Take steps
106 16-year-old's want
107 401(k) alternative

by John Wolting

ACROSS

1 Political V.I.P.
5 Where roads meet: Abbr.
9 They're full of beans
13 "My Dinner with Andre" playwright
18 "Love Is a Hurtin' Thing" singer
20 Tinny-sounding instrument
21 "He fain would write ___": Browning
23 Jazzman Chick
24 Frequented, as a restaurant
25 Tickle
26 Magna ___
27 Troublemakers, at times
28 Beginning of a quote
32 Speech bobbles
33 Sound barrier breaker, for short
34 Newt
35 Poetic preposition
36 Oft-burned item
37 Nutritional amt.
38 Quote, part 2
45 Mars: Prefix
47 Closing document
48 Do a vet's job
49 That, in Toledo
50 Sudden
52 Hacienda room
54 Some default consequences
58 A fl. oz. contains six
61 Flourless cakes
63 Maryland athlete, for short
65 Pig ___
67 King of old comics
69 Quote, part 3
74 After-dinner offering
75 Two-syllable foot, in poetry
76 Something to pass

77 Old college building feature
80 "Major" animal
82 Quote, part 4
83 ___ avis
85 Guido's high note
86 Capital on the Missouri
88 Hit
92 Sch. subject
93 Quote, part 5
100 Robt. ___
101 Undersides
102 "Cheerio!"
103 Four-time Oscar-winning composer
105 "Puppy Love" singer
107 Don Pasquale and others
109 Schmoozes
111 Strainer
112 Tree decoration
114 Get ___ (access)
117 Snack bar drink
119 Shot up
120 Quote, part 6
128 Thurman of "Henry & June"
129 Strange
130 The New Yorker illustrator Irvin
131 Put in stitches
132 "___ Haw"
135 VCR button: Abbr.
136 End of the quote, and its author
142 1964 role for Audrey
144 Hood of "Our Gang" comedies
145 Threepeater's threepeat
146 Like the sea lion
147 Pass on
148 Kind of mentality
149 Get around
150 Nostalgic, in a way
151 Cha cha cha, e.g.
152 1963 Newman co-star

153 Artist Magritte
154 Rhône's capital

DOWN

1 Unwanted children?
2 Swearing
3 Kind of deal
4 Thick piece
5 Drop abruptly
6 The 45th of 50
7 Political journal since 1865, with "The"
8 Battlement openings
9 Agreement
10 Colorful fish
11 Conductor Antal ___
12 Disagreements
13 Least adequate
14 Doll
15 Main conduit
16 Flake
17 City ESE of Miami
19 Pricey
20 Family room pieces
22 Long-tailed parrot
29 "The Lineup" grp.
30 Golf club part
31 Onetime Davis Cup coach
39 Blood line
40 "Cool!"
41 Lazybones
42 Way-off
43 Pupil protector
44 Register key
45 Hrs. in Halifax
46 Frat letters
51 Trouble
53 Old flatboats
55 Reach on the road, perhaps
56 Unmentioned
57 Convene
59 Investigation
60 The Trojans, for short
62 Record holders?
64 Vatican period

66 Game declaration by Ivana?
88 Stew ingredient
70 Took place
71 Sounds
72 Breaks up
73 Bar orders
77 ___ dixit
78 Quartet member
79 Mideast land
81 Sanctuaries
84 French friend
87 Smell like
89 Applications
90 Medicinal shrub
91 Like some parties
94 Driver's lic. stat
95 Actor Keach
96 Prohibited
97 Fake
98 Untrustworthy, to 60's–70's collegians
99 Split
104 Unfamiliar
106 Urban passages
108 Publicity
110 Washed with lots of water
113 Coach Karolyi
115 Poi, essentially
116 Like a brigadier general
118 "Zip-___-Doo-Dah"
120 Doctors
121 Cheese ___
122 Glib
123 Finishes a book?
124 Hold
125 Access
126 Certain case, in Latin grammar
127 Pet provider
133 Diciembre follower
134 "The Return of the Native" heath
137 Gymnast Korbut
138 Dumbarton denizen
139 Shelley's alma mater
140 Ballet movement
141 Critic Pauline
143 Kill with a click

by Rich Norris

ACROSS

1 Like gazpacho
5 "Pronto!"
9 Put
13 Kindergarten lesson
17 Actress Cheri of "S.N.L."
19 Clouted
20 Cubemaker Rubik
21 College appointment
22 Food for thought?
24 Fair
25 Ares' mother
26 Comparable to a pancake
27 Pain killer?
30 Bakery product
31 Kind of jet
32 Sprang
33 Plea for a TV cop?
40 Clio hopefuls
42 Lead for a Lab
43 Ryan known as "The Ryan Express"
44 Short cut
45 Blacken
48 Tanked (up)
51 Where they tell off-color prayers before meals?
55 Elect
56 Ribs
58 Half of the "Rich Girl" duo, in 70's pop
59 Snake, for one
60 Salted away
62 Famed reproach
63 Springs
64 Julia Child using miso, e.g.?
70 Actress Swenson and others
73 "___ be in England"
74 About which
78 Short wave?
79 Semidiameters
81 Donahue of "Get a Life"
84 Year in Vigilius's papacy
85 Wit in need of washing?
88 Junta, say
90 Faulkner title start
91 They precede kisses
92 "Ivan IV" composer
94 Son of Judah
95 Army refusal
97 Do well as a temptress?
101 One of the King Sisters
103 Lunks
105 Eloise's ilk
106 What one used to do in Kremlin heat?
111 Bribe, informally
114 "Oliver!" choreographer White
115 Picnic pest, in this puzzle?
116 Balding lion's lament?
119 Windows picture
120 Neolith, e.g.
121 Whopper creators
122 Overall stuff
123 Permits
124 "My treat"
125 Kind of child
126 Make over

DOWN

1 Part of an ear
2 ___ cosa (something else)
3 Gamboling places
4 "Up on the Roof" singers, with "the"
5 Bowling alley inits.
6 Remote post?
7 Suffix with symptom
8 See 104-Down
9 Tenant
10 Reason to ask "What's cookin'?"
11 Piece of the Rock
12 Start with step or stop
13 Stick
14 Result of a video viewer's spill?
15 Worries
16 Catch
18 Do parquetry
19 Bank robber Willie
23 Singer Almond or actor Singer
28 Hard wood
29 Extinguishes
33 Things like Audi's rings
34 Customize
35 Spain's ___ Brava
36 Swarms
37 Popular fashion magazine
38 Holstein abode
39 Sum of the parts
41 Stops running
44 Waited (for) until long after dark
46 Bit
47 Merlot, Médoc, etc.
49 Belief system
50 Judge
52 Ancient Germanic invader
53 Pro ___
54 Idaho, slangily
57 Town that's home to Ohio Northern University
61 Honored Hindu
62 Mil. arena abroad
63 Cubic meter
65 Difficult situation
66 Kind of stitch
67 Suffix meaning inflamed
68 Botanical beard
69 Restaurateur Toots
70 Itself, in a Latin phrase
71 New Jersey hoopsters
72 Bad photo of a shoelace problem?
75 Minneapolis suburb
76 "___ River"
77 Ogre
79 Commercial prefix meaning "convenient to use"
80 Worship
81 Release
82 One of Judy Garland's girls
83 Rapper in "Tank Girl"
86 Japanese-American
87 It goes around the middle
89 Light and filmy
93 Chicken choices
96 Large amounts
97 Popular car, again
98 Tempe sch.
99 TV actor Katz
100 Flip
101 Bubbling
102 Thrusting weapon
104 With 8-Down, Asian capital
107 Peace-keeping grp.
108 Town on the Vire
109 Hebrew letter
110 Touchable
112 Compos mentis
113 Lady in Arthurian legend
117 Assay
118 Funnyman Philips

by Cathy Millhauser

ACROSS

1 God "the most merciful"
6 Bird of myth
9 Slanted: Abbr.
13 Blacksmith's tools
18 Prefix with grain
19 Show presenter, for short
20 Pioneering Russian spacecraft series
21 Lawn game
22 Sight off the coast of Salerno
24 Bugs
25 Be creative
26 Spanish weeks
27 Expo '70 host
29 Saw red
30 Last-minute ticket acquirer, maybe
31 "Well done!"
32 Broadly
34 Certain annuity plan
36 1998, e.g., in fancy language
41 Piglike animals
44 Cleveland team, for short
46 Minneapolis-to-Fargo hwy.
47 Man, in old Rome
48 Rock's Burdon and Carmen
49 Transmit via computer
50 Seventh-century date
51 Some porcelain
53 Worker ___
54 Math ratio
55 Orchestra member
58 Gulf of ___ (arm of the Baltic)
59 No longer in enemy hands
62 Heather lands
63 Footnote word
65 A new look at an 18th-century English writer

69 Fabric with nubby yarn
72 First name in stand-up
73 Big name in computer games
77 Like a wayward G.I.
78 Nautical passageway
80 Bustles
82 Mouths
83 "From Here to Eternity" wife
85 Oil driller's setup
86 On again
88 Sing like Bing
90 Non-P.C. suffix
91 Express
93 Institution since 1701
94 Close and Ford
95 Nurses and police officers, e.g.
98 Neighbors of Ethiopians
100 Enemies of the Iroquois
101 Consider, with "over"
103 Kind of set
107 Place to go with a flashlight
110 He coached 347 N.F.L. wins
111 Menu section
112 Like our numbers
113 Apocalypse
114 1773 Tea Party, e.g.
116 Survey respondent
117 Let go of
118 Back muscle, for short
119 TV actress Taylor
120 Jacket choice
121 Sushi supplies
122 Poetic preposition
123 Seconds: Abbr.

DOWN

1 Collect
2 "12 Angry Men" director
3 Pack animal

4 Monopoly avenue next to the B.&O. Railroad
5 Sellers of record players
6 Brownish
7 Sugar ending
8 Feature of classical architecture
9 Kind of artery
10 Bomb
11 "Crazy Love" singer
12 Song syllables
13 Vases of a "La Bohème" character
14 ___ radical
15 Fast shuffle, so to speak
16 Sandwich base
17 Very beginning
21 Item that's often stubbed
23 Composer Saint-___
28 Not a good person with secrets
32 Democrats fight it
33 "___ long . . ."
35 Representation
37 Writer Welty
38 Roundish
39 Forehead feature
40 Source of an omen, maybe
41 Zoom
42 Drury Lane composer of the 1700's
43 The Panthers of the Big East Conference
45 Success for a returning space shuttle
49 "Do you ___?"
52 Target of many a wound
54 1991–92 U.S. Open champ
56 Not streamlined
57 Parts of 69-Down
60 Catlike

61 ___-Tiki
62 Tiny model
64 Casey of County General Hospital
66 Pilgrimage sites
67 Lean
68 Berlin's "___ Lost in His Arms"
69 See 57-Down
70 Soaked
71 Sculpture subjects
74 In a minute
75 Maker of a brand name?
76 Lacking
79 Early wheels
80 O.K.
81 Per ___
84 Insouciant
87 Chart holder
88 The 1990's, politically speaking
89 Vintner's cache
92 William or Henry
94 Sparkle
96 Weak
97 Train
99 Carol starter
102 Mountains, so to speak
104 "Difficult years"
105 Position
106 Met singer Simon
107 Kirk, e.g.: Abbr.
108 Straight, after "in"
109 Low tract
110 Recovering from a charley horse
113 Onetime Presidential inits.
115 Dory feature

by Charles Deber

ACROSS

1 Playwright Norman
7 1943 Bogart film
13 Where suits are put on
20 Colorless ketone
21 Canadiens and Canucks
22 Milieu
23 He should have written "What Makes Sammy Run"
25 TV role for Penny
26 Kind of chance
27 Suffix with human
29 Toot
30 Fork-tailed flier
31 He should have written "Fear of Flying"
35 Handle, as insurance claims
38 Like some heads
39 Explorer Vasco da ___
40 ___ Lobos
43 Sprang
44 Magnate
45 Sight at post offices
47 Robbins and Russert
48 Coach
49 "Yikes!"
51 ___ vie
52 What candles may signify
53 He should have written "Green Eggs and Ham"
56 Social reformer Jacob
57 O.R. workers
58 Erskine Caldwell title character
59 Seaman's description
60 Start
62 Blade attachments
64 Tommy Dorsey's "___ Always You"
65 Seeress
66 Wasted
68 Rancher's enemy
70 Stuffy
72 Frequent direction givers: Abbr.
75 Challenge, metaphorically
76 He should have written "Postcards From the Edge"
79 Certain fighter
80 Many a Gary Cooper pic
82 Canadiens or Canucks
83 Crash locale in "Alive"
84 V-chips block it
85 Strong objections
87 Oodles
88 72-Across recommendation
89 José or Juan
90 Kind of collar
91 Where Jimmy Carter taught after his Presidency
92 Nosebleed seats
93 She should have written "On the Beach"
95 Lorelei Lee's creator
96 Communicate
99 U.S.N.A. grad
100 Piece of dust
104 Gang of Four members
106 He should have written "Arrowsmith"
110 Cabalist
111 Temporarily away
112 More virtuous than thou
113 Common cleanser
114 Eats one's heart out
115 Barbecue offerings

DOWN

1 They report to lt. cols.
2 Reynolds film "Rent-___"
3 Civil War major general Jesse
4 Business undertakings
5 Most popular
6 "Java" man
7 Blab
8 B.T.U. producers
9 Chop down
10 Friend of mon frère
11 Fix some origami
12 Marxlike
13 Disney Store purchase
14 Bart Starr's alma mater
15 Libation
16 Touch up
17 Social misfit
18 Sister of King Arthur
19 Suffix with pun
24 Cape ___
28 Grunt: Vietnam :: ___ : W.W. II
31 Foreknowledge
32 Muscateer?
33 When dark comes o'er the land
34 He was lost in books
35 Hitching post
36 Condescend
37 He should have written "Hotel"
38 1928 hit with the lyric "I'm in heaven when I see you smile"
40 He should have written "Love Story"
41 Song of the past
42 View à la Shakespeare
44 They have their own lines
46 Telephone user
48 Moon of Neptune
49 Fades
50 Square dance partner
53 TV's Peter
54 "Paradise Lost" character
55 Pops, e.g.
61 Over in Germany
63 Coastline feature
64 Mosque V.I.P.
65 Pumps have them
66 Goes to market
67 Miss's accessory
68 Be prophetic
69 John's "Pulp Fiction" partner
70 Hoax
71 Plain-speaking radio talk show host
73 ___-ground missile
74 Ford predecessor
77 Sea ___
78 Little Richard's hometown
81 Mentions
84 It gets a licking
86 On the schedule
87 Wee, to Burns
88 Tree trauma
91 Sect member during the time of Christ
92 Ark contents
93 Ways of walking
94 Benefit from
95 Not in the profession
96 Baby sitter's banes
97 ___ fide (in bad faith)
98 Combine
100 Parker and Waterman
101 Minty Mexican plant
102 Soup vegetable
103 Slips
105 Title for Mrs. Perón
107 Panama City's home: Abbr.
108 Pro
109 Didn't hold

by Randolph Ross

ACROSS

1 They emerge in the spring
8 1997 Peter Fonda title role
12 Haunted house décor
16 Mil. award
19 Reprimander's reading
20 Settled, as a quarrel
22 Explorer of the Canadian Arctic
23 Parent's ploy
25 Sue Grafton's "___ for Alibi"
26 Kind of fire
27 Chemist Remsen, discoverer of saccharin
28 Soupçon
29 Displays displeasure
31 Old-fashioned cold remedy
32 Racer's path
33 W.W. II gen.
34 Ear-piercing pooch
35 Irritate
41 Shepherds' woolen plaids
42 Rhône's capital
43 Chromatin component
44 Overcome utterly
46 God-___
49 Royal irritant of lore
50 Motor-driven
52 Raised-eyebrow remarks
55 1940 John Wayne drama
60 William ___, the Father of Photography
62 Cause for a shootout
63 Red-blooded
64 "___ soit qui mal y pense"
66 Word in four French department names
67 "Momo" author Michael
69 Stand in an atelier
70 Neoprene gasket
72 It's served in shreds
73 More than desires
75 Stuff
76 Ad-lib
78 Dockworker's org.
79 "Sex for Dummies" author
81 Typewriter feature
84 Fed. stipend
85 Mimics 113-Across
87 Appetite
88 "The best ___ to come!"
89 Tre ___ (piano player's direction)
91 More, in Madrid
92 Stephen King's home
95 Creation of Burr Tillstrom
97 Completely mistaken
103 In heaven
105 Sloth, for one
106 Refuse visitors
107 Part of some E-mail addresses
109 "Master of the World" director William
110 Disney's "___ and the Detectives"
112 Hydrocarbon suffix
113 Cloven-hoofed animals
115 Content of some pits
116 Exert oneself to the utmost
120 ___-Manguean (Indian language group)
121 Hypnotized
122 Mideast entity
123 Cyst
124 Cold war force
125 Grand duke's father
126 Like a golf ball

DOWN

1 Receive
2 Disney's Michael
3 Dr. in an H. G. Wells novel
4 Checklist part
5 With 36-Down, like some service uniforms
6 Broomball surface
7 Tried hard
8 College in East Orange, N.J.
9 Ballad
10 Impress clearly
11 Spiny anteater
12 Certain boxer, informally
13 Shogun's capital
14 Classic gangster nickname
15 Surveillance equipment
16 Climbing the corporate ladder
17 Breezed
18 Abbr. preceding multiple surnames
21 1953 movie that shares the name of a Texas town
24 Participates in a vigil, maybe
30 Hydrophane or isopyre
32 "Look here!"
36 See 5-Down
37 Steve of Aerosmith
38 One with pin tales?
39 Picnic pest
40 Part of the Net, for short
45 Indignant, with "up"
46 Sits in on
47 They cant
48 British P.M. during the American Revolution
49 Spanish specie
50 Average American, they say
51 Holding
53 Where Puff frolicked
54 Eisenhower appointee to the Supreme Court
56 Nemesis
57 "___ le roi!" (Bastille cry)
58 "Eight Men Out" star
59 Like peacocks, among all birds
61 Start of many French titles
65 "Splendor in the Grass" screenwriter
68 Part of some E-mail addresses
71 Card player's cry
74 Hutch
77 One of the Power Rangers
80 Cached
82 No-hitter king
83 Certain plaintiff, at law
86 Colonial leader?
90 Actress Lena
91 Little sucker
92 "___ Mrs. Jones" (#1 hit of 1972)
93 Let down, perhaps
94 Contingencies
95 Bow (to)
96 Eastern Christian
98 Familiar with
99 Indonesian island
100 Chief river of British Columbia
101 Not of the cloth
102 Philanthropize
104 Spotted ___
108 Russian politician Alexander
111 "Breezy" star, 1973
113 Thick of things
114 Dr. Johnny Fever's station
117 Adderley of hard bop
118 Victrola mfr.
119 Last words of Little Jack Horner

by Frank Longo

ACROSS

1 Discrimination
6 1967 U.S. clay court champion
10 Divine
15 Two caplets, e.g.
19 Persian Gulf sight
20 Dreadlocks feature
21 Had a row?
22 Party times
23 Mother a pasty vassal?
27 Got on
28 D.C. body
29 Art Deco illustrator
30 Not cultured
31 Sudden burst
32 Deal preceder
34 Cookie ___
37 Not fooled by
38 Prevent from practicing
40 Sots
45 Easily tamed bird
48 Command for D.D.E.
49 Toast topper
51 Poet Thaxter
52 Straw-colored
55 Mother a pane in the backside?
58 Rotten
59 Part of a pilot's plan: Abbr.
60 Big display
61 Computer typesetter
63 Hand holder?
65 Suffix with hotel
66 "Is that a ___?"
70 They're big in boardrooms
71 CD-___
73 "No sirree"
74 City in central Israel
75 Edvard Munch Museum site
76 Scout groups
77 Salty sauce
78 Pontiac classics
80 Whaler's wear
82 Aquarium fish
84 Absorbed, as a cost
85 Record making
86 Mother someone who's really awful?
92 Doings
93 Basketwork fiber
94 Near ___
95 See 17-Down
96 It's often heard on Sun.
97 Crimson
99 Brought (in)
102 Cup part
106 Physicist who pioneered electromagnetism
108 Holliday partner
110 Make over
111 Eats voraciously
115 Ferocity
117 John in court
118 European auto import
119 Mother a small fry?
124 Parodies
125 Bequeath
126 Top-drawer
127 Glide
128 Rock and roll prerequisite
129 Mothering sort
130 Stamina, so to speak
131 Phosphate, e.g.

DOWN

1 Island southeast of Grenada
2 Hand tool that uses compression
3 Like the fox among all beasts
4 Mother too much?
5 Work unit
6 Add
7 More sloping
8 Is down with
9 Follower of Jean?
10 "Ragtime" writer
11 Like many an old bucket
12 Twisted
13 French possessive
14 Draws out
15 Already in Paris
16 Kaput
17 Parts of a 95-Across
18 Ferrara family name
24 Inits. on a rocket
25 Soprano in "Louise"
26 Kind of belt
33 Prize
35 "M*A*S*H" logo, e.g.
36 "Bye!"
39 Lake activity
41 Javits Center architect
42 Cheer at the end of a dance
43 Up to, informally
44 Deplorably poor
46 1970's P.M.
47 Like the Titanic
50 Golf ball position
52 Loose
53 Jessica or Hope
54 Dutch landscapist ___ Mauve
56 Gunfire sound
57 Pack-'em-in children's game
62 Hires, e.g.
64 Cheat on
66 Mother some babblers?
67 Greet warmly at the door
68 First name in westerns
69 Graspers
72 Lots and lots
79 More than forgetful
81 Nothing on the court
82 Hot under the collar
83 Reno and Kennedy, e.g.: Abbr.
86 Tease
87 Soundless communication: Abbr.
88 Four-time Japanese prime minister
89 ___-mo
90 Parade decoration
91 Working, in a way
98 Like antiques at an auction
100 Leg up
101 They have no sting
103 Meaning of two dots and a bar, in music
104 Conceive
105 One that sheds
107 Collector's stash
109 Classify
111 Sign of healing
112 Superhero accessory
113 See 114-Down
114 With 113-Down, a roadside sight
116 List ender
120 Rock's ___ Speedwagon
121 Remained
122 Ground breaker
123 Literary inits.

by Nancy Salomon, Marjorie Richter and Kelly Clark

ACROSS

1 Street boss
6 Exchange activities
12 Russian Revolution figure
19 Enlighten
20 Ushers
21 Longtime magazine subscriber
22 Early Virginia settler
23 The obstetrician had ___
25 Plant with a bitter fruit
27 Pretentious
28 800-year-old work on mythology
29 Nationality suffix
30 -to-be
32 Senator of Watergate fame
36 Fighting force
38 The allergist's monologue drew a ___
44 Legal proceeding, at law
46 Verdun's river
48 Gripes
49 Words before Z
50 A surgeon was the ___
54 Hostess Perle
55 Series opener?
57 Bernhardt contemporary of old theater
58 At the highest development
61 1977 Broadway hit
62 Leaf pore
64 Engine sound
65 Song words before "a rock" and "the walrus"
68 Actor Fernando et al.
69 The gastroenterologist got many ___
71 W.W. II battle site
72 Hoops legend, familiarly

73 Completion of Robt.'s signature
74 Expansion of a sort
75 Hajji's destination
76 Least typical
79 Mark McGwire, e.g.
80 ___ water
81 Miracle worker?
83 The orthopedist went on stage after a ___
88 French links
89 May birthstone
92 "You ___ Beautiful"
93 Beer name since 1889
95 The anesthesiologist's shtick was ___
97 Big name in fashion
100 Engine sound
101 Shed ___
102 Fed. property overseer
105 Mangel-wurzel
108 Prunes, in a way
112 Place for posers?
115 The dermatologist came out with a ___
120 Kind of bean
121 It's a relief
122 Capital of ancient Assyria
123 Following
124 Gretzky and Ewing
125 Get ticked off
126 Rubberneck

DOWN

1 Certain Ford, briefly
2 Dig, so to speak
3 Fictional Marner
4 The cardiologist's routine was a little ___
5 Summit refusal?
6 Tittered
7 Actress Charlotte
8 Swinging, perhaps

9 A lot of bucks
10 Formerly, formerly
11 Frequent fliers
12 Historic beginning
13 Elusive one
14 Singer DiFranco
15 Golf score range, with "the"
16 Knocked out
17 Hardly a hipster
18 "___ Little Tenderness"
20 Carved pillar
24 Tannery employee
26 Get out the tough dirt spots
31 Woman's garment
33 Handle, in a way
34 A Batman before George
35 Words from Caesar
37 With 85-Down, part of Western Sahara
38 Glitch
39 Comparison's middle
40 Calendar abbr.
41 Another surgeon had the audience ___
42 Six-time home run champ
43 Hush-hush D.C. org.
44 Yorn Kippur congregant
45 The podiatrist told a few ___
47 Kind of territory
49 Edgar, e.g.
51 50's failures
52 Small cashews, say
53 Buttermilk's companion
56 Easter fleur
59 Belong
60 Some film ratings
63 Country next to Yugo.
64 Log-towing barge
66 "Jo's Boys" author

67 Deep ditches
69 Wax producer
70 Some reunion gatherers
71 Bit of Indonesian money
75 1949–51 N.B.A. top scorer George
77 Bull's-eye
78 Brand with "churning power"
81 Quagmire
82 Common Latin verb
84 "Bali ___"
85 See 37-Down
86 TV dog
87 To bits
90 Southeastern Conf. team
91 First name at the U.N.
94 The plastic surgeon's humor gave the audience a ___
96 Next
98 Put up
99 Quagmire
101 Grant portrayer
103 Dancer director?
104 Flower with a showy head
105 Bric-a-___
106 Nonchalance
107 One place to get scores
109 Burrows
110 Onetime rival of Bjorn
111 Antler's point
113 They often itemize
114 Upset
116 Valuable rocks
117 Seasonal purchase
118 Switch ups?
119 Time before

by David J. Kahn

"OH, HORRORS!"

ACROSS

1 Esteemed smoke
7 Table linen fabric
13 Calls for Pavarotti
19 Spanish sherry
21 John's "Grease" co-star
22 Nagging pain, perhaps
23 Halloween music?
25 Like the Columbia River
26 Fools
27 "Able was I ___..."
28 Bath item
29 High-powered personality
30 ___ vez (again, in Acapulco)
32 Far from glitzy
34 Athos, to Aramis
35 Halloween pub offerings?
40 Guarantees
44 "Venus" singer
45 Word from a pointer
46 Bret Maverick's brother
48 Dolly ___ of "Hello, Dolly!"
49 ___ Cove, "Murder, She Wrote" locale
50 Part of Caesar's boast
52 Place to sing
53 Lab slide objects, often
55 Burden
56 Halloween event?
59 Spots before your eyes
60 Detroit debacle
63 Kind of bag or chest
64 Deli request
65 Vietnamese New Year
66 Appetizer often eaten with the hands
69 Good party

71 "The Merchant of Venice" maid
73 Play-___
74 Fizzle
75 Place for jewelry
76 Red Bordeaux
77 Giuseppe's God
78 Halloween topic?
82 ___ law (1840's discovery)
86 Foot part
88 Possibilities
89 Brooding sorts
90 Show obeisance
91 Suffix with spinner
92 Classic street liners
94 Mme., abroad
95 Oddball
96 Startup funds?
98 Halloween workers?
101 Laugh, in Lyon
102 ___ Pepper of the L.P.G.A.
105 Break an Xmas rule
106 Irish seaport
108 Tailor's line
109 One-seventh of a semana
110 Money in the news
115 Christmas in Catania
117 Halloween note?
120 Exaggerate
121 Songlike
122 Peak in the skyline
123 Sterile
124 Dreyfus trial locale
125 Solar ___

DOWN

1 Comic's favorite sound
2 One of a Latin trio
3 Part of R.S.V.P.
4 "Rule, Britannia" composer
5 So-so
6 Faulkner's "___ Lay Dying"
7 Capitol feature
8 Porter

9 S. J. Perelman's "The Road to ___"
10 Escapes
11 Move obliquely
12 Danny and Stubby
13 Letters found in underwear
14 Rodeo equipment
15 Football mascot
16 Halloween sprees?
17 Double-curved molding
18 Club ___
20 Distinctive individuals
24 Be rude at the dinner table
31 It's perfect
32 Catty remarks
33 Salt
35 City on the Brazos
36 Wall Streeter Boesky
37 Banned: Var.
38 Expert dealmaker
39 Pat Nixon's maiden name
41 Not going anywhere
42 Gives the slip
43 Sleep time
46 Special Forces trademark
47 Jimmy Stewart syllables
50 Mrs. Marcos of the Philippines
51 Fa follower
52 Bodybuilders' targets
54 Way to go, in Paris
57 Prop for a ball scene
58 Doubleday and Yokum
61 ___ City, oater locale
62 7-Eleven cooler
66 Swirled
67 Explore
68 Halloween correspondent?
69 Kicks

70 Hightails it
72 Like a symbol
76 Gamepieces
79 Cheerleader's characteristic
80 King Cole's fiddlers, e.g.
81 Shade of blue
83 Mainz Mr.
84 Persian's foe
85 Deliberate
87 She had a "Tootsie" role
90 "One Flew Over the Cuckoo's Nest" author
93 A turn-on
94 Be sparing with
95 Fate of Wednesday's child
97 Wagnerian heroine
98 Remain at home
99 Sword-and-sandal flick
100 League members
103 Reason for a spring ceremony
104 Our planet, to the French
106 For whom nothing's good enough
107 Basalt source
109 Goes out, in a way
111 Applies
112 Spellbound
113 Emulate Groucho Marx
114 Appear
116 Ages
118 "The Waste Land" inits.
119 Dolls of the 80's

by Nancy Nicholson Joline

ACROSS

1 ___-Ashbury (hippie district)
7 Native Israelis
13 Hunted
20 Like some sports
21 R-rated
22 Not carried, as a burden
23 Giza resident falsifies travel documents?
26 Sci-fi author Lester ___ Rey
27 Fashion
28 Ragtime dance
29 Garbo's "The Mysterious Lady" co-star
30 Blazing
32 Some platters
34 Spring addressee, for short
35 Fellow fears following strict code of conduct?
44 Sandwiches for dessert
45 Earlier form of a word
46 Mouth part
47 "Slither" star
48 Amigo
50 "Reflections on Ice-breaking" poet
52 Composer Schoenberg
56 History of short-lived indiscretion made public?
61 Certain grace
62 Not 82-Down
63 ___ Tunas, Cuba
64 Comment from the fold
65 Wagner's father-in-law
68 Discovery
70 Decision
72 Jezebel
74 Astonish
75 Wrigley field?
76 Fullest, slangily
77 English Channel feeder
79 Rising star's insecurity eased by weight loss?
87 Imbue with spiritual awareness
88 German coal-producing region
89 Friction reducer
90 Hanks role
92 Some are green
94 Coca-Cola brand
97 Hitchcockian
98 Emcee will never be forgotten?
102 "Hurrah!"
104 Composition of some sheets
105 Number next to a plus sign
106 Drill
109 Where "Otello" premiered
113 Contemporary of Duchamp
114 First private engineering school in the U.S.
117 Hubris alienates devoted comrades?
121 Late riser
122 Like some glances
123 Old Blood and Guts
124 Make an officer
125 Overseas hunt
126 Simon Legree

DOWN

1 Made tracks
2 Seraph of Sèvres
3 Charming scene
4 Elephant group?
5 Open military conflicts
6 Battlefield sorting
7 Application datum: Abbr.
8 If everything goes wrong
9 Hash house
10 Barely done
11 Woodstock gear
12 Part of S.S.S.: Abbr.
13 One with a line
14 Little or young follower
15 Israel's first U.N. delegate
16 Bar staple
17 With 98-Down, Oedipus and Willy Loman
18 Key word
19 Has to do (with)
24 Auel heroine
25 Kruger National Park terrain
31 Designer Simpson
33 Summer ermines
35 Amerind shoe
36 Bahraini, e.g.
37 Imminent
38 German war admiral Karl
39 "___ impressed"
40 It's half the faun
41 P.D. employee
42 Joyful dance
43 Sidi ___, Morocco
48 U.S.M.C. one-striper
49 Clever
51 Campus building
53 Shelley's eyes
54 Pastoral expanses
55 "Saving Private Ryan" reenactment
57 Have a date
58 Syndicate head
59 Cabinet part, briefly
60 Antipasto ingredient
65 Stevedore
66 Cry after a coin flip
67 Witnesses
69 Sitters' headaches
70 Kind of wheel
71 Let go
72 Toots
73 Newly made
75 Ristorante desserts
76 Folkways
78 Montagne's opposite
80 The Wizard's unveiler
81 Emerald and ruby
82 Not 62-Across
83 "The Alienist" author
84 Explorer Amundsen
85 Timothy Leary, to some
86 Desert dignitary
91 Capital of Poland?
93 Shut off
95 1964 Manfred Mann hit
96 Body
97 Contract tactic
98 See 17-Down
99 Medallion meat
100 Best part
101 Transported
102 Old manuscript marks
103 Prepare to check e-mail, perhaps
107 Was at the forum?
108 Faulkner's ___ Rivers
110 Radiator sound
111 Job legislation estab. in 1973
112 From
114 Poet Dove
115 Menial
116 The Platters' "It ___ Right"
118 Canoodle
119 Kamoze of reggae
120 Missive: Abbr.

by Robert Malinow

ACROSS

1 Disagreeable sort
5 Smeltery waste
9 "Shank," in prison lingo
13 Eritrea's capital
19 Colosseo site
20 Word with rush or credit
21 Rock's Mötley ___
22 Conked
23 Valhalla V.I.P.
24 Functioning in all respects
25 Heckle
26 Not at sea
27 Break a tie in a shocking way?
31 Came after
32 1995 earthquake site
33 Occupational suffix
34 News org. founded in 1958
37 Kind of pit
40 Not adhere to promises
43 Land of poetry
44 Shocking 1980 movie sequel?
50 Plant shoot: Var.
51 Rig
52 Tom Sawyer's younger half brother
53 Trump's line
54 Bygone Dodges
56 Boxer-turned-actor Tony
59 ___ Ivory Wayans
61 Ready for publication
63 Ward of "The Fugitive"
65 Vein yields
66 Suffix with meth-
69 Mark the beginning of Lent in a shocking way?
74 Part of CBS: Abbr.
75 Corporate giant named for a mythological character
76 Certain column
77 Restroom wall, often
78 Stomachache reliever, familiarly
80 One on the dark side
83 Ending for most odds
84 Cry at an awards ceremony
87 Clobber
89 Jack of old oaters
91 "No returns"
92 Shocking 1966 song lyric?
97 Foreign title
98 Star in Aquila
99 60's–70's Italian P.M.
100 Prov. east of New Brunswick
101 Apr. addressee
103 Speaker of note
105 Lovelace's "To ___, from Prison"
110 Shocking bank offerings?
116 Old photos
118 Bring into resonance
119 Moonfish
120 Country road features
121 Bit of regret
122 Tennis score
123 Baseballer Martinez
124 End of a fitting phrase
125 Sluggish
126 Schismatic group
127 College major, slangily
128 Towel stitching

DOWN

1 "Time in a Bottle" singer
2 Monster of a 1956 film
3 Screwed up
4 Swahili's language group
5 Iran, once, and others
6 Piercing place
7 Burns title starter
8 Classicist's field
9 Journalists, jocularly
10 Fishermen's spears
11 Autobahn cruiser
12 "It's ___ real!"
13 Heavenward
14 Title for Wences
15 Spree spot
16 White key
17 TV pooch
18 Say further
28 Part of any Verdi composition
29 Heart
30 Sideshow performer
35 Early Brit
36 Black
38 Floored it
39 Blood: Prefix
41 Composer Satie
42 One of the judges in Judges
43 Longtime Israeli ambassador to Washington
44 Opportune
45 Civics, e.g.
46 Pioneer computer
47 Dentist's request
48 Country singer Tubb
49 Deems proper
50 One "C" in C.C.C.
55 Panoramic photos
57 Energy
58 Oriental incense
60 Prior to
62 Chinese discipline
64 Visitor to Siam
66 Melodic pieces
67 Au pair: Var.
68 Beats by a hair
70 Cousin of calypso
71 Like some teas
72 Prefix with -plasty
73 "Half ___ is better . . ."
78 Second in order
79 Make a break for it
81 Styptic pencil stuff
82 Defense acronym
84 It's a deal
85 Beep
86 Land on the Red Sea
88 Like some relationships
90 Unusually long
93 Land under Down Under: Abbr.
94 Blowhole
95 Ripened cheese
96 Hang loose
101 Spin doctor's concern
102 Up
104 Whopped, old-style
106 Holy scroll
107 ___ couture
108 Cry from within
109 Fools
111 Buck's mate
112 Educ. helpers
113 "How ___!"
114 Big story
115 Prefix meaning "one-billionth"
116 N.L. cap monogram
117 Merino mother

by Fred Piscop

33 ON YOUR MARK

ACROSS
1 Make itinerary changes
6 Strip on the Mediterranean
10 Gov. Bush of Florida
13 One of about 2,400,000 in the United States
18 Isn't just given
19 Was in the hole
20 Instrument, in jazz lingo
21 More than whimper
22 Medical resident of 60's TV
24 Rapa ___ (Easter Island)
25 Fruitlessly
26 Café Américain visitor
27 "Later!"
28 Computer ___
30 Run at the curb
31 Honey
32 Vaulters' landing places
33 Charge with a new responsibility
35 Stoolies, at times
37 Make a denial
41 Antiquity, in antiquity
43 What's more
44 Millionths of a meter
45 She played Julie in "Julie," 1956
46 Ploy
48 Suffuses
49 Put on a pedestal
51 Serves
52 Ploy
53 Abuses the throne
54 "La vita nuova" writer
55 Kind of engineer
56 It's a cover-up
57 Some nouns: Abbr.
58 Kelly McGillis's debut film, 1983
62 Diagnostic proc.
65 Furies
66 E-mail option
67 Author Sinclair
72 Service stations?
74 Burlesqued
75 Hanging loose
76 Marauds
77 Emmy-winning Tyson
79 Camp activity
80 "Uncle Vanya" role
81 Muslim generals
82 Natural neckwear
83 Flattens
84 #1 hit of 1956
88 Deli hanger
90 Stay dry
91 Fool
92 They may be split
95 Be visibly elated
98 Deadly nerve gas
99 Leader in Israel
100 Bust ___ (laugh uproariously)
101 Household pest
103 Piece-Arrow contemporary
104 Heroics
106 Vortexes
107 Uris protagonist
108 "___ Mable" (W.W. I best seller)
109 Some kind of a nut
110 Nonrecyclables
111 It may make you see things
112 Corset part
113 Didn't hit the snooze button

DOWN
1 Made over
2 "Harlem Nocturne" composer Hagen
3 #1 hit for the Chordettes
4 Capital since 1923
5 ___ particle
6 Father of modern rocketry
7 Looks for
8 There are two per hundred
9 Fruity drinks
10 Novel published under the alias Currer Bell
11 Growing population areas
12 American University locale
13 Primogeniture beneficiary
14 Mahalia Jackson autobiography
15 "___ no idea!"
16 Drudgery
17 Grind, maybe
21 Flight engineers?
23 Speaks elegiacally
29 ". . . ___ quit!" (ultimatum)
33 Paul Newman's directorial debut
34 Biblical witch's home
36 Padded envelope
37 Attends as a visitor, with "on"
38 Voice lesson topic
39 S and M
40 Sugar suffixes
41 "By gar!"
42 Hot stuff
44 Purple dyes
47 Touch
48 Buyoffs
49 Big name in vegetables
50 "Of course!"
53 Torpedo, in British slang
55 Baseball's Flood and others
56 Holds off
59 Democracy since 1937
60 Lift
61 Fur resembling beaver
62 ___ Park, Calif.
63 Ark's first disembarker
64 Anticipatory exclamation
68 L'Enfant Plaza designer
69 Reprimand
70 City founded by Harald III
71 Loch ___
72 Seven up, e.g.
73 "It's ___!"
75 Long Island university
77 Jeweler Pierre and family
78 Horned lizard, e.g.
82 Hagfish relative
85 Worsts
86 LAX letters
87 Get one's head together?
88 Environmentalists' magazine
89 Piddling
91 December forecast
93 Gussies (up)
94 That's a wrap!
95 Deepened
96 Helen's mother
97 They may be against you
99 Goes on
102 Part of a name
105 Magic org.

by Robert H. Wolfe

ACROSS

1 Superman's father
6 Assess
11 Pang
16 Small ammo
19 ". . . in ___ tree"
20 Absorb the cost, in slang
21 Actor ___ S. Ngor
22 Certain investment, for short
23 Her car broke down
26 Short, for short
27 Horses
28 Hardly flighty
29 Supply
31 Mystical character
32 "___ Girl Like You Loved a Boy Like Me" (old song)
34 Sketch-based TV show, briefly
35 Deep-six
37 Mystic
38 "Whew!"
39 "___ Mio"
41 Amtrak stops: Abbr.
42 He's exploring new terrain
47 Nationality indicator
51 Sweet-sounding Horne
52 Mandela's org.
53 Fizzles out
55 Licks
56 Cats
58 Spiral shell
59 Paper deliverers have them: Abbr.
60 Blink rapidly
61 Time keeper, at times
62 Uses mouthwash
64 Codgers' replies
65 He has mood swings
69 The Everlys' "When Will ___ Loved"
70 Helps with
72 Latin foot

73 Choice words
74 Nightmare
75 Certain sing-along
76 Genetic research aid, often
79 Branch of Islam
80 In the past, in the past
81 "Chuang-tzu" principle
82 Intensity
83 "Stay!"
84 He's gotten carried away
88 Tater
90 Soprano Lehmann
91 Practice
92 Goya subject
96 Yenta's quality
98 "Sleepy Time ___" (1925 song)
101 Speech with a lesson: Abbr.
102 Drafts, maybe
103 Value
104 Unveiling cries
106 Beethoven contemporary
108 ___ Z
109 He's always asleep by midnight
110 Rag
114 Modern cartoon genre
115 Actor Jonathan of "Brazil"
116 Four-time Masters champion, to fans
117 Babe's abode
118 Challenges for college srs.
119 Strained
120 Inspirations

DOWN

1 Comics
2 Unclear
3 Get in sync again
4 Not so strenuous
5 Scientology guru ___ Hubbard
6 Makes a lot of progress

7 What to say to a doctor
8 Sporty trucks, for short
9 Basic ideas
10 Patriot Allen
11 Cousin of plop
12 "Alfie" lyricist David
13 Purge
14 Ballroom dance
15 Everglades bird
16 He has a lawyer
17 Londoner, e.g.
18 They fix locks
24 Longtime Playboy artist LeRoy
25 ___ Olay
30 Entry
33 Low socks
35 Long ___
36 A util.
40 Gambled
42 Classic sports cars
43 The deep
44 Prov. on Hudson Bay
45 What science fiction writers do
46 Trim
47 Made a muff
48 "Let's wait"
49 She likes having children around
50 "___ De-lovely"
54 "Whole" thing
56 Barbara, to friends
57 Charged item
58 Cornfield sounds
60 "Hopalong Cassidy" actor
62 Fit for a King?
63 Prefix with comic
65 African language group
66 Displace
67 Tiny bit, in France
68 Globs
71 Much sought-after author
74 Jollies
76 Admits nothing?

77 Three times, in prescriptions
78 Groovy
79 Golf course purchase, maybe
81 W.B.A. outcomes
83 Timber trouble
85 Author Samuel
86 70's detective series
87 Sent smoke signals, maybe
88 Some sportswear, slangily
89 Tacky note
92 Capital of Lesotho
93 The Coneheads, e.g.
94 Actress Garth
95 Sotto voce remarks
97 Gurkha's home
99 Embrace
100 1944 Preminger film
104 Very, in Vichy
105 Where Archilles was bathed
107 Ersatz
110 ___ Maria
111 Ambulance V.I.P.
112 More than pass

by Nelson Hardy

MONEY CHANGING

ACROSS

1 Classic soft drink
5 Exaggerate
11 L.I.R.R. stops
15 Illustrator Silverstein
19 Wharton grad, maybe
20 ". . . upon receipt ___"
21 First name in mysteries
22 Mata ___
23 Part of the Musketeers' cry
26 Neighbor of Britannia
27 Prefix with sphere
28 1956 Charlton Heston role
29 Expressed
30 Rip off
32 Buffalo
34 Kind of bobsled
36 "See ya!"
37 Troubled capital
41 "'Neath the ___" (Wellesley school song)
42 Refined
44 Sandwich filler
47 Third party label: Abbr.
50 Big blaze
54 1998 Wimbledon winner Novotna
55 Flap, so to speak
56 Stir up
57 Capital built around Kyongbok Palace
58 Less covered
59 Positive
61 Four-time Super Bowl-winning coach
62 1973 Rolling Stones #1 hit
63 Classic whodunit
69 More than brighten
70 Hebrew letters
71 Annoys
72 Places for plants
73 Acidic prefix

75 "Beat it!"
76 "Didn't I tell you?"
77 Lighthouse locale
78 Game requiring no equipment
82 What a mess
83 KFC order
84 Ultimate challenge
85 Judy Garland's real surname
86 Like some cows
87 Suffix with techno-
91 Partner's part, maybe
97 "On the Beach" novelist
98 Starts over
99 Hercules fell in love with her
100 London's ___ Road Studios
104 Make
105 Leaning against
106 It began in 1337
110 Twice tres
111 Farm complaint
112 Second of two
113 ___ point (makes sense)
114 Crosses, e.g.
115 Languishes
116 Deprecatory reactions
117 Saw

DOWN

1 Most fresh
2 Betting option
3 Baseball announcer's phrase
4 I, abroad
5 Cry of horror
6 Side dishes: Abbr.
7 1910's–30's Harper's Bazaar designer
8 Old-time cars
9 Family head
10 Compensate for
11 Part of a letter
12 Traffic
13 Washday brand

14 Identical
15 Polishes
16 Part of some palaces
17 "Steppenwolf" wife
18 Shade of white
24 "The Bottle ___" (Stevenson tale)
25 Klutz
31 Norse god of discord
33 Like some Fr. nouns
34 Back stabber
35 Guffaw
37 Wisconsin city or its college
38 Climatology subject
39 Type spec.
40 Judaism, e.g.: Abbr.
43 "Bad Boys" actor, 1983
44 1930 tariff act co-sponsor
45 Not playing with ___ deck
46 City ESE of Calais
47 Gulfweed
48 Long odds
49 Expressions of love
50 One of the Fates
51 Don Quixote, e.g.
52 As a rule
53 Signs a lease with
54 Girl with a gun, in an Aerosmith song
58 Some people are stuck with them
60 Lord, say
64 Old town on the Hudson River
65 "Two Treatises on Government" writer
66 Cato's clarification
67 Arrival phrase
68 Prepared to hang
74 ___ a time
75 One righting a wrong, perhaps
78 Tries to get by leaping
79 Meridian

80 Shopper's favorite
81 Longing
83 Joke target
85 Rock variety
86 Fishhook attachments
88 Fashion show locale
89 Lounging
90 Foursome
91 Get
92 Richards of tennis fame
93 TV/film actor Mackenzie ___
94 Smiling
95 Dies, with "out"
96 Hunter's quarry
97 Arab League member: Abbr.
100 Starting stake
101 Data amount
102 Tuborg, e.g.
103 Canal sites
107 Latin metropolis
108 Golfer Woosnam
109 That vessel

by Matt Gaffney

ACROSS

1 You can get a grip on it
5 Thunder sound
9 Jitterbug, e.g.
15 Uttered with contempt
19 Filmmaker Wertmüller
20 Mediterranean city known anciently as Ptolemaïs
21 Joe Orton play "Entertaining Mr. ___"
22 Ready, to Shakespeare
23 Medical suffix
24 Feature of some skirts
25 Memoirs of a psychology lab maze builder?
27 Libido
28 Implied
30 Famed aviator
31 Book about gold medalists who dump their spouses?
36 Imitative behavior
37 Quirk
38 Author of "The Female Eunuch"
39 It gave out nos.
40 Television plugs
43 Tale of a frightening encounter with a lion?
51 Persons taking testimony
53 Take in
54 Light-feather filler?
55 Waugh or Guinness
56 Indigo-yielding shrubs
60 Like most fine wines
63 Perennial trouble spot
66 Running a few minutes behind
69 Makeup items
70 Study on anthropoid regimentation?
73 Literally, "way of the gods"
76 "Don't ___ anything!"
77 Twin sister of Apollo
81 Tapioca sources
83 Yellowish brown
85 Individual
86 The Braves: Abbr.
87 Tropical Asian palm
90 Seven-time Orange Bowl champs
93 Story of a Fed. narcotics inspectors' raid on a sauna?
99 Neighbor of Isr.
100 Takes too much
101 When repeated, a 1963 hit
102 Morse code click
104 Mirror ___
107 Confessions of a drag queen?
113 Prying
116 Muscat resident
117 Bird shelter
118 Basic training manual for Marines?
122 Have ___ for
123 Burden
124 Smell ___
125 Least wild
126 "Soap" family name
127 Portend
128 Bill's opponents
129 Compact
130 Cartoonist Drake
131 Harness-racing legend ___ Hanover

DOWN

1 Kind of light
2 Rocket fuel ingredient, for short
3 Florentine : spinach :: lyonnaise : ___
4 Multicolored dog
5 Bit of this and that
6 Razzle-dazzle
7 "If I Were ___ Man"
8 "This isn't worth arguing about!"
9 Brit. award
10 Politician Landon
11 Jean Paul, e.g.
12 Kind of terrier
13 Noun-making suffix
14 College in Portland, Ore.
15 Gap between neurons
16 Military chaplain
17 Tanks and such
18 Wee
26 Disconcert
29 Drive-___
32 It's good to have these about you
33 Fabric name suffix
34 Bonds
35 Big oil supplier
39 First-rate
40 One of TV's Cartwrights
41 Place for a hero
42 Flew
44 A Muse
45 Bank acct. datum
46 Kind of chip
47 Rap's Dr. ___
48 Meter reading
49 Junkie
50 Physics units
52 Vast amounts
57 Breeds, so to speak
58 Parts of a code
59 Solidly built
61 Fluff
62 Activist Davis
64 Records
65 Neighbors of Ukrainians
67 Soprano in "Louise"
68 Misrepresent
71 Like warehouse goods
72 Like a child's drawing of the sun
73 "Get out!"
74 "Hell ___ no fury . . ."
75 Welcome sight after a shipwreck
78 Bryologist's study
79 Blackened
80 Blacken, in a way
82 "Men ___ from Mars . . ."
84 Anchorage-to-Fairbanks dir.
88 Waveless
89 In good time
91 Sheets and pillowcases
92 Air alternative
94 Request on some invitations
95 Gland: Prefix
96 Batman and Robin, e.g.
97 Anti-Nazi leader of W.W. II
98 Stay-at-homes
103 Holder of the highest career batting average in baseball history
104 Alpaca tender
105 Fate, in Greek myth
106 Analyze
107 "This ___ of those things . . ."
108 Bother
109 Santa ___
110 Ten or higher
111 Chopin piece
112 Put back
114 In the past, in the past
115 Duel souvenir
119 Mens ___ (criminal intent)
120 S.F. setting
121 Hog's home

by Marjorie Richter

ACROSS

1 Clog kin
6 Come clean
12 Diner bottle
18 Harangue
19 Carol opening
20 Property receiver
22 Cook on the screen
23 "Three's Company" co-star
24 Harder to plow, perhaps
25 Finish last in a renting contest?
27 Luster on display?
29 This side of
30 Plunge suddenly
32 Thirst quenchers
33 Genealogy word
34 Deseeders
35 Spider-Man creator Lee
36 Have relevance
38 Fools
40 Top gun
41 A nephew of Donald's
42 Beat
43 Commodities exchange area
44 1899 warrior
45 Dodge
46 Breastwork
50 Took wing
53 Panel of tiresome people?
56 Manchurian border river
57 Collegiate starter
58 Seeger of song
59 Witch's place
60 Team number
61 Put away
62 Brand of sauce
63 One of the wealthy
64 Jackson 5 member
65 Bough
66 Sound off
68 Mane area
69 Chairperson?
70 Abu Dhabi bigwig
71 Ship perfume?
73 Many chords
74 Rally
76 Bob in the Olympics
77 "The Grapes of Wrath" name
78 Alliance for Progress grp.
79 Sound of a step
81 Rein in
82 It ends in Oct.
85 U.S. Open champ, 1985–87
88 Roger Rabbit et al.
89 Suffers
90 Builder's choice
91 Profitable extraction
92 Sectional
93 Recipe verb
95 Orbital point
96 Bridge-support combine?
100 Payoffs to chart makers?
102 Nominal
103 Self-important sort
105 Fit for farming
106 Another
107 Undivided
108 Stirred up
109 Searches blindly
110 Become whole again
111 Two of Henry's six

DOWN

1 Containing element #34
2 Daughter of Minos
3 Chorus section
4 Significant person?
5 Shade of blue
6 Remote
7 Inventor of the stock ticker
8 Scrap
9 J.F.K. arrival
10 Western tribe
11 As the case may be
12 1974 Oscar winner
13 Bitter drug
14 Castilian kinsmen
15 Genesis son
16 Workers' protectors
17 Little fellow
18 Source of caviar
21 Sea flock
26 $C_4H_8O_2$, e.g.
28 Groundless
31 VCR button
35 Sought damages
37 Annapolis frosh
38 Go public with
39 Remain sober?
41 Groundbreaking person
42 Like Galahad
43 Sky pilot
44 Group of beer drinkers?
45 On the portly side
46 Put to the test
47 Ornamental film
48 On a high
49 After-class aides
50 St. Louis Browns Hall-of-Famer
51 In installments
52 Kind of clock
53 Get one's feet wet
54 Present
55 Go with the flow
58 Origami supply
62 Tournament flora
67 City in the Ruhr
68 Can't do without
69 Grumbler
72 Phylum subdivision
73 Rocky peaks
75 Batman after Michael
77 Dixie drink
79 Hot and sour soup ingredient
80 Oven pan
81 Stronghold
82 Put out of commission
83 Represses
84 No longer green
85 Numbers game
86 Astray
87 Like "it"
88 Australia's ___ Strait
89 Sky lights
90 Turn badly?
92 It may be blank
94 Longhorn's rival
95 Soil sci.
97 Japanese sport
98 Hardly haute cuisine
99 Point at the dinner table?
101 ___-kiri
104 Nonacademic degree

by Richard Silvestri

ACROSS

1 Actress Valli of "The Third Man"
6 New York, e.g.
13 Feeling
18 Noisy bed-partner
19 Smallest of HOMES
20 Wedding march skipper
21 Start of a verse
24 Kind of witness
25 Fam. member
26 Certifies
27 Nasty biter
28 "Give the dog ___"
30 Fellows
31 Relishes
35 Prepared to propose, perhaps
36 Brit. W.W. II heroes
37 "___ Want for Christmas"
41 Ooze
42 Tops
43 Antitoxins
44 Not bare
45 Part 2 of the verse
51 Directional suffix
52 Pulitzer-winning writer Sheehan
53 Hose woes
54 11th-century cathedral city
55 Punish, in a way, as a student
57 Florence's ___ Palace
58 Baker's supply
59 Storehouse
62 South African antelopes
65 Put through a furnace
68 "The Violent Land" author
70 "___ Dance" (Grieg favorite)
74 Hut
75 Give a mighty blow
76 Composer ___ Carlo Menotti
77 Doña ___, "The Violent Land" lady
78 Part 3 of the verse
83 Edge of a rampart
84 Tolkien tree-men
85 Pike
86 Garlands
87 Regarding
88 "Yay!"
89 Prepare, in a way
91 Jinx
93 Like Falstaff
94 Praying figure
95 Apiece
96 Former "S.N.L." comic
100 Bump's place
101 Portended
105 End of the verse
110 To Shakespeare he was "high in all the people's hearts"
111 Smashed
112 Bear up under
113 Jardin zoologique inhabitants
114 False names
115 ___-Prayer

DOWN

1 Pilaster
2 Like Lucy Locket's pocket
3 "Dies ___"
4 Florida beach name
5 Actor George of "Disraeli"
6 Sully
7 H.S. class
8 Olympics entrant: Abbr.
9 Pound a beat
10 Get fixed
11 Rob
12 French pronoun
13 Coagulates
14 ___ Sound, Fla.
15 Work
16 Leftovers
17 W.C.T.U. members
18 Actor Alastair
20 "Anything for You" singer Gloria
22 Sound at the door
23 George of "Route 66"
28 Part of A.D.
29 [Out of my way!]
31 ___ Park
32 1940's–60's world leader
33 Informal wear
34 Go (for)
35 Schroeder's predecessor as chancellor
36 Jackson known as "Mr. October"
37 Most sore
38 Fine fleece
39 Lollygags
40 Phrase of explanation
42 Top of a platter
43 Scythe handle
46 In a sluggish way
47 Department store department
48 Fraternity letter
49 Musical vamp
50 Whatever
56 Site of a 1943 Allied victory
57 Academy head
60 Super Bowl III hero
61 Awry
63 Puppeteer Bil
64 ___ even keel
65 Queen's land
66 Chess log
67 Flip, in a way
69 Easy chair site
71 Flattened
72 W.W. II beachhead
73 Word
75 A.L.'er until 1960
76 Trans-Pacific stopping point
79 Celestial beings
80 Flatten
81 Binge
82 Worldwide workers' grp.
89 Blue ___
90 Scrappy fellow?
91 Like shoes
92 Nicholas III's family name
93 Zero in (on)
94 "Sunset Boulevard" actress Nancy
95 Experienced
96 Soft drink Mr. ___
97 Regarding
98 Porn
99 Biological suffix
101 Academic types
102 "___ pinch of salt . . ."
103 Frenchman
104 It begins "In the first year of Cyrus . . ."
105 Not a grade to be proud of
107 Call ___ day
108 Rita Hayworth's Khan
109 Relig. school

by Frances Hansen

ACROSS
1 Clown's supply
5 Tore
9 Border
13 Comedian's supply
18 Part of F.D.R.: Abbr.
19 "Your ___"
20 Sewed up
21 Root of government
22 Pest-removal word?
24 Scott Turow book
25 Molasses cookie
27 Practice area, of a kind
30 Sound for Old MacDonald
31 Lansing-to-Flint dir.
32 Safari sight
33 R.&B./jazz singer James
34 One abroad
35 Still-life subject
36 Hipsters
38 Gum predecessor
41 Tanning lotion abbr.
44 Found a new tenant for
46 Richie's dad, to the Fonz
47 Extremely easy shot
51 Applied, as a patch
53 Come to
56 George Sand, for one
57 Worth
58 "The wicked flee when ___ pursueth": Proverbs
60 Give out
62 Augur
63 During the knight-time?
65 Inn crowd
66 "Human Concretion" sculptor
67 Stiff, hot drink
71 President Madison: Abbr.
73 Drive off

76 How some papers are presented
77 Item for a Mexican pot?
78 Only insects that can turn their heads to look behind them
80 In ___ (unborn)
81 Some shirts
82 Climber's spike
83 Acts frugally
85 Tea source
88 Stall call
89 Black civil rights org. since 1912
90 Well-wisher's word
91 Col. in a profit-and-loss statement
92 "Nashville" actress
97 Narc's find
99 Certain rainwear
102 Much-used
103 Dept. of Labor division
104 Not too swift
107 With 112-Down, a pale shade
108 1930's comics girl
109 One of six, usually
113 Winter Olympics event
116 Madre's baby
117 ___-toothed
118 One who pulls strings
119 Triple-edged sword
120 They may be put on pedestals
121 Keyboardist Hess
122 Give rise to
123 Origin
124 Jr.'s exam
125 Stratagem

DOWN
1 Puff
2 Provoke
3 Circumference
4 Interference
5 Alert subject
6 "Turandot" tenor

7 Conquest of 5/29/53
8 Erase
9 Military communications expert
10 Here, in Le Havre
11 Condemned publicly
12 Trim
13 Ding-a-ling
14 Two-time U.S. Open winner
15 Strength
16 Clan chief of old Scotland
17 Extremely
23 Source of many calls
26 Sufficient, in verse
28 Written down
29 In-flight P.A. announcement
35 Prolonged separations
37 Pavement caution
39 Trouble
40 Yawning
41 1928 movie subtitled "The King of the Beasts"
42 Doom
43 Subject of numerous 70's lawsuits
45 Lassitude
48 Lamb chops accompanier
49 Chief who negotiated peace with the Pilgrims
50 Language ending
52 Never, in Nuremberg
53 Oriental nurse
54 "O Babylon!" playwright Derek
55 Actor Bruce
59 Some E.R. cases
61 Chop ___
63 Cries of disgust
64 Gardner and others

68 Vein pursuits
69 Partner of away
70 Flying group
72 1960 Everly Brothers hit
74 They have big bills
75 One of an old threesome
77 Person in a race
78 AWOL pursuers
79 Fire hose water source
80 Open
81 Granules
84 Like Brahms's Piano Trio No. 1
86 Perfect
87 Hotel force
90 Some Olympians
93 Capacity
94 Runs off (with)
95 Sun Devils' sch.
96 "Don't be discouraged"
98 Artery connection
99 Caravel features
100 Invite, as to one's apartment
101 20th anniversary symbol
105 Soothsayer
106 When the año nuevo begins
108 Squander
110 Ballerina Pavlova
111 Scorer's mark
112 See 107-Across
114 Marlowe's "The ___ of Malta"
115 Wedding page word

by Rich Norris

40 PROVERBIAL CONFLICTS

ACROSS

1 They're seen at going-away parties
6 Cuba or Mallorca
10 It may be dominant
15 Word of possibility
18 Jacques's pen pals, maybe
19 Envelope closer
21 1945 newsmaking site
22 Some Latin, for lovers
23 An eye for an eye, but also . . .
26 Avian chatterer
27 Kind of prof.
28 Cannes cleric
29 Little hoppers
30 Long woven scarf
32 Verdi's "Caro nome," e.g.
34 Theater souvenir
35 Works of 103-Down
36 Good things come in small packages, but also . . .
42 When doubled, a Washington city
43 ___-eyed
44 Comet, e.g.
48 UFO crew
50 Took off
52 Moravian, e.g.
53 1959 pop/folk hit
54 "___ had it!"
55 Two's company, three's a crowd, but also . . .
60 Title role for Jodie Foster
62 N.C.A.A.'s Cavaliers
63 Narrow way
64 Mount
65 The squeaky wheel gets the grease, but also . . .
72 Intangible qualities
75 Set the pace
76 Last names separator
77 Crafty
81 Don't judge a book by its cover, but also . . .
88 "Have some"
89 Mekong native
90 Kind of cloth
91 Per ___
92 Lake Michigan port
94 Old-fashioned
97 Like earnings in some reports
99 Ones getting a licking?
100 Do unto others as you would have others do unto you, but also . . .
105 Tolerates
108 Farm females
109 Do, say
110 Screen blinker
111 Foreign attire
112 Kind of center
114 Parts of a military defense
118 Temper
119 He who hesitates is lost, but also . . .
123 Snort
124 Big flop
125 Lady's beau
126 Ice station attire
127 Figured out
128 Not so nice
129 Choice word
130 Faint

DOWN

1 Going away statement
2 Easily tamed birds
3 Affectation
4 Like an attractive apartment
5 Euroflier
6 First aid equipment
7 Pig
8 Delayed
9 Lucky tip?
10 Tommy Lee Jones portrayal, 1994
11 Encouraging sounds
12 Bass ___
13 Like most cable news programs
14 Break
15 Kind of party
16 Blow away
17 They can sleep while you watch
20 Australian port
24 Reagan Secretary of State
25 Rake
31 Shuttlecock
33 Gleeful
34 Wrangler's concern
35 Miff
36 The Finn man
37 Bisect
38 First name in architecture
39 Jenna of TV's "Dharma and Greg"
40 Hershey brand
41 Contemporary of Agatha
45 Gulf leader
46 Part of French "to be"
47 Unusually excellent
49 Rebbe's locale
51 Put down
52 Chase flies
56 Joanne Woodward Oscar-winning role
57 Carol contraction
58 Letters in a line score
59 Gossipy Barrett
61 Professional school hurdle: Abbr.
66 Sorta: Suffix
67 Kinsmen
68 "A rat!"
69 Like a certain band
70 Polish sci-fi author
71 Valuable
72 First Amendment lobbyists, for short
73 ___ Bator
74 Latitude
78 Maria Cristina, for one
79 Beats badly
80 1950's trial
82 What juice comes out of
83 Tender spots
84 Merciless one
85 Spats
86 Port opening
87 "Stille ___" (Christmas carol)
93 Side order
95 Till fill
96 Radio antennas
98 Attic pic
101 With convenience
102 Days of old
103 "A Modest Proposal" writer
104 Two-star
105 Serving well
106 Cabinet item
107 Inched
111 TV listings
112 Asia's ___ Sea
113 Sleep phenomena
115 Designed for flight
116 Certain shark
117 Farm team
120 Sugar suffix
121 Tramload
122 Raises

by Randolph Ross

ACROSS

1 Question for Poirot
4 Do away with
9 Twinges
14 Braces
18 His greeting at the Vatican
20 ___ Gay
21 1914 battle site
22 With 115-Across, his protest about always being quoted
24 Elève's place
25 Demand at a breakup
26 "I'll get right ___!"
27 Valuable Scrabble tile
28 Some TV's
29 Sight from Messina
30 Scale notes
32 Idle talk, so to speak
34 ___-you-please (not tied down)
36 Skedaddle
37 Clangor
38 It pours but doesn't rain
39 With 68- and 97-Across, his comment while driving to Cooperstown
41 Alphabet trio
42 It makes a racket
44 Real estate account
45 Site of ancient Miletus
48 With 86-Across, his query after a sudden downpour
50 Group of notes sung on one syllable
52 Old Eur. conflict
54 Punt, for one
55 747 letters
57 Old hat
58 Carbolic acid
60 Rope with a loop
64 El océano, por ejemplo

66 "There you ___"
67 Radiation dosage
68 See 39-Across
71 Folks
72 ___ treadmill
73 "Star Wars" lovely
74 Cola choice
75 Make gloomy
77 After-theater destination?
79 Year of Clovis I's death
81 Suffix with refer
83 O.T. book
84 How some warnings are given
86 See 48-Across
91 Put on
92 Centers of interest
93 Foppish
96 Green
97 See 39-Across
99 Crackerjack
101 Devil's end?
102 Road warning
103 It may be grand
104 That girl in "That Girl"
105 Baseball's Master Melvin
106 Quash
107 Cabaret band
109 Draw from
111 Word before house or hall
113 Big troublemaker
114 Light ___
115 See 22-Across
119 Small change
120 Network, e.g.
121 Source of all the quotes in this puzzle
122 Ice cream brand
123 Gray shade
124 High-hatters
125 "Let's do it!"

DOWN

1 Passed, with "away"
2 Inquisition target
3 1992 David Mamet play

4 Flounder's cousin
5 Mil. rank
6 Mr. Rogers
7 Swept hairstyles
8 60's event
9 One of five rulers
10 Farm worker
11 Plane part
12 Major shipbuilding city
13 Dicta
14 Sonora snack
15 See 53-Down
16 His reaction to the election of a Jewish mayor in Dublin
17 Follows through on
19 Hot issue
21 Imbroglio
23 Word in many magazine titles
30 Loyal
31 Emcee's forte
33 Hospital supplies
35 Play to ___
38 Critic's pan
39 Certain terrier, informally
40 1990's Senate leader
43 Double
46 Senescence
47 Peeples of TV's "Fame"
49 Auricular problem
50 Early stargazers?
51 Make ___ in
52 What he liked best about school
53 With 15-Down, his take on why the Yankees lost the 1960 World Series
56 Kind of hours
58 Can. divisions
59 Geometric figure
61 Klee contemporary
62 Driver's helper?
63 Concert prop
65 Opposite of ham
69 Clean (up)
70 In ___ (somehow)

76 Hendrix of 60's rock
78 Horse-and-buggy ___
80 Sewed up
82 Uncommon major
85 Big name in construction
87 Numerical prefix
88 Trapper John's last name
89 Answer to an accusation, maybe
90 Copland's "Symphonic ___"
92 Brno is its principal city
94 Low-cal
95 "Steps in Time" autobiographer
96 Slip away
98 Beat at dinner
101 Civics, e.g.
103 Sir Robert Peel, notably
105 Reason for tears?
106 Still life subject
108 Containers
110 Mountainous land
112 Explanations
113 They're all in the family
116 Elephant fan: Abbr.
117 Vietnam's ___ Dinh Diem
118 Male cat

by David J. Kahn

ACROSS

1 Where Hawthorne wrote "The Scarlet Letter"
6 Verve
10 Crackers
14 Bacillus shapes
18 Blazing
19 Food fish, in scientific names
21 "My Brother ___" (Grateful Dead song)
22 The wrong stuff
23 Pecking order?
25 Money order?
27 Dynamo's pivot
28 Team coached by Bud Grant for 17 years
30 Coordinated, in a way
31 Function
33 Rare sports result
34 Bad reception?
35 Alphabetical order?
42 Litmus is one kind
43 On the main
44 Red shade
45 Disconnected
47 Skewer
48 Che cohort
49 Reverent
50 Abbr. concerning the holy or "potholy"
53 Difficult position
55 Batting order?
59 Waxed
61 Split
62 Dozer's spot
63 Cry at an old-fashioned battle
67 Tick off
70 Headed north, by Northwest
72 Interlaken's river
73 Snowfall
74 Agitate
76 Back order?
82 Sagebrush State native
87 Kind of cozy
88 Bubbling on the stove
89 Tree thicket
91 Moth with translucent spots on its wings
92 Red flag
93 It's deadly for Bardot
95 Skip
96 Aura
98 Benedictine order?
102 They hold cones
104 Had a cone
105 Not orig.
106 Regard
107 Neighbor of the larynx
110 Impresario
115 Side order?
117 Suborder?
119 Poop out
120 It's often on the house
121 Pioneer in calculus
122 Levels
123 Returned MS holder
124 Many ages
125 Encouraging
126 Squirreled supply

DOWN

1 New York merchant Horace
2 Throw ___ (go ballistic)
3 One of the Simpsons
4 Word with while
5 Computer buyer's concern
6 Atty.'s title
7 Like some vents
8 Et ___
9 Guitar part
10 Implored
11 One way to buy an item
12 McDonald's lid?
13 Tree with tiny red berries
14 Cultivated
15 Cheviots and merinos
16 Strip (of)
17 One-way transports?
20 Japanese pooches
24 Switch suffix
26 Antidemocratic belief
29 Mozart's age, when he wrote his Fifth Symphony
32 DuPont brand
34 "The fault, dear Brutus, ___ in our stars"
35 Beer-brewing mixture
36 Analogy words
37 Shipshape
38 Cotton ball applications
39 P.M. counterpart
40 Countryside cylinder
41 Proverbial loser
46 Decimal starter
48 Meter reading, maybe
49 Wrestling falls
50 White stuff
51 Protein source
52 Pull a switch
54 Word with drop or roll
56 El Greco's homeland
57 Football Hall-of-Famer Strong
58 Suffix with computer
60 Glen Campbell title city
63 Shed
64 Crime motivation
65 Suburbia, e.g.
66 Public image, for short
68 Winter air
69 Eclipse, for one
70 Make tracks
71 O.T. book
75 Line of clothing
77 Equipped à la raptors
78 U.K. award
79 Melodious Mel
80 Opera opener
81 Horse color
83 Big baseball surname
84 Half-witted
85 Dye source
86 Hoopster Archibald
90 Cluster in Taurus
92 Property recipient, at law
93 Greek salad ingredient
94 Old Hollywood star with a mustache
96 Hearth goddess
97 Essential oils
99 Black and Valentine
100 Rooftop fixture
101 Water rompers
102 Leans (on)
103 Stroll
107 Certain Fed
108 Time
109 Cockney greeting
111 Latin learner's verb
112 One of the five chief cities of the Philistines
113 Regards
114 Hebrew "beginning"
116 ___-hoo
118 Venture

by Cathy Millhauser

43 CROSS WORD PUZZLE

ACROSS

1 Jumble
5 Gut feeling?
10 Put one past?
14 70's–80's Mercury
19 ___ Rios (Jamaican resort)
20 Cole Porter title city
21 Rumble
22 Ethical Culture Society founder Felix
23 Certain corner square
26 Noted 60's radical
27 First name in horror
28 Stopping points
29 "Darn ___!"
30 Tree that sprouts roots from its branches
31 Actress Bergman
33 "Popeye" creator
35 Brit. honor
37 ___ Accords (1998 peace agreement)
38 Nabors role
39 Stock holder?
41 Staple Le Carré feature
45 Sense-ability
47 Dun
49 "___ a borrower . . ."
50 Tanker
52 Blind as ___
55 Booty
58 Part
61 Quickly, mailwise
63 Einstein, e.g.
64 Least suave
65 Roller
67 Hoodwink
68 Horsefeathers
69 Lenten treat
74 Family members
75 Handy
78 Makeshift punishment device
79 Yasir Arafat, originally
82 Teens, e.g.
84 Standard axes
86 Targets appear on them
87 More awesome
89 Santa ___
90 Sites for dates
91 Blew a gasket
93 Rhein port
95 Went downhill fast
99 Bit of embroidery
103 T.G.I.F. party request
105 Salinger orphan
106 Atmospheric beginning
107 Enzyme suffix
108 Holdover
110 All eyes
112 Part of a Shriner's attire
115 Cousin of a raccoon
117 Gossipy Barrett
119 Forest female
120 Subject of strike talks
121 Write something, even if not the final draft
124 Arrowsmith's wife
125 Collectible illustrator
126 "Who can that be?" response
127 Fuss
128 Cedric ___ of "Little Lord Fauntleroy"
129 Those caballeros
130 "The Entry of Christ into Brussels" artist
131 Hospital work

DOWN

1 Nickname for a good kisser
2 NATO, e.g.
3 Roof, in a way
4 Proceed on one leg
5 Flips
6 Court material
7 Military danger
8 Literary contraction
9 Do further archeological work
10 Jockey who won 17 Triple Crown races
11 Hip
12 Ring locale
13 Dr. of rap
14 Castro calls it home
15 Gulf port
16 Not speak seriously
17 Communications satellites
18 Actress Papas and others
24 Year in the apostle Paul's travels
25 Native village, in South Africa
30 Retro car
32 Range order
34 Apodes member
36 Radar sighting
40 Partner-in-crime
42 Frees
43 Cronies
44 Kidney enzyme
46 Italian cabbage
48 Photo ___
51 Flog
53 "Peace be with you" and others
54 Sounds from the masseur's room
56 Wandering
57 Like some pieces
58 Rugby formations
59 Alluring
60 Back
62 Union opposer
66 Notorious 30's–40's criminal
70 It comes in black and white
71 Bordeaux output
72 Harrah's locale
73 Turner and others
76 Oral traditions
77 TV's Gray and Moran
80 Réunion and others
81 Daredevil
83 Attacks
85 Blab
86 Bob Cousy's alma mater
88 "Phooey!"
92 Garment workers
94 It's a wrap
96 1960 dance biography
97 Authorize
98 1970's policy
99 Actress Lombard
100 High provider
101 Jalopies
102 The "H" in Hanukkah
104 Toot
109 Feudal lord
111 "Emerald Point ___" of 80's TV
113 "My ___!"
114 Shrinking sea
116 Comics canine
118 Hydrox competitor
121 Cousin of "hmmm!"
122 Took the title
123 Mil. pilot's award

by Robert Malinow

44 GAINING WEIGHT

ACROSS

1 Gold count
7 Calif. daily
14 See 17-Down
19 Mark of a ruler
21 Upset and then some
22 Dreadlocks sporter, for short
23 Take the algae out for a stroll?
25 Lord's attendant
26 Public transport
27 "Rah!"
28 "And this is the thanks ___?"
29 Ax politely
31 Penta plus three
32 Juan-___-Pins (Riviera resort)
33 Sports trophy since 1927
35 Sapporo sash
36 A question of timing
37 Pants problems
39 It has shoulders
40 Trading partner of ancient Tyre
41 Vandalize part of Ohio?
45 Weight lifter
46 Annual TV event, with "the"
50 "You have to see this!"
51 Is worthwhile
52 Fate
53 Pin spots?
55 It comes with sections
58 1958 movie chiller, with "The"
59 Standard varieties
60 Old magazine billed as "America's Aviation Weekly"
63 Introverts
64 Deviation
65 Our church's blond caretaker?
68 Aqueous
69 Lazybones's declaration
71 ___ point (never)
72 Corp. magnates
73 State of the union
74 Buyer, in a phrase
75 Solderer's activity
77 Text
78 Singer Coolidge
79 Confessional account of a sensational nature
81 Naval position
82 Twinkle-toed
84 Abide a W.W. II general?
87 It doesn't get far from home
88 Color of the Seine
89 Flying ___
90 What tots are taught
94 Blink of an eye
95 Liqueur brand
99 Nothing at all
100 Excoriate
101 One way to pitch
103 "The Joy of Cooking" writer Rombauer
104 Motor attachment?
105 Cross
106 Like movies
107 Storage spot for a midget?
111 Across-the-board
112 Holds one's interest
113 Fiasco
114 Scotsman's nickname
115 Bacon servings
116 Pass along greetings

DOWN

1 Bow (to)
2 Old-style revolutionary
3 Empathize
4 1993 Super Bowl M.V.P.
5 Big bang maker
6 Research types
7 Wee
8 Have ___ of (display)
9 Lemon-flavored, maybe
10 Upset
11 Concern
12 It may block a compromise
13 Like many classical aphorisms
14 Fathom
15 Kind of shift
16 Equal to Isaac?
17 With 14-Across, certain crystal
18 Brie base
20 Its main street marks Last Chance Gulch
24 Flies or gadflies
30 Sch. meeting room
34 Fleece
38 Patronizes
40 Indo-European speaker
41 Choral syllable
42 With 83-Down, "new socialist man" advocate
43 Everywhere
44 Nuzzles or nozzles
45 "An American in Paris" co-star, 1951
46 "No problem here"
47 Bow
48 Give top honors in New Jersey?
49 Diplomat: Abbr.
51 Pullovers
53 Go flat?
54 Class of submarines
56 Launderer's challenge
57 Purim honoree
59 "Butterfield 8" author
61 Carnegie Hall event
62 Team components
65 Government issue
66 Just for laughs
67 Dress (up)
70 Inclined
73 Coffee maker
76 Small intake
77 "Miró, Miró, on the wall," e.g.
79 Particular
80 Kindergarteners' art, e.g.
81 Succeed
82 Takes in
83 See 42-Down
84 Stir
85 Verdi's Alfredo Germont, e.g.
86 Followed
88 Cold call?
90 Fracas
91 Measles mark
92 King of 70's pop
93 2000 Olympics site
95 1941 #1 Sammy Kaye hit
96 Whom King David sent to be killed in battle
97 Campaign concern
98 Faster's opposite
102 Pored over
108 "___ moment"
109 Naval letters
110 Denver Nuggets' orig. league

by Manny Nosowsky

45 HIDDEN ZOO

ACROSS
1 El ___
6 It helps you see plays
11 N.L. batting champ, 1964, '65 and '67
19 Dish sometimes served with bacon
20 Kind of roll
21 House style
22 Active again
24 Way out, computerwise
25 Kind of strength
26 It won't hold water
28 Odd cat
29 Figure of Arthurian legend
30 Strains
32 ___ ha-Shanah
35 La Fenice productions
38 Wrap
40 Somerset Maugham's "___ Betters"
43 Raillery
45 Diner owner in "Beverly Hills 90210"
46 One of the newly rich
50 Eur. nation
51 North Carolina county named for a Revolutionary War commander
53 "A Doll's House" wife
54 Peak resort time
56 Twos in the news
58 Ring-shaped
61 ___-high
62 They're done for tests
63 Describe
65 Persian Gulf emirate
67 Cross out
69 Korean autos
70 Bon mot
73 Pop's Celine ___

74 Gave a rest
77 "Beloved" director, 1998
78 Woman's shoe
81 Synthetic fiber
82 Some TV drama sets
85 Pan-fry
87 Peels
88 Much-discussed sociopolitical phenomenon
90 Like the White Rabbit
92 Movie following, maybe
93 Pennsylvania ___
94 Legendary fashion editor
99 Scottish river known for its salmon fishing
100 1986–87 Mets All-Star Fernandez
101 N.Y. Knicks venue
102 Some dummies
103 Sunken ship explorers
105 Trading letters
108 Raised
110 "Hand it over!"
111 Holidays overseas
114 Kind of manual
116 Unremarkable either way
120 Settle
124 Place to crouch
126 Member
127 "A Passage to India" woman ___ Quested
128 "The House of Blue Leaves" playwright
129 Cry of disagreement
130 Arrested
131 Satisfactory marks

DOWN
1 Superabundance
2 Ready
3 Sen. Bayh
4 Church vessel

5 Second, e.g.
6 Scintilla
7 John of London
8 Cross to bear
9 Keep track of
10 Hospital figure
11 Hospital amts.
12 Unglued
13 Dash
14 Melancholiac
15 Calendario part
16 Suffix with neat
17 ___ kwon do
18 Bishop of ___ ("Henry V" character)
23 Novelist Lurie
24 Width specification
27 Penthouse feature
31 Like a depth finder
33 Skinny-dipping
34 Employ
35 Walking ___
36 Nursery school need
37 Head of a noted clan
38 Went boldly
39 Destroy
41 Anesthetized
42 Staff positions?
44 Pauciloquent
47 Tad
48 The Beatles' "___ Loser"
49 More rubicund
52 Like modern messages
55 Like a Puccini aria
57 Not going anywhere
59 Start of a bridge declaration
60 They may be rattled
64 Ship's dir.
66 1996 French film "___ Vep"
68 One of eight Eng. kings
71 Necklace piece
72 Some are precious
74 Continuing stories

75 Noted peripatetic conductor
76 "Cotton-Broker's Office" artist
79 Goof-off
80 ___ Park
83 Missile stat
84 Bath installation
86 Traveler's info
89 Confines
91 French ___
95 Flashed signs
96 It may be found in a pit
97 "CHiPs" star of 70's–80's TV
98 Fork off
104 Middle of a suit?
106 Retains
107 Like "The Shining," e.g.
109 "For you there's rosemary and ___": "The Winter's Tale"
110 Cartoonist Wilson
112 Ness, for one
113 Meets
115 W.W. II gun
117 "___ le roi!"
118 Staple of many video games
119 Union busters?
120 Hullabaloo
121 Rock composer Brian
122 The ___ Man
123 Family tree word
125 Year in Antoninus Pius's reign

by Nancy Nicholson Joline

ACROSS

1 Followings
6 "___ Luxemburg" (1986 film biography)
10 E-mail
17 Joined
18 Carried furniture
19 Epoch from 10 to 2 million years ago
21 50's–90's jazz singer
23 Circumstance of living
24 Foreign currency
25 Cheer
27 Plastic ___ Band
28 Downhill slope
29 Times old and new
30 Daimler-Chrysler products
31 Loses it
33 Indian tourist stop
34 Turkey helping
35 Pair at sea
36 Ship danger
37 Skips bail
38 Thieves
41 Kind of ball
42 Key letters
43 Like a certain key: Abbr.
44 False, like some talk
45 Imported vodka
49 Appliance brand
51 Throw
52 Taxes
54 Like Chopin's Scherzo (Op. 54)
55 Criticism, so to speak
56 Continental abbr.
57 "___ me down to rest me" (old prayer start)
58 Bond-issuing org.
59 On the line
60 Whodunit solver: Abbr.
61 Lilly, the drug maker
62 Holy person
64 But, in Bordeaux
65 Fr. holy women
67 Tabula ___
68 Celebrity's opposite
69 Year in Louis VII's reign
70 A goner
71 Book of prophecies
72 In accord
73 Horizon
75 Extrinsic
77 German article
78 Big Apple inits.
79 Center of Beaujolais country
80 Elegant one
85 Denounces
87 Bagel purveyors
88 "Excuse me . . ."
89 Stagewear for Madonna
90 Reflecting no light
91 Start of a caution
92 "Dynasty" actress
93 Some cereal
94 Physicist's study
95 Kitty
96 Fix the walls
98 Cast one's lot (with)
99 Ones sitting tight?
102 Pop singer known as "The Delta Lady"
104 Ticket dispensers
105 Top echelon
106 Like many a Western bandit
107 Most populated
108 Québec's Levesque
109 Amplified

DOWN

1 Singer's locale
2 Offense
3 Vichyssoise needs
4 Puppets, e.g.
5 Where the Blues Brothers debuted: Abbr.
6 Summaries
7 Offenses
8 Highway department supply
9 Author whose novels span 6,000 years
10 Dashboard inits.
11 George and others
12 Warnings
13 TriBeCa neighbor
14 Univ. of Md. competes in it
15 Singer with Parliament and Funkadelic
16 Guarantee
17 Popular packs
18 Bad looks
20 Small heaters
22 "That's not what ___!"
26 "(You don't Know) How Glad I Am" singer
30 "Steppin' Out" singer
32 Born
33 To boot
36 V.I.P.
37 Come clean, with "up"
39 Valuable strings
40 Legal scholar Guinier et al.
41 "L'Arlésienne" composer
44 "How Sweet It Is" singer
45 Battery type
46 Singer with an Oscar-nominated song from "Robin Hood"
47 Like some beds
48 All choked up
49 Paroxysm
50 "Happy Birthday, Mr. President" singer
51 Becomes a whiter shade of pale
53 Inventor Howe
55 Actress Emma
58 Hollywood sisters
61 Kind of chair
63 Primary goal
66 Menlo Park monogram
67 Torrents
70 Uncontrollable motions
74 Boston suburb
76 Loafer
79 Football Hall-of-Famer Dawson
80 Lottery ticket
81 Slowly, to Masur
82 Cut
83 Rough
84 No longer pale
85 Believer
86 On
87 Grandparents, traditionally
88 Fly
91 Beneficiary
92 Dine at home
93 Lose one's nerve
95 Show of hands?
97 Good amount of money
98 Jai ___
100 Opposite of remove
101 Atl. crosser
103 Man with a law

by Elizabeth Gorski

ACROSS

1 Not much
5 Indy 500 data
10 Great man?
15 Like some track meets
19 Coney Island's ___ Park
20 Sister of Euterpe
21 Lake that feeds the Truckee River
22 "She Believes ___" (Kenny Rogers song)
23 Broadway musical about a $1,000-a-night vacation?
25 Stood
26 E-4's, E-5's et al.
27 Winner of eight Norris Trophies
28 Poetic periods
29 Broadway musical about a wrestling free-for-all?
32 File box filler
34 ___ rubber (shoe material)
35 Electrical unit
36 "How Can ___ Sure" (1967 hit)
37 Prefix with centric
38 ___Kosh B'Gosh (kids' clothing line)
40 Cheese base
42 Certain sweater
44 Series of 30 requiems, to Roman Catholics
47 After-dinner selection
49 Dodge
50 Tiny cars' paths
52 Impressionist
54 Comedienne Ullman
56 Sawfish kin
57 James Dean type
59 Fedora features
62 Rector's income
63 Prepares to paint
65 Musical intervals
67 ". . . baked in ___"

68 Broadway musical about three guys using the same pickup routine at a bar?
70 Church section
71 Some pots and pans
73 London's ___ Hill Gate
74 Stranger
75 Factory machinery
77 Colorful fish
78 Physicist Angström
79 Person on a dais
81 Retainer
82 Glittery stone
83 Assured of success
85 Kind of appeal
87 Verbatim
89 Torments
91 Can in Canterbury
93 Attendance fig.
94 Oater sound effects
98 Airport monitor abbr.
99 Go out
101 Baseball Hall-of-Famer Bobby
103 Dupe
105 Broadway musical about a blown putt?
108 [sigh]
109 Bit of financial planning: Abbr.
110 It's sold in bars
111 Smash to smithereens
112 Broadway musical about Judge Judy?
115 Actor Calhoun
116 Trixie's pal, in 50's TV
117 Seemingly forever
118 All-inclusive
119 Figure (out)
120 Checks out
121 What a junker may be good for
122 ___ vale (farewell)

DOWN

1 Noted 1969 Harvard grad
2 Gun location
3 Old-style revolutionary
4 Decathlete O'Brien
5 Snicker
6 Affixes, in a way
7 Dining table sights
8 Season abroad
9 Kind of panel
10 "Don't go away!"
11 Town south of Elizabeth, N.J.
12 Sounds before "I've got it!"
13 "___, With Love"
14 Acne sufferer, most likely
15 Surfboard flaw
16 Straightens out
17 Pseudopod formers
18 Let up
24 Involuntary exile
30 Japanese computer giant
31 Give the evil eye to
33 Broadway musical about a duffer and his new driver?
34 Prom figure
39 Laundry supply
41 Jeanne ___
43 Broadway musical about a G.I. Joe collectors' convention?
45 Non-P.C. suffix
46 Onetime Chrysler model
48 Unisex garment
50 "Never mind!"
51 Bodega patron
53 Ostensible
55 Singer Winans
56 E.R. cry
58 Mr. Clean alternative
60 Gotten out of
61 Forbidding
63 Sachet emanations

64 More sinuous
66 Sun. talks
68 Coloratura's piece
69 Some blowups
72 "So soon?"
74 "The Zoo Story," e.g.
76 Signal to leave
78 Cabinet dept.
80 Motocross, e.g.
83 Title girl in a Ricky Nelson hit
84 Contract inkers, say
86 Whole bunches
88 Acid, at times
89 Pyle player
90 Accessory pin: Var.
92 Natural necklace
95 Relaxant
96 It's sometimes begged
97 "Camel News Caravan" anchor
100 African virus
102 Amend, as an itinerary
104 Wacky
106 Some scouts
107 Inflammatory ending?
108 Get an ___ effort
113 Roll-call vote
114 Big pooch

by Fred Piscop

ACROSS

1 Moptop
7 Dessert pastries
12 Scored in bezique
18 "1984" conspirator
19 Where lemons are picked?
20 Opium compound
21 Fixing the space-time continuum?
23 It started a little before 1000 B.C.
24 Controls
25 Baffled
26 Thank-you-___
27 Pants problem
28 Ago, in Aberdeen
29 Average
30 High priest in Exodus
32 Newcastle's river
33 Geology?
38 Migraine headaches, so to speak
39 Ability to hit a target
42 Donkey drawer
43 Inevitable
44 Lose everything
45 Part of a percussion section
47 Courses
48 ___ tree (Indiana state tree)
49 Commercial passage
50 Worth
51 Be attributable (to)
52 "Be ___!" ("Come on!")
55 Rube
56 Amtrak fares?
58 Turn about
59 Capek drama
60 Barry Sanders and teammates
62 "Nonsense!"
64 1970's–80's cause
65 Singer who co-starred in "Johnny Mnemonic," 1995

67 Limit placed on PBS?
71 Limping, maybe
73 Words from Mr. Moto
74 Efficiency symbol, in physics
75 Modern fat substitute
76 North Wind personified
77 "Aunt ___ Cope Book"
79 Dogtrot and foxtrot
80 Successor car to the Studebaker
81 Off-shore lodging
83 Set of plates
84 "The King and I" role
86 Time to play taps
87 Like a landowner
88 Arachnids that appear over the summer?
91 Some Oklahoma Indians
92 Beget
94 Fabric name ending
95 Counting method
99 Queen Eliz., e.g.
100 Attention ___
101 Experienced, old-style
103 Vow taker
104 More hot-tempered
106 Waterway named for a talk show host?
109 Like some foreign movies
110 God of death who underwent resurrection
111 Three-time Emmy-winning host
112 Bound
113 Like most store items
114 Texas oil city

DOWN

1 Strong beers
2 Key color
3 Flame throwing, maybe
4 Fall preceder?
5 Vacation souvenirs
6 Abbr. in a business letter
7 3.26 light-years
8 Spur
9 Bother for a boxer
10 Because of
11 It's a mess
12 Western landscapist Thomas ___
13 Land south of Judah
14 Football Hall-of-Famer Ford
15 Addendum to a log?
16 They might backfire
17 Like some sympathies
19 Most doll-like
20 "Later!"
22 Gridiron stat
26 First-of-a-kind 1960's TV star
30 Flower part
31 Top-notch
32 They connect to the knees
34 Ed of "Married . . . with Children"
35 Players
36 "___ goes according to plan . . ."
37 Gobble
38 Calculus calculation: Abbr.
39 Semiramis's realm
40 Communicating
41 People who study cuneiform?
44 Talk show chatter
46 Arctic explorer John
47 Coin of Pakistan
48 Little nothing
50 Woman of letters?

51 Most of the world
53 Golden
54 Ushers
56 TV event of 1977
57 Old foes of the Spanish
61 Model
63 Bratislava resident
66 Caloric cakes
68 Without exception
69 Stews
70 Like 70's fashion, now
72 Coach Parseghian
76 Judge's seat
78 Kind of school
79 Shot up
81 Blushing
82 Harmonica-like instrument
83 Comfortable ___ old shoe
84 Bikini events
85 New York's General Post Office is on it
89 Sea nymph
90 Labor
92 Hurry
93 Western friend
96 Marries, perhaps
97 "None But the Lonely Heart" writer/director
98 Sealy competitor
100 Home page
101 Motor with some oomph
102 Its flag is green, white and orange
103 Small fastener
105 "Go get 'em!"
106 "Baloney!"
107 Mother bear, in Málaga
108 Prefix with terrorist

by Dave Tuller

ACROSS

1 System of shorthand
6 Have in the past
10 Palestinians
15 Zip
19 Steinful
20 Wrinkly fruit
21 Ravel's "Trois Poèmes de Stéphane Mallarmé," e.g.
22 Times past
23 Type size
24 Squeal of delight
26 Indicator
27 Mao's successor
28 Most moist
29 Put on again
31 Big crop in Iowa
33 No-see-um
34 One in a rush
35 Merchant ship
38 Sits up on two legs, maybe
39 Tamper with
40 Unethical items in the antique business
41 A lot
42 ___ de combat
43 Identifying
45 Leapers
47 Cracked up
48 Holiday drink
51 Least at peace
52 Poorer-fitting, in a way
53 Didn't go straight
54 Singing syllables
55 Beans
56 1994 Peace Nobelist
57 Stand for
59 Sandwich holders
60 "Holy cow!"
61 Excessive ambition
62 Does many things at once
63 "Fried Green Tomatoes" author
65 Pravda provider
66 Doesn't sit tight
67 First mate of TV
70 York, for one: Abbr.
71 V.I.P.'s
72 The best of times
73 "Footloose" singer, 1984
74 "It's My Party" singer Lesley
75 Texas A&M player
76 Japanese-American
79 Race segment
80 Business suit shade
81 City of an 1854 manifesto
82 Olios
84 Brush source
85 Two-generation name in Indiana politics
86 City on the Clyde
87 Declaration before "to me"
89 Alike, in Alençon
93 Der ___ (Adenauer)
94 Addleheads
96 Words of wisdom
97 Dutch artist Jan van der ___
98 Suffix with exped-
99 Unworkable
100 Old Venetian rulers
101 Slips
102 California hockey player
103 ___ point (embroidery stitch)
104 Some molding profiles

DOWN

1 More than willing
2 Latest thing
3 William ___, Alaska's first 72-Down
4 Excel
5 Post-univ. test
6 Science fiction awards
7 Wild-eyed
8 Ones hiking through snow
9 News
10 Worse than jitters
11 Cheer
12 Enero to enero
13 Makes limp and soiled
14 Eye sores
15 Savings
16 French rocket
17 Macbeth's weapon
18 Former SAG president and family
25 Voice votes
28 Mudhole
30 Last-ditch effort
32 Went after
34 Musical professor
35 Seltzer starter
36 Horse of a certain color
37 Most awkward
38 Start up
39 Pro greats Jackson and White
42 Pardner's mount
43 Toes
44 "y," when compared
46 Stephen of "Citizen X"
47 Flocks
48 Absence of emotional complications
49 "Art of Love" poet
50 D.D.E. and others
52 Mystifies
53 Modern diversionary political tactic
55 Like some doubts
56 Like nothin'
57 Reps.
58 Crow
59 Prams
62 Manipulate
63 Computer record
64 Law degree
66 Clown's need
67 ___ details
68 Not fer
69 Scholarship criterion
71 Spring sound
72 See 3-Down
73 Some drivers
74 All choked up
76 "Sure, count me in"
77 Bear, so to speak
78 Roofing specialist
80 Pelé once played in it: Abbr.
81 Symbol of strength
83 "As ___ my witness"
84 Performed terribly
85 Kisses for Carlos
87 Fictional lab assistant
88 Breakfast name
90 Old-fashioned pledge
91 Miracle Mets lead-off man
92 Discounted by
95 Actress Peeples
96 Trouble

by Randolph Ross

ACROSS

1 "The Cosby Show" co-star
7 Priest's wear
10 "Chicago Hope" actress
15 Its symbol is an eagle: Abbr.
19 Title subject of a 1994 film bio
20 One side of a ship
21 Popular potato
22 Legal plea, for short
23 SALATA
25 Republication
27 Many wines
28 100 cents, in Sri Lanka
30 Grapefruit juice property
31 Common pasta suffix
32 LEUMI
36 Quite mad
38 Kitchen device
39 Mortgage org.
42 Goose sound
43 Nickname
45 United Nations sight
46 Typo
48 One learning method
51 Water-___
53 Alphabet run
55 Prefix with sphere
56 Big name in rap
57 Memory unit, for short
59 Throng
61 Made uniform
63 Many people lie about it
65 Gandhi, e.g.
66 Flinch, say
67 Suffix with respond
68 Abbr. above zero
69 What that is in Spain
70 Highlands tourist spot
72 Bunny man
74 Counters
76 Obstacles for marauders
78 Pressing
80 Emergency surgery, for short
81 European autos
82 "Isn't ___ bit like you and me?" (Beatles lyric)
83 "Don Pasquale" setting
84 Fullest extent
85 U.P.S.'ed
87 Bit of chill
89 Type-A
91 1997 N.L. Rookie of the Year Scott ___
93 Clock-radio switch
95 Mex. Mrs.
97 Bookbinder's leather
98 Letters at sea
99 Halo
102 High places?
106 TCHU TZIH
108 Iran-contra org.
109 Stiff drinks
111 Like some bombs
112 See 115-Down
113 Peripatetic leader
116 GHIACCIO
119 Props in a Schwarzenegger flick
120 Fuse
121 Poet Hughes
122 Reverses
123 Voice mail prompt
124 Big section of a dictionary
125 Abilene-to-San Antonio dir.
126 Sign in the middle of town

DOWN

1 Get hold of again
2 Glandular prefix
3 KÖTTBULLAR
4 Caretakers' equipment
5 Thumbs-up response
6 Periodontist's deg.
7 Tempted
8 Arose quickly
9 Sprinkle
10 Vietnam War Memorial designer
11 12-Down is one
12 WAI HUA'AI
13 Stanley Falls' river
14 First-aid item
15 Before
16 "___ goes"
17 Feint
18 Royal wish
24 Some Wall St. traders
26 "Do ___?" (scaredy-cat's query)
29 Period
32 Female octopi
33 AKKULROALIT
34 Pound sound
35 1,500-year-old text
37 Covers with fine black particles
39 LIAISON
40 These get the biggest cheers
41 Parched
44 Sign of conceit
47 Mother of Poseidon
48 Seine feeder
49 Sketches
50 Parched
52 Who shot J. R.
54 QOLI
58 MASERN
60 Kennedy follower
62 Preserver
64 Scott of the P.G.A.
71 ". . . ___ saw Elba"
73 Hightail it
75 Entr' ___
77 Going after
79 Lego, literally
80 Kind of traffic
86 They may be assaulted on the street
88 Divvies up accordingly
90 A-K or L-Z, e.g.
92 Org. that awards the Spingarn Medal
94 Year in Edward the Confessor's reign
96 What I love, in song
100 Jitters
101 Typesetting units
103 Not dom.
104 Reunion attendees
105 Clearest of head
106 Parson's place
107 Drops
109 Stupidhead
110 Nose: Prefix
112 Perry Como's "___ Love You So"
113 Project
114 Martinique, par exemple
115 With 112-Across, enthusiastic review
117 Elementary ending
118 Santa ___

by Martin Schneider

ACROSS

1 Chew (out)
5 Roost, so to speak
10 __-fi
13 Photo marrer
19 Sore
20 Lines on sonar screens
21 The "O" of Cheerios
22 Packing a wallop
23 Blessed side dish with hot dogs?
26 Bakery attractions
27 Rocketeers
28 Parts that are thrown away
29 Cleaner's challenge
30 Cattle in a cattle drive
31 Cool cat
32 Sinn __
33 German industrial family
36 Angling equipment
37 Submarine-launched missile
40 Expiration
41 Tot's hair-setting equipment?
44 Singer DiFranco
45 Woods critter
46 "Star Wars" princess
47 Site of a helix and antihelix
48 Hellenic letters
49 O. J. Simpson as a bard?
53 Portuguese king, 1861–89
54 Putterers
58 Fencing action
59 Palooka
61 Homes for struggling artists
62 "Happy Days" character
63 Chili con carne ingredient
64 Natives of Mork's home planet
65 Racer Andretti
66 Shakespeare's Duke of __
67 Garden beauty
68 Critic at Cape Canaveral?
70 __ impasse
71 Treasure on the Spanish Main
72 Twelve __
73 Color of le ciel
77 John
78 Physician at home where the buffalo roam?
83 Hospital caution
84 Money derived from an old union
86 Related on one's mother's side
87 Flummox
88 Badgers
89 Satisfying sounds
91 At the home of
92 Subordinates of 99-Down
93 New Testament king
94 Patent medicines, supposedly
98 One of the Pirates of Penzance
100 Hadrian's Wall?
102 Famous landing point
103 Jackie's second
104 Inventor Howe
105 "Phooey!"
106 Egrets and such
107 Actress Carrere
108 Past: Fr.
109 Emmy-winning Thompson

DOWN

1 Barbara, familiarly
2 "Rent-__" (1988 flick)
3 "Hold up!"
4 Keystone, e.g.: Var.
5 Hostage situations
6 Roused
7 1950's British P.M.
8 Ceiling
9 Part of a school
10 Whoosis
11 Brittle, say
12 "__ Easy" (1977 hit)
13 Takeoff place?
14 Tidbits
15 Dreamland
16 Provisions in Hell?
17 Black fly
18 Certain celeb news shows
24 Modern notifications
25 Kind of sea duck
31 Persian Gulf port
32 Like one debate side
33 Fast-food inits.
34 Uruguay, for one
35 Classic card game
36 French beverages
37 __ Noël
38 Like some defensive basketball players
39 Adolescent nickname
41 Round units
42 "Psycho" co-star
43 Some froufrou
46 Lummoxes
48 Calculus pioneer
49 Pounding parts
50 University in Worcester, Mass.
51 Musical London
52 Begin a plant relocation
53 Bed
54 "It's __!" (thumbs-up reply)
55 Kind of vows
56 Like the beasts on Noah's boat after 40 days and 40 nights?
57 Prepare
59 Battleships and war, e.g.
60 Ethnic New Year celebration
62 With 80-Down, peach center
63 Archbishop of New York, 1968–83
65 N.F.L. coach Jim
66 Wine from Verona
68 Actor Calhoun
69 Sends packing
70 __ king
73 Cantankerous oldsters
74 Smith or Taylor
75 Sushi offering
76 Beehive State athlete
78 Bookmark alternative
79 T.L.C. givers
80 See 62-Down
81 Register
82 Boys of song
83 Mysterious
85 Ready for harvest
87 Express
89 Fudge
90 Artist Toulouse-Lautrec
91 Like some cigars
92 "__ Smile" (1976 hit)
94 Gab
95 Dough for pizza, in the old days
96 Detective's need
97 Cousin of Mlle.
98 Circular __
99 See 92-Across
101 Pavement caution in California

by Lloyd E. Pollet

ACROSS

1 City north of Vallejo
5 "A one and ___..."
9 Darlings
13 Way off the highway
17 Digger
18 One of a nursery rhyme couple
19 Jordan's Queen ___ International Airport
20 Eye part
21 Emulate Cicero
22 Terrifying
24 Practice logrolling
25 Get ahead?
27 They go with the floe
28 Brewing container
30 Blended whisky brand, or a Valentine's gift
32 Ring tossed at pegs
34 Make another sheepshank
35 Shots, for short
36 Mix-up
38 Sign in a house window, maybe
41 Car of a 1964 song
43 Bébé fare
45 Period of prayer
46 Performer
48 Classicist's subject
50 Slangy hat
51 Stew
55 Cut short
57 Degrees for C.E.O.'s
59 Element form
61 Suffix on fruit names
62 Get slick, in a way
65 Author ___ S. Connell
67 His wife was a Duke
68 Avg.
69 Not a popular nextdoor neighbor
73 First-rate
74 "There Is Nothin' Like ___"
76 Extra-long
77 Blessings
78 Pres. Hoover's dog King ___
79 With it
82 Engine speed, for short
84 Luvs rival
86 Ad
87 Tout's offering
89 Model kit extras
92 Cushiness
93 Political refugee
96 Road ___ (driver control problem)
97 Econ. total
98 Ben Franklin, in some books
102 Rib
104 Those: Sp.
108 ___ coup (too late): Fr.
109 Fated (for)
111 Dean's list, e.g.
113 Advisory councils
116 Unwelcome person
118 Herbaceous ornamental
119 Like much folk mus.
120 Miniature speedway event
123 Laos's ___ Prabang
124 Merit
125 Red Brigades victim Aldo
126 Literacy volunteer, e.g.
127 Diminutive endings
128 Niuewpoort's river
129 Water server
130 Kind of arch
131 Wet septet

DOWN

1 Nativity inn problem
2 Old-style call to arms
3 Man of many words
4 "You ___ right!"
5 Shrinks' org.
6 Lou Grant's paper, in brief
7 1961 Britten composition
8 Hokkaido port
9 Kind of play
10 Yale Bowl player
11 Spec for some specs
12 Wizard
13 Flotation devices
14 Do the Wright thing?
15 "The Idylls of the King" character
16 Straw-filled mattress
17 Labor leader James
18 Taffeta trait
23 Composer Stravinsky
26 "The sign of extra service" sloganeer
29 "East of Eden" twin
31 Tent event
33 Neolith or paleolith
37 Stir up
39 Year in John XVIII's papacy
40 Some narcs
42 Made fit
44 Feature of Rome
46 Dressed to the nines
47 Mint family member
48 Old-time pianist Templeton
49 Hoopster Hall-of-Famer Bing
52 Takes turns
53 Food connoisseur
54 Principles
55 Ring figures
56 Post-E.R. place
58 Auto founded by an aircraft company
60 Henley participants
63 Einstein's birthplace
64 Nectar flavor
66 One who's earned stripes, e.g.
70 Canned
71 First-rate
72 Words with diet or roll
75 Utility company worker
80 Inflamed, in suffixes
81 Anear
83 Throw
85 Early morning course, often
88 Nappy wearer's transport
90 Mature
91 Wife of Jacob
94 Vapor form
95 Builder
97 Kind of therapy
98 Baker's specialty
99 Janet Baker's specialty
100 Baroque
101 Ste. Jeanne ___
103 Temperate
105 Beethoven's "Pathétique" is one
106 Flarewear?
107 Smelting byproducts
110 "Peachy"
112 Long looks
114 Saki title
115 Lento
117 Crown
121 Paydirt
122 Country singer David Allan ___

by Cathy Millhauser

53 THAT WOMAN

ACROSS

1 Unkind nickname
6 "Hey ___" (1963 pop hit)
11 Scrap
15 Big do
19 Word from a bird
20 Matching felony?
21 Decathlete's need
22 Shed item
23 Angel seeker?
25 Undo
26 Plane section
27 Overindulge
28 Urban alligator's home, they say
30 Without qualification
32 He wrote "The Miser"
35 Category
36 Slight amount
37 Emulates Crosby
38 Rid of the superfluous
39 Murmured softly
41 Smoker or sleeper
42 Blue Grotto cats?
45 Johnny ___
47 Unaffiliated record company
49 Criminal charge
50 Radial need
51 Something to pick
52 Geometric combining form
53 Chief
54 Bottom bottom line?
59 Photographers' concerns
61 Mixed bags
62 Worries
63 Complains sotto voce
65 Second to none
66 Peanut candy
67 Have an inspiration?
68 Cappuccino cousin
69 Norman native
70 Detect Dan's cologne?
72 + or – item

73 Thicken
75 "You Only Live Twice" scriptwriter
76 Get off the fence
77 Deli order
78 Wall Street worry
80 Lyrical lines
81 Undead in the water?
87 Pontiac of song
88 Fine furs
90 Before curfew
91 Execrate
93 Concerto movement
94 Take out membership
95 Tied up at the marina
96 Slugfest souvenir
98 Opposite of dimin.
99 Third of a Latin trio
100 Bumper sticker starter
101 Continental prefix
103 If 50% survives the heat, then . . . ?
109 Natural impulse
110 Tater
111 Digger of early TV's "The Life of Riley"
112 Stand for Steen
113 "Calm down . . ."
114 In billiards, what the English call English
115 Where Irving is
116 Expressionless

DOWN

1 ABC and NBC overseer
2 A patient may say it
3 Swing site
4 Director Leone of old westerns
5 Plenty
6 Word processing command
7 Compass drawing
8 Canteen grp.
9 Bungle

10 Roof sight
11 Toot
12 Serve sake, e.g.
13 Fatima's husband
14 Trucker's approval
15 Stick on
16 The plume that's mightier than the sword?
17 Commuter line
18 European air hub
24 Anatomical sac
29 "Beau Geste" author
31 Schleps
32 Thirteenth-century starter
33 Rue Morgue murderer
34 Kin to a kingfish?
35 Stagehand
36 It's human
38 Says the rosary
39 Acts skittish
40 Defense mechanism
43 Warm-ups
44 Resort lake
46 "The Divine Miss M"
48 Set up for service
51 Master artist's studio
53 Land in two pieces
54 Needle point?
55 Influential group
56 VCR feature
57 Eva Duarte, after marriage
58 Seeders make it
60 Rat
63 Bungle
64 Like some beds
65 Smith or Page
66 "Sic semper tyrannis" shouter
68 Arctic residents
69 Alluvial
71 Ladies' man
74 Graceful
77 "Cinderella" event
78 Divides appropriately
79 Dorm dweller

81 Hollywood crosser
82 "The Blue Max" actress
83 Surrealist Magritte
84 You can't hear if you're out of it
85 Rich fabric
86 Lacquer ingredient
89 60's dance
92 In addition
94 Destroy by degrees
95 Bursts into tears
96 "Leaving Las Vegas" star
97 Kibbutz dance
98 Dirty deposit
102 Reuters rival
104 Roman law
105 Spring training state: Abbr.
106 "___ Beso" (1962 hit)
107 Cartoon canine
108 Underhanded

by Richard Silvestri

ACROSS

1 Confirmation, for one
7 Chip company
12 Old verb ending
15 Donald, to Huey, Dewey or Louie
19 Jack of hearts feature
29 ___ Island, Fla.
21 Olive cousin
23 Russian technological achievement
25 Locked away
26 They're often kept on ice
27 Since
28 Change-making key
30 Literary inits.
31 1984 Uris novel
33 Financial considerations
36 Back-stabber
37 Spiny-rayed aquarium fish
39 Gang members
43 Present wrapper, maybe
46 Start to like
48 It may be pitched
50 In order
51 Big belly
52 Crab or turtle shell
54 Date
55 Virile type
56 Slightly gamy
57 Propelled
58 Come-___ (marketing ploys)
60 "Father Murphy" extras
62 Clinton antagonist
64 Amount of a peddler's wares, perhaps
67 Tab neighbor
68 Call to a farmer
69 "Cheers" co-star
71 ___ lark
72 Shoots

74 Seat of Orange County, Calif.
75 Prime Minister from 1947–64
78 Is left to, as a responsibility
80 Under the ___ (nautical term)
81 Banana ___ (desert)
83 "You've got mail" co.
84 Peace Nobelist Ducommun
85 ___ so weiter (et cetera): Ger.
87 Lack of enthusiasm
89 Kal ___ pet products
90 Drew on
91 Winner's signs
93 Chipper
94 Brand at the laundromat
95 It's often burning
97 Light rock songs
99 Abbr. in many company names
102 Inspired kind of thinking.
104 Parent's demand
107 Vanilla ___
110 W.W. II camp
111 "___ Union Woman" (old labor song)
114 Actress Gray and others
116 Site of an annual August 9th peace ceremony
118 Classic BBC show
121 Orchestra member
122 Running competitions
123 D.C. org. dropped from this puzzle . . . or what much of your money is
124 Fur
125 Unsweetened
126 Heavenly abodes
127 Rich cakes

DOWN

1 Walkover
2 Concerns, criticisms, etc.
3 Show
4 "Mr. Belvedere" star
5 Mohammed's favorite wife
6 French article
7 "___ shocked as you . . ."
8 Security grp.
9 Big payoff bet
10 Prefix with hazard
11 70's leader with a palindromic name
12 Stories-within-stories
13 Coffee break time
14 Pedants
15 Altdorf's canton
16 Cardinal point?
17 Head honchos
18 One of the Windsors
22 ___-Roman
24 Atlantic City destination, with "the"
29 "Step ___!"
32 Battling
34 Diet setbacks
35 Hawaii draw
37 Artistes wear them
38 California's ___ Valley
40 Be treated satisfactorily
41 Trouble
42 Criteria: Abbr.
43 Oral poetry
44 Use a 9-iron, say
45 The Clintons, the Bushes, etc.
47 Drop like ___
49 Start of many movement names
52 They come with new computers
53 ___ Gay
59 Like employees
61 Bogus: Var.

63 Casually showed up
65 Article of faith
66 Lays bare
70 P.L.O.'s Arafat
72 Made-up
73 Where to get postcards
76 Fireball sound
77 Carpus connector
78 TV's "Family ___"
79 About 1 o'clock: Abbr.
82 The way you do the things you do
86 Weakness
88 Ancient Jew
92 Yemen's capital
96 Martini's partner in winemaking
98 Lentil, e.g.
100 Group whose rock opera was once performed at the Met
101 Hole fixer
103 Magic, at one time
104 Dog reprimand
105 Hospital event
106 Between: Fr.
107 Move slowly
108 Cartel city
109 "My stars!"
112 Envelope abbr.
113 Fathers may hold it
115 Lip
117 "We ___ Family"
119 Motorist's concern, for short
120 Baseball's Mel

by Matt Gaffney

ACROSS

1 Fierce tribesmen
8 Town near the geographical center of California
16 Hip-hop repertoire
24 Best Original Screenplay nominee of 1984
25 Flawless
26 Unpredictable
27 11TH CENTURY: Olaf Haraldsson defeated . . .
30 Old shows
31 One of the Dodecanese Islands
32 Actuate
33 Former Air France fleet member
36 Actor Williamson
37 Like a violin concerto by Bach
40 Three coins in la fontana?
42 Minnesota city
43 12TH CENTURY: Notre Dame erected . . .
48 Fliers, often
50 Milne character
51 A.L. M.V.P., 1951, 1954 and 1955
52 Marathoner Pippig
53 First name of Pope Alexander VII
55 Demesne
56 13TH CENTURY: "Tristan und Isolde" penned . . .
62 Belief
63 It may be on the line
64 "___ first!"
65 Certain laundry load
66 14TH CENTURY: Tamerlane fights . . .
73 Allowance
77 Attends Exeter, e.g.
78 Effort
79 Holding
80 Shot contents
84 Wasn't serious
87 15TH CENTURY: Columbus ship chartered . . .
90 Bravura
91 Longtime Missouri Sen. ___ Symington
93 ___ tree
94 Classified offering
95 Lana's first
96 16TH CENTURY: Russia war-torn . . .
102 Cathedral of Notre Dame locale
103 Certain
104 Gung-ho about
105 Robert Fulghum's "It Was on Fire When ___ Down on It"
106 Japanese conquest of W.W. II
108 Polish place
109 17TH CENTURY: "The Night Watch" painted . . .
114 Gum arabic source
118 Sonny
120 Director Ferrara
121 ___ Lady
122 18TH CENTURY: Yale University founded . . .
130 Three-time British Open winner
132 Roll up
133 Generations
134 Corps core
135 Actress, subject of the biography "Hollywood Comet"
136 "Un ___ di" (Puccini aria)
137 19TH CENTURY: Simón Bolivar conquers . . .
143 ___-wip
146 Beach sight
147 Bad mark
148 ___-al-Arab waterway
149 Kind of job
150 Quercitol source
152 Order against the Jedi, in "Star Wars"
154 Singing parts
156 20TH CENTURY: Two World Wars take place . . .
164 Gifts that grow on you?
165 Base for shingles
166 Some Christians
167 Part of the Ottoman Empire until 1829
168 Lycurgus and Lysander
169 Aromatherapy product

DOWN

1 Gull's sound
2 Ingredient in a black and tan
3 Young ___
4 Zingers
5 Like some couples
6 Employ, in Exeter
7 "Troades" tragedian
8 With 9-Down, shavers
9 See 8-Down
10 Indian weight
11 Support giver
12 Sophisticated trader, for short
13 Picks up
14 House Speaker during Carter's Presidency
15 Tree
16 "Kanthapura" novelist
17 Maundy money
18 Quickened, with "up"
19 Response to a sneezer
20 "Liar Liar" actress Cheri
21 "Forget it!"
22 Mai tai ingredient
23 Charlie Chaplin's half-brother
28 Kind of appeal
29 Prefix with polar
33 Of the spatial relationship of atoms in a molecule
34 "Gimme a break!"
35 Japanese seaport of 300,000
37 Swedish-based furniture chain
38 One who isn't in
39 Peut-___ (perhaps): Fr.
41 "Rock" suffix
44 Chem. unit
45 It has an eye on the tube
46 Unhurried
47 Have
49 They may cover a lot of ground
53 Khalid's successor
54 What makes a chef chief?
56 Trust, e.g.: Abbr.
57 Moves a shell
58 Neighbor of Russ.
59 Spain's ___ Brava
60 Like some garments
61 One with a title
63 Observe
67 Mental grasp
68 El Greco's birthplace
69 Oft-broken promise
70 With 87-Down, Avenida Revolución locale
71 Lassitude
72 Cuts the nonsense
74 Pachacuti, for one
75 It may cause inflation
76 Part of Q.E.F.
80 The Mideast's ___ Desert
81 "Ziegfeld Follies" costume designer
82 Pull (in)
83 Picnic coolers
84 Jack beat him for the heavyweight title, 1919
85 Sympathetic response
86 Lambaste
87 See 70-Down
88 Lie
89 Singer Terrell
91 Scharnhorst commander
92 Tiger Beat alternative
97 Toast
98 Disquiets
99 Zhou ___
100 Blade
101 Kvass ingredient
102 Asia's ___ Sea
106 Toots
107 Did something with
108 Binders?
110 Down
111 Struck, in a way
112 Pulitzer winner Welty
113 Nodding
114 Jezebel's husband
115 Fearful of being shot
116 Comprised of selected passages
117 PC inserts
119 When John VI's papacy began
123 Holy ___
124 Like some legal issues
125 Rioting
126 Came out with
127 Comics dog
128 Push
129 Orthodox leader?
130 Chopin piece
131 Ham protector?
135 1994 Richard Preston best seller, with "The"
137 Showed one's hand, maybe
138 Processes grain
139 Corner
140 Artificial flavor bases
141 Relative of an alewife
142 Some South Africans
144 Famed Miami country club
145 Words before hint or line
151 Fill
153 Jewish wedding ring?
154 "The Man I Married" actress
155 Exercise options?
156 Duke's assn.
157 Constitution preceder
158 It may be a lifesaver
159 Kit ___
160 Waste watchers: Abbr.
161 Loss leader?
162 Drawer's frame
163 Wilfred Owen's "Dulce et Decorum ___"

by Frank Longo

56 "SEZ WHO?"

ACROSS

1 Junior high subj.
4 Neil Simon play locale
10 Flexible, electrically
14 Figure on the ceiling of the Sistine Chapel
18 Scale
20 Symphony with a noted funeral march
21 Ad writer's award
22 Kind of weight
23 Podded plant
24 "Hi. It's me. Mark McGwire."
26 Besmears
27 Big name in the Big Apple
29 Superlative suffix
30 Handled
31 "Okay, I pulled the plug. So sue me."
36 Reply in Rome
39 Whistler, e.g.
40 See 70-Down
41 Kind of meal
42 Response to goo
43 Farm layer
45 Literary inits.
48 "You think I'm annoying? Fine, I'm outta here."
54 Blow
55 Squatter?
56 Cabbage
57 Typewriter part
59 Old-fashioned greetings
63 Exclude
64 Whatsoever
66 Animal fur
67 He was translated into Latin
68 "To govern or not to govern. That is the question."
71 Buffalo's county
72 Record
74 First name in TV talk
75 Old car with a Turbo-Hydramatic gearbox
76 Former British protectorate
77 Sierra ___
78 Power control, for short
79 Right at one's peak
81 Western Athletic Conference player
82 "Gimme a dozen donuts. And step on it!"
91 For this or that
92 Subterfuge
93 Simpson case judge
94 Occupied
95 Chin stroker's words
97 Basketball's ___ Bol
100 People left in ruins
101 "Honey, you're wearing THAT?"
106 Club news source
107 Kiln
108 Rogaine user's hope
112 Muslim pilgrim
113 "Don't I look fetching in this dress from Warsaw? Huh, huh?"
117 Corn locale
118 Fordham's basketball conference, informally
119 Part
120 1930's–50's actor J. ___ Naish
121 Edger, e.g.
122 Tidings
123 Maryland athlete, for short
124 West Texas city
125 Insect killer

DOWN

1 All excited
2 God of discord, in Scandinavia
3 Whiz
4 Turned into
5 Mideasterner
6 Publishing sensation of 1958
7 Many a Rembrandt
8 Year in Domitian's reign
9 Actor Charleson of "Chariots of Fire"
10 Agree to
11 Skirmish
12 Soiled
13 New England catch
14 Add on
15 "After we delineate this sales chart, our stockholders will love us."
16 Trunk
17 Words repeated after "O Absalom" in the Bible
19 Fancy homes abroad
25 Temporary jobs
28 Fools
30 Twofold
32 Kind of function
33 Desire
34 Defense missile
35 Bygone ruler
36 Team V.I.P.'s
37 Least bit
38 The U.K. touches it
43 Loaf
44 Month to celebrate U.N. Day
46 Form of rock and roll
47 Anger
49 Some brass
50 Apple product
51 Like three out of four suits
52 "War's ___": Cowper
53 Boxing's Oscar ___ Hoya
58 Request
59 Transport, sci-fi style
60 Richly wrought
61 "I'm a rabbi and . . . um . . . wait, where was I?"
62 Headline
64 Williams of "Happy Days"
65 ___ Friday's (restaurant chain)
66 Math work
69 Shred
70 With 40-Across, 1944 Chemistry Nobelist
73 Stand
78 31-Across's grp.
80 Warner-Lambert competitor
83 Modern ice cream flavor
84 Nick
85 Lived ___ (celebrated)
86 "___ chance"
87 Song at the start of a church service
88 Actor's need
89 PC key
90 Musical seconds?
96 Spots
97 Accident
98 Con
99 Scoreboard figure
100 "Who's the Boss?" woman
101 "You're a Grand Old Flag" writer
102 Hold forth
103 Orleans's river
104 Like some surgery
105 Aristotelian final cause
109 Caddie's offering
110 Flat
111 Shut down
113 Excess amount
114 Army E-5, e.g.
115 Flit (about)
116 Prefix with washed

by Joe DiPietro

ACROSS

1 Art drawings
7 Bubbler
14 Bengali language group
19 Digital window?
21 Plumbing control
22 Needlepoint?
23 Upfront offerings
25 Prince Valiant's wife
26 Chemical prefix
27 Toledo Mrs.
28 Skimmer, e.g.
29 Yellowstone sight
30 French champagne-producing city
32 Not long to wait
34 Machine parts
35 It's dishwasher-safe
40 Early bird, say
43 Like grapefruit for breakfast
44 Stop running
45 Secretaries Day mo.
47 Drive-___
48 Gold deposit?
49 Suffix with persist
50 Film promo words
53 "Hell's Angels" star Ben
54 One was lost in flight
57 Approx.
58 Latticework
59 Flattering talk
60 Sires
61 No-goodniks
63 Gumps
65 Marie Antoinette, e.g.
67 Smoke trace
68 Big citrus fruit
71 Poison ___
72 Old bird
73 Conflict
77 Actress Meyers
78 Where to toot one's own horn?
83 Butler's locale
84 Corridor
86 Sister of Selene
87 Bourne of "The Bourne Identity"
88 "Or ___!"
89 Granada bear
90 Tee choices: Abbr.
91 Cardiologists' concerns
92 Zip a Ziploc, e.g.
94 Air Force One passenger
99 In
100 ___ Valley, Calif.
101 Spingarn Medal awarder
102 Cleans up, in a way
104 Stop for gas
105 Soph. and jr.
106 Like a bloodhound
111 "Dead Souls" novelist
112 "My stars!"
116 Building block
117 In general
118 Now hear this
119 Feasts
120 First bishop of Rome
121 Truman portrayer, 1995

DOWN

1 Reading place
2 Larger-than-life
3 "Le ___ Goriot"
4 Research facil.
5 Bartender?
6 Coll. major
7 Hitmen
8 Unenthusiastic responses
9 Charge
10 Comfy
11 On the nose
12 Poetic adverb
13 Baseball positions: Abbr.
14 Where many jokes are set
15 "Wide open"
16 Wing tips, maybe
17 "Suffice ___ say . . ."
18 "Behind That Curtain" detective
20 Dairy-case image
24 Mirages for money, e.g.
31 Antiquity
33 Surgery need
34 Reddish-orange
35 Barker's partner
36 Vocalist Tucker
37 Assign
38 Rebecca rejecter
39 TV's
41 Gnawed around the edges
42 Peewees
46 Pineapple skin segment
50 The Kennedys, e.g.
51 Department north of Paris
52 ___ point (embroidery stitch)
54 Try to win first prize
55 Fleur-de-___
56 Sudden upturn, as in sales
62 Arrivé
64 Dawn, to a don
65 Santa ___
66 "No sweat"
67 Press a suit
68 Post in Washington, for example
69 Pope's cape
70 Broadway premiere of April 11, 1991
72 Get it wrong
74 Some shells
75 Cheering wildly
76 Plant with tubular yellow flowers
79 "Call to Greatness" writer, initially speaking
80 Substitutes
81 British tax
82 TV interviewer
85 Appear
87 "Home Alone" actor
91 Hail Mary path
93 Areas for flight attendants
95 Stone foundation
96 Rudolf Nureyev, e.g.
97 Not participate in
98 Like bottles of beer
102 Cry of mock horror
103 Diana's lover ___ el-Fayed
107 Abecedary link
108 Physics Nobelist Isidor I. ___
109 Scratches (out)
110 Strike
112 Scale notes
113 Lufthansa direction
114 Ring support?
115 His or her: Fr.

by Jim Page

ACROSS

1 Le Carré specialty
9 Put out
16 Eagle's grp.
19 Cream ingredient
20 East, in Ecuador
21 Face-off
22 . . . on a daughter's wedding day
24 "___ New World" (Arlen/Gershwin song)
25 Subj. of the 1962 Nobel Prize in Medicine
26 Work places with tables, for short
27 Edsels, commercially
28 Crawled, say
29 Fires
32 "Hair" co-writer
34 "Lulu" composer
35 Jerk
36 Gone by
37 . . . on a long car trip
41 Direct-mail sticker
42 Rural parent
43 Actress Patricia and others
44 Social connections
45 Film director Allégret
47 Enduring
49 Silly Putty holder
50 Racing jibs
52 A bank may have one
53 . . . at a beach picnic
59 Querying responses
60 Fancy ___
61 Fat
62 Allied victory site of 7/18/44
63 Skin
65 One of a Latin trio
67 High ratings
68 Do a knight's work
69 Figure skater Kulik
70 Roommate, informally
72 High-jump need
73 House pet's plaint
74 . . . at the dinner table
78 Like Homo sapiens
81 Chucks
82 Tee, e.g.
83 Sweet Italian wine
85 "Jurassic Park" actress
86 Start of the last line in "The Star-Spangled Banner"
87 Life form
89 Hypnologist's subject
90 Dickens's Little Dorrit
92 . . . on Christmas morning
96 Cole Porter's "___ Loved"
97 Underlying
99 Common background for British P.M.'s
100 Cries after charges are made
101 Tiny, in part
102 Kind of race
103 Lionized comedian?
104 Caldwell of "Master Class"
105 Some meditation
107 Go once over lightly
108 . . . on Mother's Day
115 Grown-up elvers
116 Title woman in a 1925 Broadway hit
117 Grand Prix circuit name
118 Andre Young, a k a Dr. ___
119 Man who's wired?
120 Insectivorous creature

DOWN

1 ___ uncle
2 Mideast grp.
3 Somebody special
4 Dorks
5 "Hansel and Gretel" prop
6 80's–90's singer Suzanne
7 Christian ___
8 "A Man and a Woman" composer
9 Christie creation
10 Buffet table items
11 Sweeping
12 Fishing wires
13 Safeguard
14 Not willing to experiment, maybe
15 Egg containers
16 . . . on the first day of school
17 Bagel request
18 Poplars
21 Checker, e.g.
23 Knots
29 Cigarette introduced in 1913
30 Stone with curved, colored bands
31 . . . at a family reunion
32 Camelot, to Arthur
33 Hole producer
34 ___ tiger
35 Bear
37 Tyler and Jackson, e.g.
38 Old New Yorker cartoonist Gardner ___
39 Lit
40 Blue-pencils
46 Capons, once
48 Run through
49 Poetic adverb
50 Spring ahead
51 Threshold
54 Clearwater National Forest locale
55 Certain speech sound
56 Long-necked instrument
57 Kind of whale
58 Small amount
63 A.T.M. need
64 Scads
65 Speech coach's assignment
66 Some shoes, for short
71 Chomp
72 Music since the 40's
73 Unite
75 "Hamlet" court fop
76 Locale in a western
77 Casts off
79 It's bad on wood floors
80 Sandra Dee title role, 1961 and 1963
84 Without this, a maid is mad
86 Coming
87 Brazilian port of 1 million
88 "___ he drove out of sight . . ."
90 Degraded
91 Gambler's I.O.U.
93 Jack-tar
94 Present
95 Jeered
98 Theories
101 Prefix with red
103 Director Wertmüller
104 Penne alternative
105 Gusto
106 Robert ___
109 D.D.E.'s arena
110 Singer Sumac
111 Cio-Cio-___ (Madame Butterfly)
112 Bathroom need
113 Suffix with Capri
114 Site of many 90's experiments

by Nancy Nicholson Joline

ACROSS

1 Shakes
9 Shouting
15 Do
19 Pointed ends
23 Hardly vintage
24 The Mormons' trek, e.g.
25 ___ Kumar, "The Jewel in the Crown" role
26 Request on an order
27 Madonna role, 1996
28 Meryl Streep role, 1985
30 "Qué ___?"
31 Devil's Island escapee ___ Belbenoit
32 Pops
34 Home of the Ewoks
35 One who gets the message
37 Signs of superciliousness
40 Old railroad car, maybe
42 Up
44 Strauss opera
45 Part of an e-mail address
47 Broadcast
49 Suffix with glamour
50 Skyline features
51 Cate Blanchett role, 1998
56 Marie-France Pisier role, 1981
59 Hymenopteran
60 Prefix with form
61 Attention
62 One of Chaucer's pilgrims
63 Response to a garbled fax
65 Person of great endurance
67 Brief warning
69 Ogee shapes
71 City on the Loire
74 Certain toothpaste tubes
75 1992 A.L. Championship Series M.V.P.
78 Med. specialty
79 Son of Judah
80 Chicken
81 Sub components
83 Alternatives to 32-Across
85 Year after Augustine became the first Archbishop of Canterbury

86 Center opening
89 Sir, in Portugal
90 Words repeated in "___ is above the law and ___ is below it": Theodore Roosevelt
93 Beau
95 Early record label
98 Ingrid Bergman role, 1948
100 Salad ___
101 Stopped
102 Our, in Augsburg
103 Ship's dir.
104 H.S. event
105 Rights org.
106 Dinosaurs' open mouths, e.g.
108 It's hardly welcoming
111 Flood
116 Dixie school
117 Final
118 Strata
119 Chamber pieces
122 Saw
124 Québec peninsula
126 Real estate ad abbr.
127 Burly types
128 Rod
130 Glow
133 W.W. II Mosquito pilots
134 Ancient Irish capital
135 Castaway site
137 Greer Garson role, 1943
139 Sigourney Weaver role, 1988
142 Quakers
144 Benevolent one
145 It's a natural
147 Ice, with "up"
148 Celebrities get these
149 Some quarters
151 Gumshoes
153 They open up at night
158 Showed off
160 Bel ___
162 Nursery school item
164 Check
165 Miffs
166 Sissy Spacek role, 1980
169 Judi Dench role, 1997
172 To ___ (perfectly)
173 Lasting attachment
174 Like a crystal chandelier
175 Effort
176 Computer ___
177 They've come out
178 Soprano Mitchell et al.
179 Tossing

DOWN

1 Holds
2 Fact
3 Vacant
4 Native Americans might raise a flap about this
5 Get on
6 Beat
7 Servant of Antony in "Antony and Cleopatra"
8 Council
9 Pasta go-with, perhaps
10 Second-rate
11 Title of respect, abroad
12 Spy's equipment
13 Military weapons
14 Corporate operations
15 Cling to
16 Intl. assn. since 1948
17 Burned up
18 Maneuvers adroitly
19 Place near Vesuvio
20 Vanessa Redgrave role, 1968
21 People who watch their bags
22 Least lavish
29 Broadway concerns
33 Gossip
36 It helps the medicine go down
38 Columbia competitor
39 Words of concurrence
41 Place for cards, perhaps
43 Ram
46 Gettysburg figure
48 Lot for Wednesday's child
51 "Paradise Lost" and others
52 Writer Jones
53 Favorites
54 Knocks
55 Lover's keepsake, perhaps
57 Message ender
58 Rainy day provisions
64 Think creatively
66 State, once
67 Oater feature
68 Fleece providers
70 Round-table sessions
72 Bestows lavishly
73 Pet
76 Mediterranean resort site
77 From
82 Settles
84 F.D.R.'s mother

87 Work with feet
88 Threatened
91 Air
92 Longtime TV western star
94 Reveals
95 "The Hot Zone" virus
96 Jennifer Jason Leigh role, 1994
97 Part of E. I. Du Pont
99 Man's name meaning "champion"
101 Whizzed through
107 Jaded
109 Way to produce a champion animal, maybe
110 Tel Aviv native
112 Foes of the Romans
113 Spheres
114 À ___ (ashore): Fr.
115 Elianic work
118 Home to Shining Path guerrillas
120 Horse colors
121 Blew
123 Extremely
125 Collector
129 Like corn on the stalk
131 Olympics event
132 Bribe
135 Salt lake
136 Ancient Semitic goddess
138 They don't stand on ceremony
139 Transfers ports
140 Signs
141 1942–45 stat. disseminator
143 Completely clean again
146 Schubert's birthplace
150 Calcium, e.g.
152 Break off
154 Place to run aground
155 Do the honors, so to speak
156 Miscellanies
157 Leads
159 Shade of gray
161 East End greeting
163 Sailor's rope
167 Grayback
168 Female principle
170 Small music-makers
171 New Year's, abroad

by Nancy Nicholson Joline

60 CO$_2$

ACROSS

1 Action film sequence
6 TV monitor?
9 Kind of car
13 Twist
18 Until, in Tijuana
19 Solid backing
21 Sauce
22 Suggestions
23 Deep red garnet
24 Not skimpy
25 One who wants the crème de mint?
27 Steak, e.g.
29 Relations
30 Bewail
31 He's a doll
32 Tilts
33 Simple sack
34 Failures
37 Basted
38 Macaroni shape
41 Pro ___
42 Very smart
44 Professional suffix
47 Sound of thunder
48 Where a suit may be pressed
51 Large-print edition of the Bible, e.g.
53 Do-nothing
55 Pulls down
56 The T in M.T.M.
57 Brezhnev, to Khrushchev
58 Yacht centers
60 Veneer
61 Slicker
62 Subject of environmentalist study
63 Pass out
64 Plantations' stations
66 "___ stirreth up strifes": Proverbs
67 Heavy
70 Some clarinets
71 Street clearer
72 Greenish blue
73 Nostril wrinkler
74 Ice pack?
77 Love symbol
78 "Go on . . ."
79 Fit
80 Bounce
81 Operative
82 Tricksters
84 Passes on principle
87 Do a takeoff on
88 Brownie topper
91 Department in Provence
92 ". . . sat down beside ___"
93 Actor Vigoda
96 Where U.P.S. is headquartered
98 Visitor from the sticks
102 Furniture ensemble
103 Didn't flare
105 Crime scene evidence
106 Gardener's gadget
107 Hoosier neighbor
108 Plains Indian
109 Ships
110 Major finale?
111 Pepper, for one
112 More reliable

DOWN

1 Peeper
2 Tonkin Delta capital
3 Like a fly reel
4 Phaser setting
5 Suffer embarrassment
6 Parking lot sign
7 Occurred
8 Loon
9 Fallen apart
10 Slammer
11 Poet's time of day
12 Stag party?
13 Boxer's sparring partner, at times
14 School without dorms
15 Subject of sailors' knowledge
16 Big splash
17 Stimulates
19 Heavy blow
20 Prepares for a hand
26 No longer hot
28 Button in Bond's car
33 Avoiding a clash
34 Dolt
35 Blyth of "Mildred Pierce"
36 Looked down on
37 Participants in 32-Across
38 Sweeping
39 Follower of the news?
40 Birds fly back and forth in it
41 Fool mistake
43 Barbarous brutes
45 Diamond ___
46 Counterfeit cops?
48 Hands over
49 "Give me your answer"
50 "Educating Rita" star
52 A little work
54 Burrows
56 Running figure
58 Committed a hockey infraction
59 Tenochtitlán resident
60 Bat eyelashes
63 Detour
64 Chairman of note
65 Two-time Emmy winner as best actor in a comedy
66 Rise
68 Barge ___
69 Jay's home
71 Sounds of unhappiness
72 Anagram of 71-Down
74 French royal name, 987–1328
75 Wake attendees
76 Expensive gift
81 Opportune
83 They go for the gold
85 Undergo natural selection
86 Hit 70's sitcom
87 Truman's nuclear agcy.
88 Bags of diamonds
89 Liszt's "La Campanella," e.g.
90 Set straight
92 Noted park name
93 One of 3.5 billion
94 Pig out
95 Computer command
97 "___ forgive our debtors"
98 Western weapon
99 H.S. subject
100 Let out
101 Major animal?
104 Bit of repartee

by Harvey Estes and Nancy Salomon

APOSTROPHES IN THE HEADLINES

ACROSS

1 Half of a 1955 merger: Abbr.
4 Florida footballer
9 "Zip-___-Doo-Dah"
13 Mallow family plant
17 Strive
18 Horror film director George
19 Like relaxed-fit jeans
21 Conch shell effect
22 VIOLENCE ON THE ICE GETS OUT OF HAND!
26 Some Iroquois
27 Burdens
28 Releases
29 Great bargain
30 Shoe strengthener
31 Does something appealing?
32 Ending with Smurf or Rock
35 Dormmate
38 Word on the Great Seal
42 CONCERT ENDS WITH DISH ON FAN'S HEAD!
48 Partially
49 "The Sound of Music" song
50 Hibernia
51 Do in
52 Half-and-half half
54 Dudley Do-Right's beloved
55 ___ Tan (cigar brand)
56 Paesano's land
57 Clueless
59 Ref. room offering
61 Chapeau's perch
63 INSURGENT'S PARKA IS GUNFIRE CASUALTY!
71 Michigan college
72 Blue shade
73 Section of Queens
74 Five-iron, once
78 Year in the life of Constantine

81 Figures on Pharaohs' headdresses
83 Afoam
84 Basket material
85 Symbol on a phone button
86 Works with measures
88 Back-to-sch. times
89 OPERATING PHYSICIAN HAS TROUBLE WITH STATIC CLING!
93 Squid squirts
94 Back-baring top
95 Autocrat
96 Church center
97 Juanita's "those"
100 Not upright
105 Dancing man in "Dancing Lady"
109 Zealous
111 Don't mind
113 ONE PART OF EMPLOYEE RETURNS TO JOB!
116 As old as ___
117 Postembryonic
118 With class
119 A.A.A. recommendation
120 Bank take-back
121 Campaigner's stand
122 Kind of mail
123 Teakettle sound

DOWN

1 One of the Three Musketeers
2 Attack locale
3 French school
4 "Tauromaquia" artist
5 Rockers' equipment
6 Part of AT&T: Abbr.
7 Electioneer
8 Shade of blue
9 A lot, maybe
10 First of two related lists
11 German resort

12 Overflowing
13 Lunchbox treat
14 Brown and Williamson brand
15 Large number
16 Pounds' sounds
18 Colorful partridge
20 Union member
23 1990's car
24 Prefix with version
25 "The Nanny" network
30 "___ off to see the Wizard"
31 Ancient Semite
33 Pro ___
34 Window over a door
36 Chit writer
37 Medley
38 ___ cosa (something else): Sp.
39 Kind of time
40 Lucie's father
41 Ready to go in
42 Somewhat, slangily
43 "Er . . . um . . ."
44 Poet/dramatist Larry et al.
45 Country towers
46 One who makes a bundle
47 Checks to make sure
48 Fraud
53 Heavy sweaters
56 Oft-misused contraction
58 Something underfoot?
60 Criticize, slangily
62 Catholic Reformation writer
64 Feeling
65 Animal with striped legs
66 1997 boxer of the ear?
67 Extinguish
68 Corinthian, for one
69 Gossamer
70 Those opposed

74 ___ operandi (ways of working)
75 ". . . unto us ___ is given"
76 Like some jokes
77 "___ a Rebel" (1962 Crystals hit)
79 Four-striper: Abbr.
80 Rock's Mötley ___
82 Gnats, rats, etc.
85 Drooled
87 Married mujer: Abbr.
90 Zhivago portrayer
91 Ragú alternative
92 Lush, in a way
96 Biomed. research agency
98 Lord's workers
99 Alan of "Havana"
101 Throw, as a grenade
102 Certain girders
103 Sunnites and Shiites, e.g.
104 Wee ones
105 At a distance
106 Pro or con
107 Kisser
108 Shots, for short
109 Morales of "La Bamba"
110 Hand-held holers
111 Vier preceder
112 "___ show you!"
114 Posting at SFO or LAX
115 Old Spanish queen

by Cathy Millhauser

ACROSS

1 Doesn't stop cold turkey
10 Chooses.
13 First call?
17 Hesitant
23 No longer painful
24 Like a chandelier
26 Kind
27 It may pick up in the afternoon
28 Like most bottles
29 Turn out
30 Hear
31 Fished in crevices
32 Performer of complicated operations
34 Toulouse time
35 ___ Day
37 Pertaining to church taxes, old-style
38 See 83-Across
40 Ground for a claim
43 Unbalanced
47 Testify
49 Tighten
51 Cavern
52 Utter
54 Descendant of Muhammad the Prophet
55 Spread out
58 Like some traditions
60 Mount Vernon, e.g.
62 Treasured instrument
64 Dwight Eisenhower's mother's name
65 With judgment
67 Flushed
69 Windy City rail system, briefly
70 Noted Russian shrine
73 Isn't cautious (with)
76 "Buy" or "sell," say
77 Word in Kansas' motto
79 Like
80 Hopper
81 Mathematician Hein
82 Legalistic adjective
83 With 38-Across, popular entertainment
85 5.5-point type sizes
87 View
90 "Description of the World" writer
92 Connected
93 Mescaline source
94 Kind of vaccine
95 Work on
96 With the bow, in music
97 Shade of green
98 Year the Roman writer Persius died
100 Fictional lawyer
101 Tell-tale weapon?
106 Reason for coyness, maybe
110 Exercise
112 Liaison
113 Subject of Project Blue Book
114 Put on the shelf
116 Kid
117 Blatherskite
118 Early game score
120 Milking area
121 Nut
124 "Ah'm ___ it!"
125 New Jersey ___
126 Bridge comment
130 Childish doings?
132 Earthquake aftermaths
134 Isolate
136 Duplicate
137 More subtle
138 Crayola shade
140 Verse style
143 Debussy subject
146 Shows level-headedness
153 Feuding
154 Can
155 "An Old-Fashioned Girl" author, 1870
156 Entertaining thoughts
157 Cooks
159 Top
160 Fertilizer ingredients
161 Like most paparazzi
162 Volleyball player
163 Wraps up, so to speak
164 TV drama settings
165 Place for verbal expression

DOWN

1 Soupçon
2 Whistle, maybe
3 Old-time entertainer
4 "Chicago" lyricist Fred
5 Goes back over
6 Shooter's supply
7 1887 La Scala premiere
8 Hats with tassels: Var.
9 "The Godfather, Part II" character
10 Tough luck, in Britain
11 Medicare cutback proponents?
12 Hit hard
13 "Immediately!"
14 Up
15 Bringing down
16 Crane
17 John Huston's film-directing debut
18 Opposite of smooth
19 Big bird: Var.
20 Chapter
21 "A Loss of Roses" playwright
22 Fantail, for one
25 "It ___" ("Who's there?" response)
33 Cry before disaster
36 Colorado natives
39 Kind of valve
41 Onetime military engineer for Cesare Borgia
42 Seat of Humboldt County, Calif.
44 Examine thoroughly
45 Starve
46 Gave birth to whelps
47 Buyouts, e.g.
48 Actor M. ___ Walsh
49 Log carrier
50 Show fear
53 Kids
56 Was moved by
57 Take over
59 Lily, in Lille
61 The Euphrates crosses it: Abbr.
63 Site of a black hole
66 Web site?
67 Capitalist's concern
68 It's tied at the back
71 Manet, at times
72 Fundamental
74 "Symphonie espagnole" composer
75 Tangy ethnic food
78 One of the Channel Islands
83 Group with Grammy's 1982 Record of the Year
84 Word with sing or string
86 Mailing to a casting director
87 They don't take turns
88 Some canines
89 Nonsense
90 Wing, say
91 Model
92 Upstairs, in Uruguay
93 Igneous rock far beneath the earth's surface
94 Dear people?
96 Intermission ender, maybe
99 Part of a football play diagram
100 Like some bedsheet corners, in Britain
102 Bind, as grass stalks
103 Setting of many Stephen King novels
104 Instrument lens
105 Detaches, in a way
107 Printing amount
108 Poet's eye
109 Rupture
111 Fliers with wedge-shaped tails
115 Sad feeling
119 Six-time Rose Bowl winner, for short
122 Billion years
123 Major fishing area in the Pacific Rim
127 Blows away, so to speak
128 1979 Duvall title role
129 ___ month (moon phase recurrence)
131 Roy Orbison classic
133 How complainers complain
135 It can put you to sleep
137 "The French Lieutenant's Woman" author
139 Appalachian feature
141 Apology preceder
142 Alpha, beta, gamma, etc.
144 Top dogs
145 Order to a typographer
146 Family dogs
147 Latin pronoun
148 Macintosh, e.g.
149 Plug
150 Anvil locations
151 ___ stroke
152 Spot
158 Rounder than round

by David J. Kahn

63 LE PUZZLE

ACROSS

1 Eritrea's capital
7 Heart contraction
14 "The ___ Williams Show" of 1960's TV
18 Bearers of calves
19 Many a Floridian
20 Dressed (up)
21 Alaska denizens
23 Fiasco at the bar?
25 Trial
26 Rural tracts
28 Lecterns
29 Hosts
30 Minimally
32 The Baron, of college basketball
34 Bleaching solution
35 Maximum
36 Direct
38 Jupiter and others
40 "Dream-Land" poet
41 Conscription problem?
43 City or province of Spain
47 Ornamental attire
48 Dick
49 Fire
50 Crepe de Chine, e.g.
52 Actor Erwin
53 "___ fliegende Holländer" (Wagner opera)
55 Part of a classical trio
57 Inexpensive cigar
59 Black
61 A little knight life?
65 Actress Benaderet
66 Desktop problem
68 Unconventional
69 Effective
71 Pop musician Ocasek
72 Tom's fishing gear?
75 Sound units
76 They can be twisted
78 Nerve opening?
79 Bubblehead
81 It's bigger than a med.
82 Lighten up?
83 "Le Coq ___"
84 Summit gatherers, for short
86 Locale in the game Clue
88 Lampoons
91 Pop stars turned versifiers?
95 Publisher Ballantine
96 How to give a reprimand
98 ___ nous
99 Unruffled
102 PC component
103 Kid's ball material
105 "Leaving Las Vegas" actress
106 Opening at an opening
107 March
109 River to the Colorado
111 Inuit: Abbr.
112 Little laughter while still on the runway?
115 Suggest
117 Dentist's request
118 Column feature
119 Amazed onlooker, e.g.
120 Vaulted church area
121 Yields
122 Yield

DOWN

1 Opposite of smooth
2 Marksman
3 Did some quick metalwork?
4 Ryan's "Love Story" co-star
5 "Get ___!"
6 Poser
7 S.A.T. takers
8 Shrill cry
9 Cop's contact
10 Do some craftwork
11 Saturnalias
12 Princess who observed the Force
13 Yet, in poems
14 Ancient Incan capital
15 Cooper's tools
16 Sign a new lease
17 Summer quaffs
20 Became faint
22 Fahd, for one
24 Stench
27 Light arrays
31 Fallback position
33 Diving maneuver
35 Very soon after
37 A.C.L.U. concerns: Abbr.
39 Infant's need, for short
42 Oft-framed document
43 ___ Grande, Ariz.
44 Bear, in Bolivia
45 Hypothesis about the origin of bracelets?
46 Property recipient, in law
49 "The Life of the Insects" playwright
51 Poet who wrote "A thing of beauty is a joy for ever"
52 Steinbeck's birthplace
54 Light brown
55 Union locale
56 Cougar, briefly
57 60's–70's hallucinogen
58 Yardarm attachments
59 Jettison
60 Cigar end?
62 Judicious
63 1984 Peace Prize recipient
64 Some deer
67 Replies of confusion
70 Spray alternatives
73 Queue before Q
74 End of a trip
77 Actor Cariou
80 H. Rider Haggard adventure
83 Buggy terrain
84 According to
85 "Buddenbrooks" author
87 Rue Morgue culprit
89 One of the Lennon sisters
90 Filled
91 Show
92 Full of feeling
93 One on a board
94 Pleasure ___
96 Benchwarmers
97 Lozenge
99 Old money
100 Formal jackets
101 Put out
104 Dentist's suggestion
106 City on the Yamuna River
107 So
108 Surveyor's work
110 Architectural pier
113 11-member 19th-century org.
114 MS. preparers
116 Vocal objection

by Rich Norris

ACROSS

1 "Much Ado About Nothing" friar
8 Long Island town with a weather station
13 Diversified
20 Lake of the Four Forest Cantons
21 Queen topper
22 Quite a while back
23 Without change
24 Pianist Claudio
25 To the extent that
26 Chat
27 The
29 Film frame
30 Kin to blackguards and knaves
32 Some coal carriers
33 Opening run
35 Bill passers
36 Boulez's New York Philharmonic successor
37 Psalm ender
42 Pulitzer playwright Akins
43 Carry out
45 "I'm so glad!"
46 Biblical question
47 Overlooked
49 Purple shade
51 Heavy-duty hauler
52 Pretend
53 Gather with difficulty
57 "Batman" sound effect
58 Language of Mexico
61 A castle of Blackbeard overlooks its harbor
63 ["Oh my!"]
66 Russian name meaning "holy"
68 "___ your disposal"
69 Where Davy Crockett was born: Abbr.
70 Ghostlike
75 Word that's an accidental acronym of a Hemingway title
77 Santa Fe-to-Roswell dir.
78 Overwraps
79 Oversight
83 Home with a view
85 Great times
87 Showed off, as biceps
89 Substantial
90 Finish completely, with "up"
93 Juice providers?
95 "___ then I said . . ."
96 Doesn't work
97 Become a member
99 Shot maker
100 Race place
101 Phony
102 Experience
103 Wedded
104 Slips, e.g.
110 Uncomfortable
114 Gourmet sprinkle
115 ". . . ___ in the affairs of men": Shak.
116 Offender
117 Driving force
118 Mission in "The Thin Red Line"
119 Short solo
120 More lathered
121 Downing Street family, 1955–57
122 Is displeased and then some

DOWN

1 One way to fall
2 Stratagem
3 Soufflé ingredient?
4 Fit together
5 Barbaric
6 ___ the finish
7 Kind of shorts
8 "That makes sense"
9 Begets
10 1968 British comedy "Only When I ___"
11 Poker player's declaration
12 Potbellied
13 Get way too thin
14 Stravinsky and others
15 Skillful
16 Morales of "La Bamba"
17 Bust maker
18 Alike: Fr.
19 Two teaspoons, say
28 Itty-bitty bit
31 Car co. bought by Chrysler
33 Blue, in Baja
34 Cut to the ___
35 Can
36 Big drawer?
37 When early-bird specials often end
38 Emergency PC key
39 At risk
40 Transport of song
41 Offers?
43 Sicilian spouter
44 Rear end
48 Zing
50 Be off
51 Beats in a pie contest?
54 Got off
55 Little dog, briefly
56 Pennsylvanie, e.g.
59 "I love you, Juanita"
60 As well
61 Like some transactions
62 Like a rat in ___
63 One of a Christmas trio
64 Appropriate
65 Panoramas
67 Roscoe
71 They rise above sea level
72 Tee follower?
73 Flynn on screen
74 Whom "she saw . . . on a seesaw," in a children's ditty
76 Where to find Aletsch Glacier
80 Our world
81 Cause to go
82 Swirl
84 Short order, for short
86 Mount in 1980 news
87 Clones, e.g.
88 "Who am ___ judge?"
90 Many a dinosaur
91 Doing kitchen duty, to a G.I.
92 Set up
94 Caustic cleanser
98 Preached
100 Sulking
101 Kind of heart or teeth
102 Was sustained by
103 Stan's man
104 Goddess in "Aïda"
105 "Little ___"
106 Spanish appetizer
107 "The Bronx ___ . . ."
108 French Sudan today
109 The Owls of the Western Athletic Conference
111 Come-on
112 Whereabouts
113 H H H

by Manny Nosowsky

65 PERSONAL SCORE

ACROSS
1 Brute
7 Pregame fixture
13 Joke
20 Embodiment
21 Solar wind source
22 Property receiver
23 I (1946)
26 Reactions to baby pictures
27 Big bang creator
28 Sci-fi extra
29 Cancún kinsman
30 Curlew's cousin
31 Drive gear
34 Chicago's ___ Expressway
36 Anticipatory exclamation
39 "My Mama Done ___ Me"
40 Burning heat
41 1998 report producer
43 It (1961)
47 Misfortunes
51 Charles de Gaulle's birthplace
52 Cell component
53 Capitulate
55 Employ a therapeutic technique
59 Fed. grant giver
62 Red dye no. 1?
63 They may get a licking after dinner
64 From the heart
67 Frostflower
68 Serb, e.g.
71 He (1975)
74 Person with vows
75 More than flinches
77 Features of a face
78 1930 Triple Crown jockey
80 Viola d'___
81 Part of B.C.E.
82 Flivver
85 Movie that Khrushchev watched being filmed
87 Fritter away
91 Kind of sprawl
93 Accordingly
94 They (1951)
100 Cabbage
102 1990 stage and film biography
103 Renowned British runner
104 Marxist?
105 After-bath application
108 Sleep inducer
110 Recycled item
112 Itinerary abbr.
113 Refuse
115 Old Plymouth
117 Itinerary word
120 You (1977)
125 Triumph
126 Does more than see
127 Relative of jujuism
128 Revolution's enemy, maybe
129 Fixes firmly
130 Novelist's need

DOWN
1 Roman-fleuve
2 Testify
3 Distillery items
4 Letters in a long-distance company's number
5 Cartoonist Wilson
6 Recluse
7 With intensity
8 Prohibition
9 National debt unit
10 Dearie
11 Insect study: Abbr.
12 Muslim messiah
13 De Niro's role in "Raging Bull"
14 The Morlocks ate them
15 Beam
16 Confident solver's tool
17 Bind
18 Kerensky's successor
19 Building toy
24 Flavor
25 Remove a slip?
30 We (1945)
32 Slangy suffix
33 Demond's co-star, in 70's TV
35 She (1989)
36 Night stalker
37 It grows on you
38 Mideast peace talks site
42 Kind of welder
44 Yaw
45 "The Beggar's Opera" writer
46 Buttinsky
48 Slow, to Salieri
49 Shroud of Turin material
50 Lewis Carroll animal
54 "Gotcha!"
56 Bike part: Abbr.
57 Baggy
58 Moore co-star
60 Discretion
61 Negotiate, as a loan
64 Successor to the Prophet, in Islam
65 Cry of pain
66 Road houses?
68 Parker's need
69 Missouri town where Truman was born
70 Onward
72 It's a drag to fishermen
73 "___ momento"
76 Part of a Hemingway title
79 Oil container
82 Copy cats?
83 "East of Eden" girl
84 Picnic hamperer
86 York, for one: Abbr.
88 "Comin' ___" (1981 3-D western)
89 Close
90 Air
92 Vocal opposition
95 Without interest
96 Oversight
97 Straight, in a way
98 Laplander, e.g.
99 Corrupt
101 Part of a Hemingway title
105 Proffer bait
106 Fur seal
107 Morning alarm
109 Ship that brought the Statue of Liberty to the United States
111 Join securely
114 This pulls a bit
116 Endorsed
117 Middle of a famous boast
118 ___ a secret
119 Worked up
121 1960's singer Little ___
122 Flight
123 Ballot abbr.
124 Provincetown catch

by Robert Malinow

66

FOURLOCKS

ACROSS
1 Buñuel collaborator
5 Satan, at first
10 Brought on board
15 Stadium that seats 55,000+
19 Orwell's alma mater
20 Dog or hound
21 Accustom
22 Jacks take them
23 Big boom boxes?
25 Smoking settlements?
27 Forger
28 What dispensaries dispense
30 Suffuse
31 ___ Lingus
33 Stands for
34 Items for those seeking closure
35 Like some candles
39 Cub house
40 Secular
41 Bach wrote over 200 of these
43 1773 jetsam
46 Moscow resident
50 Baseball's Vizquel
51 Strip joint instruction?
55 Like some fears
56 Singer Clark
59 Madonna, originally
60 They're exclusive
61 Sodium or chlorine
63 Insurance co. employee
64 List abridgements
66 Like Life Savers
68 A deliveryman may have one
69 Outstanding
73 Hindu honorific
75 Readies, in a way
80 Car owner's headache
81 Brush
84 First-aid item
85 Sleipnir's master
86 Clucking clairvoyant?
88 Machu Picchu worshipper
89 Drink
91 Flexible fish
92 Toy for indoor play
95 Jumpers, informally
96 Pride
99 Puck stoppers
100 Swinger
103 Michelangelo's marble source
107 Maui's ___ Crater
108 Oriental nursemaids
109 Uses a shortcut
111 94-Down's faith
115 Binary language?
117 F.B.I. director's side of the story?
119 Pole, e.g.
120 Papal court
121 Skater Stojko
122 Cubic Rubik
123 Newcastle's river
124 Bridge guardian
125 Studio stock
126 Ocean

DOWN
1 G.O.P. opposers
2 First half of the files?
3 Burt's ex
4 What many a baby throws?
5 Overpower
6 Convention
7 Classic 1925 Von Stroheim film
8 Undercut
9 Basic amino acid
10 "Start playing!"
11 "Seven ___ blow" (boast in a children's story)
12 Hicks
13 History chapters
14 Christmas time: Abbr.
15 Spare tire eliminator?
16 Seasonings
17 Finish
18 Boobs
24 Kind of radiation, in science fiction
26 Paramecium fringe
29 Happy
32 Like Gen. Schwarzkopf
34 No-goodniks
35 Aim improver
36 Great Pyramids sight
37 Related through a mother
38 Cassette type: Abbr.
40 Black-and-white engraving
42 Break down, in a way
44 Ship's heading
45 Sign to look elsewhere
47 Methane's lack
48 Goya's duchess
49 Noun suffix
52 Dry run
53 Kind of nut
54 Stevenson's "Prince ___"
57 Admit
58 Quotation notation
60 Gregg grad
62 Locks
65 Needle case
67 Pitch-dark
69 Make a splash
70 Fix up
71 Drop a line?
72 Royal records?
73 People in photos, usually
74 Ocasek of the Cars
76 Mealtime prayer result?
77 Site of 1967 fighting
78 Tom or Sam
79 Carillon sounds
82 Letters on a scoreboard
83 Female lobster
86 Novel creation
87 Like certain battery terminals: Abbr.
90 Crow
93 Unnamed litigant
94 Dervish
97 Muster
98 Brooks Robinson, e.g.
100 Biblical verb
101 "Our Town" heroine
102 Heathen
103 Where the Mississippi meets the Ohio
104 Use
105 Kind of gland
106 Get ___ on (hurry)
109 Innuendo
110 Like Darth Maul
112 One-time capital of Rome
113 Top-notch
114 The L train?
116 Be in a cast
118 Slalom curve

by Greg Staples

ACROSS

1 Stone of some Libras
5 AM selections: Abbr.
9 Tussle
14 Raising a sweat, perhaps
19 Pitch
20 Foot: Prefix
21 Verse from Villon
22 Do some campaign work
23 When to slop in the mud on the farm?
26 Kind of joint
27 Gray, for one
28 Maryland athlete, for short
29 Almost purée
31 "___ dreaming?"
32 Like some apartments
33 Council of ___ (1409 assembly)
35 With bite
37 Took action
38 60's coll. radicals
39 Wisest of the centaurs, in Greek myth
41 Brown shade
42 Not be alert
43 Tale of a tiny bellower?
45 Talk effusively
49 Alpine sight
50 Hot to trot
51 Priest of I Samuel
52 Shoulder piece
54 20's beer barrel busters
55 Like some shopping
59 Homecoming visitors
60 Acted like
62 Apple product
64 Shortly before?
65 Traitorous intruder?
68 What an ass declares in cards?
71 Berlioz's "Les Nuits d'___"

72 Beloved subject of Thomas Campbell
73 Jaywalking, e.g.
74 Home run, slangily
75 Not at all like
78 Newswriter's specialty
80 Exploitative employer
82 Rough stuff
83 Tot toter
84 Stitch souvenir
86 Abbr. starting some corp. names
87 Bedtime reading in the forest?
93 Place for a run
94 Call upon
95 Canine cover
96 Calendar abbr.
99 Roaster, maybe
100 Nonabrasive
101 Cross with a loop
102 They exist from hand to mouth
104 It's often left hanging
105 "Got it"
106 Warrant follower
108 High point
110 Takes off life support?
112 "Time to have a foal"?
115 Gold standard
116 Pal
117 Profusion
118 Prince Albert, e.g.
119 Doesn't fold
120 Like cancan dancers
121 Noise pollution
122 Play opener

DOWN

1 Them
2 Held jointly
3 Troublemakers, never
4 Potted plant place
5 1974 Sutherland/Gould spoof

6 Airborne faultfinder
7 Botheration
8 Separates
9 Prodder
10 Tight
11 "Radio Free Europe" rock band
12 Red-white-and-blue
13 Green gem
14 Comfortably inviting
15 New England state sch.
16 One who accepts charges
17 Use Schedule A
18 Put down
24 Common aspiration
25 Singer Lennon and others
30 Essayist Day
34 Smooth
36 Stick-to-it-iveness?
40 Blood pigment
42 Seat of honor location
43 Handy digit
44 Scratched (out)
45 Big cheer
46 Ready, with "up"
47 Burning the midnight oil, so to speak
48 Makes veal, maybe
53 Shaq's alma mater
54 "That's ___ sure!"
55 Source of 85-Down
56 Germanic tribesman
57 Familiarize
58 Tube-nosed seabird
60 7th-century Arab caliph
61 Brown, in a way
63 Phone button trio
66 Set aside
67 Test for a college sr.
68 Part of an E-mail address
69 So far, on a pay stub: Abbr.
70 Hindu habits

73 Handle
76 Sci-fi writer Frederic
77 It makes one hot
79 Item that's often hidden
80 Athens attraction
81 Voice stretcher
83 Like many a sports report
84 Comparison basis
85 Stopper
87 Center strip cuts?
88 Gorge
89 Trumpet blast
90 Barely enough
91 One step
92 Flubbed
96 Affixed
97 Boot
98 A matter of will?
100 Nubs
103 Author Jong
107 "When I was ___ . . ."
109 Seasoned hands
111 Word from a con
113 Fix
114 A crowd, for Caesar?

by Nancy Salomon

68   JUST FOR OPENERS

ACROSS

1 Arises
6 Florida fruit
12 Officer of the Ottoman Empire
15 Jerk
19 Private sector?
20 Hit actor of 60's TV
21 The Jets or the Sharks
23 Home of the Black Bears
24 Florida fruit
25 One of the "three faces of Eve"
26 House detective's item
27 They get their kicks
28 Opera featuring the "Prisoners' Chorus"
29 Au courant
31 Eric Dickerson's alma mater, for short
34 Try
35 Crooks' patterns, to cops
38 It may be due
39 First name in erotica
41 Computerniks push it
45 O'Neill masterwork, for short
47 Singer Jackson
48 Scratch
49 Like rich desserts
51 Semiotics study
53 Assassinated Swedish P.M.
54 Like a combination lock
55 Battery type
57 Three-ply snack
58 Kaffiyeh wearers
59 Request from an ed.
60 Directional suffix
61 Tails
64 Lush
65 Allowed

67 Hydrocarbon suffix
68 Spooks
70 Evelyn who played Scarlett's sister
73 Gizmos
75 String of pikake flowers
76 Set foot (on)
80 Forest clearing
82 "The Postman Always Rings Twice" wife
83 Burns's birthplace
84 Painter Veronese
85 First name in TV talk
86 Tipped off
89 Arrive angrily and abruptly
91 ___ de Castro (storied noblewoman)
92 Soccer score, perhaps
93 Party dance of old
94 Mountaineers' wear
97 "The Maids" playwright
98 Excites
100 Draft org.
101 Project
102 Vote in the Senate
103 Dwindles
106 ___ "Le Morte d'Arthur"
110 Iceberg's location
111 Noted heart surgeon
115 Individually
117 Poet Levertov
118 Yves St. Laurent fragrance
119 Thanksgiving aftermath
120 Run on
121 Utah's ___ Mountains
122 Latin trio member
123 Draft org.?
124 Judge
125 Append

DOWN

1 Word with chop or sweat
2 The O'Haras' home
3 Asteroid discovered in 1898
4 Test group?
5 What CBers watch for
6 Some addresses
7 Rodeo item
8 Bridge supports
9 Like some rewards
10 What solar flares are measured in
11 Ship's log entry
12 "So that's it!"
13 Make the rounds?
14 Still serving
15 Vehicle for Blanche DuBois
16 Part of a pump
17 Amahl's visitors
18 Melville novel
22 Added to the database
30 Rajah's spouse
31 Medic
32 Restrained mood
33 In vain
35 They'll knock you out
36 Neighbor of Silver Springs
37 Hingis rival
40 Jean or Jacques
42 Greece, to the Greeks
43 Macho military type
44 Where Hemingway wrote "A Farewell to Arms"
46 German wine valley
47 Dan Beard's org.
50 Variation of the samba
52 Pea-___ (dense fogs)
53 Spread
56 Treasury of sorts
60 Prefix with friendly

61 1990's dance craze
62 In tune
63 George ___
66 Julian calendar date
69 Ringo's original surname
70 Best boy's colleague
71 Turgenev heroine
72 Lyricist Carole Bayer ___
74 Part of E. I. du Pont
77 Easy wins
78 Hodgepodges
79 They'll bray for you
81 Spinners
83 Suffix with 24-Across
84 Lost momentum
87 ___ loop (skater's jump)
88 Contest hopefuls
90 Sound of impact
95 Emanations
96 "A Tidewater Morning" author
98 Purse items
99 Exodus commemorations
104 Gentry
105 Mathew Brady shade
106 First name in espionage
107 Astringent substance
108 Byron poem
109 It's shown to the usher
110 The Red and the Black
112 Cherry type
113 Aries of Taurus
114 Essential company figure
116 M.P.G. determiners
117 Means of ID

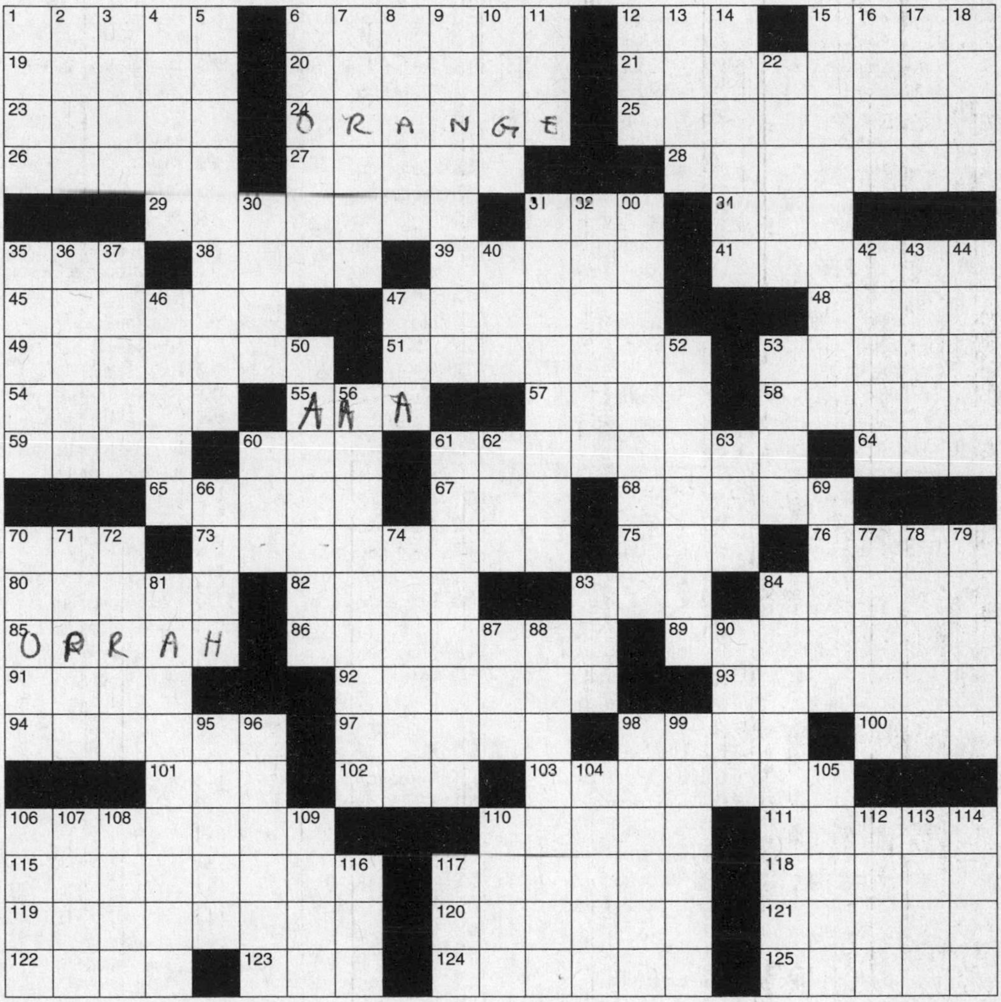

by Nancy Nicholson Joline

ACROSS

1 It "passeth all understanding": Philippians
6 Mark for life
10 Moselle tributary
14 Shore souvenir
19 Dumas swordsman
20 One of Chekhov's three sisters
21 Fiend of dreams
22 Home of Creighton University
23 Nixon's first Commerce Secretary Maurice ___
24 Garr of "Close Encounters"
25 Microfilm unit
26 Odd-toed ungulate
27 DRAB
29 DESSERTS
31 CBS News's "___ America"
32 Prefix with political
34 Baby talk "words"
35 Baseball Hall-of-Famer Duke
38 PAN
41 I. M. Pei's alma mater
44 Feted with alcohol
45 MADE
47 Advertising sign
48 Thai title
49 Quantities: Abbr.
50 God: Sp.
51 Hounding group, often
53 U.K. honour
54 PAWS
57 Smoked delicacies
58 SUNG
60 Perch
61 Speculate
62 Kind of cycle
63 Twit
64 More Machiavellian
65 Like some rebates
67 Perfume
68 Small songbirds
71 Journalist's idea

72 OMEN
74 Overly
75 Metallic mirror
77 Vacation location
78 Dynasty of Confucius and Lao-tzu
79 SLIPUP
80 Simplicity
81 Smokejumper's need
83 WETS
84 "Guinness Book" suffix
85 STOOL
87 Squashes
88 Assist, in a way
89 Needlefish
90 Like the Beatles in "Help!"
92 LIAR
97 REVILED
102 Newbies
103 E or G, e.g.
104 Abbr. on a mountain sign
105 Cliff hangar?
106 Japanese cartoon art
107 Hidden valley
108 Big Island bash
109 U.S. notable
110 Strained
111 Get smart with
112 Revenuers
113 Lispers' dread

DOWN

1 Overtake
2 Words to a traitor
3 Starbuck's superior
4 Admits
5 Tried
6 ___ voce
7 Rated G, so to speak
8 Cultural intro
9 Parjanya, in Hindu myth
10 Somewhat
11 Ending with golden or teen
12 Sphere of study

13 Very devout
14 OPRAH
15 Actors Epps and Gooding
16 Valley of vintages
17 Stylish
18 Carol start
28 According to
30 High times
33 Charlotte-to-Raleigh dir.
35 Overload
36 Halos
37 DNA
38 Alternative to plastic
39 Turmoil
40 "What thou ___, write": Revelation
41 MINED
42 Motivate
43 Café cup
45 Solution's strength
46 Large mythical birds
48 Flatmate
50 "Max ___ Returns" (1983 film)
51 Bullfight attendants
52 Bloom of "Limelight"
54 1973 Elton John hit
55 Winches
56 Put up
59 Put off guard
61 Reflect badly?
63 Prickly-leafed plant
64 Said, old-style
65 Tricky billiards shot
66 Is in
67 "The French Connection" highlight
68 Rush-hour subway rarity
69 Went after
70 Hot items for colds
72 Materials for venetians
73 TRAMS
76 Twins share them
78 Hens
81 Fin. adviser

82 Actress's cameo role, perhaps
83 What some fabrics resist
85 Cast down
86 Nash and others
87 Classic LeMans series car
88 "Oh, give me ___"
90 Leading
91 Word on the Great Seal
92 Homme d'___ (statesman)
93 Talkative starling
94 Grand finale?
95 "Germinal" author
96 Summers in la cité
98 It may be found with a magnifying glass
99 81-Down's recommendations
100 Have pheasant under glass, say
101 Three are a match

by Charles M. Deber

ACROSS

1 Wags
7 Jack-tars
12 Like some tickets
19 Song on which "Love Me Tender" is based
20 One trying to avoid charges?
21 Cheese with holes
22 Golfing?
24 People stand for this
25 U.S. trading partner
26 Thundering group
27 Water under the bridge
28 Palindromic diarist
29 Share a role?
34 A charming way to look at things?
37 Arizona tourist locale
38 "Deuce Coupe" choreographer
39 It's for good measure
40 Walking the dogie?
45 Brown ___ (old musket)
46 "The Sound of Music" figure
49 Smell bad
50 Boy who's bowed
52 Cleaning cabinet supplies
53 Assassins have them
56 Like 007
61 Sale item abbr.
62 Former monarchy
64 G.I.'s superior
65 Cause of an immune response
66 Irrelevant to Don King?
71 Upright
72 Initials on a toothpaste box
73 Supreme leader
74 The Rams of the Atlantic 10 Conf.

75 Aquanaut's place
76 Proved valid, in a way
79 "ER" order
80 Actress Virna
82 Impulse transmitter
83 Kind of tree
85 Mirth
89 An event to honor the best hospital patient?
93 "___-Cop" (1988 film)
95 Aimée from Paree
96 Crème de ___
99 An angry place to live?
101 Rearranges the lettuce?
105 Broadcaster in many langs.
106 Bowlers
107 Start of a prayer
108 Pres. Davis led it
109 Prepare, as a fancy invitation
111 Two good N.F.L. plays?
117 Carpet cleaner
118 Scotland yard, approximately
119 Puts down
120 Lab employees
121 Like the surf
122 Hunter's trophy

DOWN

1 Bourbon drinks
2 Wise counsel
3 Senator Hutchison
4 High priest at Shiloh
5 Half a cartoon duo
6 Part of a line: Abbr.
7 More likely
8 Halt
9 Brightly colored
10 Summer shade
11 Regular: Abbr.
12 Do about as expected
13 Venae ___
14 Embodiment

15 Cartographic fig.
16 Snug snack item?
17 Ballet headliners
18 White House affairs
19 Monkeys' uncles
23 "Got ya!"
27 Black-and-white diving birds
30 Benches
31 Web site?
32 Anthologies
33 Walk softly
34 Massage reactions
35 Jazz man
36 Essence
38 N.F.L. draft move?
41 March marchers
42 Safety device
43 Piece of stage lighting
44 Neil and Loretta
46 Dress designs
47 How some learn
48 "Big" girl
51 Muchachas: Abbr.
53 Lanford Wilson's "The ___ Baltimore"
54 M.I.T. or N.Y.U.
55 Little one
57 Chest protector
58 Rodent that menaces sugarcane
59 Kind of pathway
60 Thing
62 Dietary
63 "All the perfumes of ___ . . .": Shak.
65 "___ is as good as a wink"
67 Actor Wheaton
68 Where the successful go
69 Words of commitment
70 Singer Cara
76 Some bar features
77 Can
78 Anderson's "High ___"
79 Rocker Patty
81 Home-run hitters
83 Rivals
84 Visitor to Siam

85 Like a worst-case scenario
86 French poet ___ de Lisle
87 Tees off
88 Verdun was in it once: Abbr.
90 Scrape
91 Press for payment
92 Marseilles Mrs.
94 Sad news
97 Witch's deity
98 Not so punishing
100 Relief pitcher
101 Ballerina Shearer
102 Title name
103 Travel word
104 Marino and others
107 Its HQ is in Brussels
110 Tattler
111 Group the Surgeon Gen. addresses
112 Part of the 25-Across: Abbr.
113 Jazz grp.
114 Lamp site
115 Knack
116 ___ Friday

by Randolph Ross

ACROSS

1 Rolls up
8 Carbo-loading meal
13 Jalopy
18 Country with modern Africa's first female head of state
19 Stick to
20 Undercut
21 Feminine jazz group?
24 Buffoon
25 "Already?"
26 Silo contents, for short
27 Grp. that holds an open house
28 Recently
31 French business partner, maybe
32 A prof. may have them
33 New girl on the block?
39 Twiddled one's thumbs
40 On target
41 Old terr.
42 Socially challenged person
43 Beat on eBay
46 Swab
48 First bishop of Paris
51 Comfort
52 "___ Tu" (1974 hit)
53 Emmy-winning Lewis
55 Run out
58 Shoe specification
59 Classic role-playing game, informally
61 United
63 Like Shelley's "sister of the spring"
65 Unbelieving lady?
70 Beef on the hoof
71 It may be laid down in church
72 Part of a religious title
75 Smidge
78 Charge
81 Unpopular kids
83 Times Square sign
84 Lake of the Ozarks river
86 Engaged in a coven's rite
88 Conceive
90 Certify
92 Yours, en français
93 Dutch city NW of Amheim
94 Personification of the sea, in myth
95 Address abbr.
96 Common woman?
102 Personification of the sun, in myth
103 Many truckers
104 Saved, in a way
105 It may be tapped
106 Old curiosity shop stock
107 Classic Caesar/Gershwin tune of 1919
110 Street fleet
114 Handy miss?
119 Sudden
120 Bottom of a ring
121 Like some Asian-Americans
122 Novelist Frances Parkinson ___
123 China ___
124 Keeps going

DOWN

1 "When I was ___"
2 Mr. Minderbinder of "Catch-22"
3 Genesis name
4 Bell ringer
5 Overseas title: Abbr.
6 Article in Stern
7 Inept person
8 It shows the head of José Morelos
9 Designed for flight
10 Attention ___
11 Washing instructions site
12 Costume
13 Doughnut filler
14 Swindle
15 Not fixed
16 Not final
17 Classical literary works
19 Big name in Top 40
20 Early stage
22 Old photo print
23 Where 17-Down originated: Abbr.
29 Pooch
30 Ballet practice
31 N.J. post
33 Gossiped
34 "Hänsel und Gretel," e.g.
35 Wait on
36 O. Henry surprise
37 Protection from a storm
38 "Rule Britannia" composer
39 Metro map abbr.
44 Cybername
45 Low grade
47 A PC may use it
48 Like a Mel Brooks movie
49 High-tech suffix
50 Sent unwanted E-mail
54 Like Hitler
56 ___ Walton League (conservation group)
57 Land of 147 mill.
60 Servant's list
62 J.F.K. guesstimate
64 Related on one's mother's side
66 Stein of the Comedy Channel
67 Immobilize
68 Distinctive profile
69 Poor soil ingredient
73 When some news shows air
74 River through the Savoy Alps
75 ___ good turn
76 Old navigation instrument
77 "Geronimo," e.g.
79 Burns
80 "See ya"
82 It's usually played first
85 "Is that so!"
87 Holiday preparation
89 Actor Johnny
91 Writer's block?
93 Actress Getty
97 Sign of secrecy
98 Beethoven symphony
99 Bacteriologist Salk
100 Like Nash's lama
101 "Macbeth" witch
102 Wheel man
103 Brilliant feats
107 Off
108 Worked like Arachne
109 Some miles away
111 Tennis score
112 Bit of sweat
113 Workers need them: Abbr.
115 What's what in Spain
116 TV's "Emerald Point ___"
117 Press hard on
118 Bunk

by Brendan Emmett Quigley

ACROSS

1 Awestruck tourists, e.g.
7 Not more than
13 Not as quiet
19 Eyepiece
20 One hit
22 "Era la notte" opera
23 "Monday Night Football" scene at Texas Stadium?
26 Ernst contemporary
27 Nibble
28 Understanding comments
29 Desert sight
30 Send on
33 More than disquiet
35 Difficulty
36 ". . . and __ yours!"
37 "Jerry Springer" topic?
43 From the beginning, in music
45 Lifestyle
46 Yelling
47 Big Ten Conf. member
48 "The Addams Family" cousin
49 __ acid
53 Enlightenment, in Zen
55 Drop off, maybe
56 Alternative title for "My Three Sons"?
61 Gang leader of 70's–80's music
62 Safire subject
63 "The door's open"
64 Loses it
67 Kind of cap
70 Reprimands
73 For the full band, on a score
76 Mediterranean tourist destination
79 Bring (out)
81 Why "The Brady Bunch" girls do well on exams?

87 Rock's Bon Jovi
88 Rumbled in the wee hours?
89 Hard sell, maybe
90 Gulager of TV's "The Virginian"
91 Decide to leave, with "out"
92 Alley __
93 Kind of degree
95 Had space for
97 Part of an action sequence on "N.Y.P.D. Blue"?
104 Musical dir.
105 Hook shape
106 Toyota model
107 Training sites, for short
110 Off-road transports: Abbr.
112 Start of many California place names
113 Funny one
114 Dig in
115 Effect of laryngitis on "The Nanny" star?
123 Deepest of the Finger Lakes
124 Sea cow
125 Book that's not read much
126 Quick round of tennis
127 Everett of "An Ideal Husband"
128 "Villette" novelist

DOWN

1 Be a success in life
2 Find __ for the common cold
3 1994 Best Original Screenplay winner
4 Room extension
5 Cheering word
6 Hit letters
7 Group
8 Hemingway setting
9 Coffee orders
10 Circus cry

11 Jeanne, e.g.: Abbr.
12 Piece of pipe
13 Gym shapes
14 "Respect for Acting" author Hagen
15 Inhabitually
16 Ignes fatui
17 Dash
18 "Oliver Twist!" girl
21 Weather, in a way
24 Nullify
25 Discredited, as a theory
31 Actress Bartok
32 Some used cars
34 It glistens
35 Indo-__
36 __ Island, Fla.
38 Driving passion?
39 Hogshead
40 Many Guinness listings
41 Future atty.'s challenge
42 Western agreement?
43 Gumshoe
44 Friend of D'Artagnan
50 Lac contents
51 "__ Over" (1964 hit)
52 Bloke
54 Water tester, maybe
57 Subdivision maps
58 It's big in corporate management
59 Like old cigars, maybe
60 Sister of Calliope
65 Annoys
66 Court worker
68 Muscles on 13-Down
69 Hoopsters' targets
71 Rehearsal
72 Architectural column support
74 Sweltering
75 Frequent negotiator with the P.L.O.

77 Blast
78 Jackie's O
80 Result of a failure
81 Campus figure
82 Mediate
83 Subject of wishful thinking?
84 1999 Ron Howard satire
85 Consumer Reports report
86 Slippage preventer
87 Scribble (down)
94 Guys
96 Fire
98 Angles
99 Office break time, maybe
100 Mineral named for a French physicist
101 Judge, at work
102 Draft proposal for a treaty
103 Stuff
108 Charged
109 Newspaper section
110 Mr. Moto reaction
111 81-Down, often
112 Thwack
116 First-class
117 Old political alliance: Abbr.
118 Safari sight
119 Fortune
120 Executive Fed. agcy.
121 38-Down benchmark
122 "Is that __?"

by David J. Kahn

ACROSS

1 "Prima Ballerina" artist
6 Hill of law
11 Chester Arthur's middle name
15 Marvel Comics superhero
19 Betel nut tree
20 Confined to one part of the body
21 U-shaped instrument
22 How some things strike
23 Using tape on a bulletin board?
26 Part of the eye
27 Charades, basically
28 Most clever
29 Pell-___
30 Be near bankruptcy
31 Early 70's sitcom
32 Logo
34 Kind of twist
38 Some Brahms works
39 They probably don't think much of you
40 Convex molding
41 Furniture material
42 About 1% of the atmosphere
43 Headline about the Rolling Stones' leader's recovery?
46 Noted work?
48 Way out
52 Order at the George & Dragon
53 Sea bordering Kazakhstan
54 Huge
55 Come into one's own
57 Certain chord
59 Library material
60 Memory
61 A-mazing animals
64 It involves many sharp turns
65 Big paperback publisher
66 Hit the big time
67 Chucks
68 Color wheel display
69 Kitchen tool
70 Neighbor of Mont.
71 It's said with a wave of the hand
72 Compass heading
75 Catch
76 Fleece
77 Blows to the head?
80 Wallace cohort
83 Woman from Bethlehem
86 Sit up for
87 Dog treat
90 Brimless bonnet
91 Nixon policy
93 1980's Sandinista leader
94 Director's option
95 Lister's abbr.
96 Gloomy
97 Having less shading
99 Game resembling pinball
104 "Civilization" director Thomas
105 Soft drinks revealed?
107 She found success with Caesar
108 Purcell's "___ and Welcome Songs"
109 #2 Bill Withers hit of 1972
110 Like some stocks
111 Acetylacetone form
112 Common mixer
113 It may reflect well on you
114 Driving problem

DOWN

1 "Hi and Lois" family pet
2 Old railroad name
3 Contracts
4 One more than sieben
5 Towering desert plants: Var.
6 Certain gene
7 Silent votes
8 Here, but not here
9 Serving of 52-Across
10 Atlas Mountains locale
11 Pop star Morissette
12 Université preceder
13 Synagogue chests
14 Kitty
15 Cardsharp's technique?
16 Shantytown composition
17 Food that may be folded
18 Spheres
24 ". . . ___ You Ain't My Baby?" (1944 hit)
25 Pavarotti's football feats?
33 What Mr. Brown can do, in a Dr. Seuss title
34 Tomato variety
35 Ungodliness
36 Viva ___
37 Source of a bugle call
38 "Do ___!"
39 Centimeter-gram-second unit
41 Wrapped up
42 Advance amount
44 One taking orders
45 The Depression and others
47 Org. with many rules
49 Kind of thermometer
50 Hungry look
51 Lean (on)
54 Fancy home
55 Previously
56 Simple
57 "The Breakfast of Charlatans"?
58 Teen party
59 "We're constantly attacked" and "the stockades are rotting"?
61 Punishment unit
62 Janis's comic strip mate
63 Get-up-and-go
64 Influence
65 Philistine
67 Locks
68 Language with mostly monosyllabic words
71 Covered with many small figures, in heraldry
72 View electronically
73 Stage presentation
74 Italian duchess Beatrice d'___
76 Red or black, e.g.
78 Incubator activity
79 Cow, maybe
81 Hot time: Abbr.
82 Bombs
84 Like the oceans
85 Beat in yardage
87 Lace site
88 Affixable, in a way
89 It may be laid on thick
90 Mother ___
91 What thunder may do
92 Make permanent
94 Like many gardens
98 Fuss
99 Fleshy fruit
100 Favorite one
101 Palm used for basketry
102 Tree trunk bulge
103 Ghoul
106 Small peg

by Raymond Hamel

74 TRADEMARKS

ACROSS

1 Congressional matters
5 Risking dizziness
10 Winner's feeling
14 Salon supply
19 Like some speeds
20 Rich kid in "Nancy"
21 Schleps
22 See 33-Across
23 London Magazine writer
24 ___ Heights
25 This and that
26 "The Age of Anxiety" poet
27 Cable talk show trademark
31 Acid neutralizers
32 Smart stuff
33 With 22-Across, Federal law enforcement matter
34 ___ Royale, Mich.
35 See 2-Down
36 Shrewd
37 E.M.S. course
40 Clubs: Abbr.
43 Subjects for forgiveness
44 The Thinker, for all we know
45 Tongue locale
46 W.W. II military trademark
51 "Aladdin" prince
52 Aggregate
53 Astronomical figures
54 Beat, so to speak
55 Improve
57 "Our ___ Sunday" (radio soap)
58 Bit of a draft
59 China's ___ Piao
60 TV comedy trademark
67 Singer Acuff
68 Palacio feature
69 "I guessed it!"
70 Welsh emblem
73 Quick notes?
76 Pink-slips
78 Driven types
81 Phenom
82 Art world trademark
86 Plodding sort
87 Controls
88 Actual existence
89 Composer Bruckner
90 Noted cathedral town
91 Truck treatment
92 Prefix with sphere
93 Drake Stadium site
95 Kind of block
96 Cornstarch brand
97 "Good night, sweet ladies. Good night, good night" speaker
100 1940's film trademark
105 Running errands, say
106 Ring dance
107 Month after Adar
108 Band
110 Lodge member
111 Like most proverbs: Abbr.
112 Diaphanous linen
113 1997 Oscar-nominated title role
114 Last Supper attendee
115 Care for
116 Quite a bargain
117 Choice word

DOWN

1 You may stand in it
2 With 35-Across, a sign of spring
3 Hardship
4 Short result?
5 Historic Scottish county
6 Novice
7 Author Havelock ___
8 Verve
9 Many years ago
10 Certain print
11 Eye-openers
12 Sponsorship
13 Pill passage
14 Hardly plentiful
15 Bluenose
16 Hitch, in a way
17 Part of A.B.A.: Abbr.
18 Driving needs
28 Mix it up on the mat
29 Stylish music
30 Breathless
35 Perjurer
36 "High Hopes" songwriter
37 Circuitry site
38 "The Dunciad" poet
39 Symbol of slimness
40 Man in a garden
41 Coastal catch
42 Appealing
43 Lips service?
44 Leaves off
45 Kind of column
47 Inflamed
48 For the boys
49 Check
50 Small belt
56 Glean
58 Sign by a ticket window
59 Columbia squad
61 "Return of the Jedi" girl
62 Some investments
63 ___ Minor
64 Amiens is its capital
65 Chinese dynasty before the birth of Christ
66 Push back, perhaps
71 Come back
72 Insightful
73 Salinger girl
74 Stake driver
75 Any NATO member
76 Top of a range?
77 "Judith" composer
78 Gymnastic finishes
79 Bygone sign on U.S. highways
80 Not so newsworthy
83 Long green
84 Free
85 Veggieburger, to a hamburger, e.g.
91 Play varsity ball
92 Businessman Hammer
93 Ex–New Jersey college, founded 1893
94 French fashion figure
95 No-goodnik
96 Moses' brother
97 Davis in Hollywood
98 Totally
99 Film "___ of God"
100 Extinguish
101 "O" in old radio lingo
102 Cheer
103 Single
104 Brawl
109 Comment before "I don't know"

by Lou and Fran Sabin

ACROSS

1 One of a study group?
7 Strengthen
13 Checked for heat
20 Potential tennis opponent?
21 Can't take
22 It may be represented by a tree
23 Chevy Chase and others
24 Like a 54-Across
25 Like standard music notation
26 Somme time
27 Start of an idle question
30 Lip
32 Can't take
33 Old lamp fill
34 "My Friend Flicka" author
37 Key material
39 Face of time?
43 Question, part 2
49 Gathering point
50 Beethoven's Opus 20, e.g.
51 Washed away
52 Finger board?
53 "King ___" (1950–65 comic strip)
54 Boot part
56 Athenian H
59 Prospector's dreams
60 Cold development
62 "Apollo 13" subject
64 Knighted dancer ___ Dolin
66 Pilothouse abbr.
67 With 69-Across, asker of the question
69 See 67-Across
71 Push-up aid?
74 Muff
75 Actor Andrews
77 Psychopharmacologist's prescription

79 Donnybrook
82 Wasn't off one's rocker
84 Nodding one, sometimes
86 ___ mundi
87 Cloudiness
88 Propeller holder, perhaps
90 1954–76 national capital
92 Helps with a con job?
93 Question, part 3
96 Nordstrom rival
97 Work time
98 Like a 117-Across
99 Bow
100 They're heard when Brits take off
103 Sound from a pen
107 End of the question
116 Soccer ___
117 Encircling ring of light
118 Like AB negative, of all major blood types
119 It was defeated in 1588
121 Reedlike
122 Pilot
123 Unsubstantial
124 Service providers?
125 Time-___
126 Superlatively slick

DOWN

1 Loafer's lack
2 "West Side Story" girl
3 Memory units
4 King of France
5 From the top
6 Musician John
7 "King of Hearts" star
8 Up
9 Cheese place
10 Preoperative delivery, once
11 Start of a break-in
12 Helen's mother

13 Smooth
14 How baroque architecture is ornamented
15 Digging, so to speak
16 A-line line
17 Intoxicating Polynesian quaff
18 Major Hoople's outburst, in old comics
19 Take-out order?
28 They may be lent
29 Twelve
31 Infatuated with
35 Get a move on
36 Masters
37 ___ lamb
38 Dwell
39 Botherer
40 One way to serve coffee
41 Plot, Perhaps
42 Big name in chips
43 Autocrats
44 Toast beginner
45 Archilochus work
46 It doesn't sting
47 Hero of medieval romances
48 They might get drunk in the summer
49 His "4" was retired
55 It's good to meet them
57 Red ___ (Japanese food fish)
58 Vantage point
61 North American dogwoods
63 Shade provider
65 Unliquidated?
68 "Tuning in the U.S.A." broadcaster: Abbr.
70 68-Down's medium
71 "You are correct!"
72 Talk a blue streak
73 It may precede other things
74 Some are lean

76 In ___ way
78 Head set?
79 Corp. recruits
80 Portoferraio's place
81 Vichyssoise ingredient
83 Schussboomer's transport
85 Took away (from)
89 Accident-assessing areas, briefly
91 Wonderment
93 Dispute subjects, perhaps
94 Beekeeper's exclamation?
95 "Now ___ you . . ."
97 Greeter
100 Spelling and Amos
101 Skip ___
102 Focus of some tests
104 Effigy
105 Meeting points
106 It's headquartered in Troy, Mich.
107 Stinger
108 Molokai show
109 Vultures were sacred to him
110 Carnival sight
111 Winged one in Wonderland
112 Latin I word
113 Collapsed
114 Highland toppers
115 Oblast on the Oka
120 What "5" can mean

by Elizabeth C. Gorski

1

L	A	V	A	S	█	B	E	E	F	E	D	█	A	T	T	I	L	A
O	R	A	C	L	E	█	A	N	N	E	X	E	S	█	T	R	I	T	O	N
S	O	L	T	I	F	A	R	E	D	W	E	L	L	A	M	I	D	O	W	N
E	C	L	I	P	T	I	C	█	█	E	C	L	A	T	█	L	I	N	E	S
S	K	I	N	S	█	R	A	C	E	R	S	█	V	O	I	L	E	█
█	█	G	O	B	█	R	O	Y	█	█	S	E	N	S	█	S	L	E	W
D	O	M	I	N	O	S	O	L	E	F	A	T	R	E	L	A	T	I	V	E
A	K	I	N	█	W	E	L	L	D	O	N	E	█	R	E	V	█	K	E	N
T	A	X	█	N	E	Y	█	O	C	T	O	█	A	M	E	N	D
U	P	E	N	D	E	D	█	E	S	T	H	█	F	U	S	T	Y	█
M	I	D	O	R	I	T	I	R	E	S	O	F	A	N	L	A	S	O	L	O
█	S	Y	N	O	D	█	A	C	R	E	█	F	O	R	T	R	A	N
M	A	C	H	O	█	S	E	E	A	█	L	A	O	█	D	Y	E
A	L	I	█	F	M	S	█	P	E	L	L	I	C	L	E	█	T	I	E	R
L	A	T	I	F	A	H	S	O	L	D	O	N	A	D	M	I	R	E	R	S
L	I	E	N	█	R	A	H	S	█	W	E	D	█	S	N	O	█
█	F	A	V	R	E	█	C	A	S	S	E	S	█	G	L	O	A	M
S	T	A	I	D	█	I	B	S	E	N	█	M	O	L	E	L	I	K	E
L	A	R	E	D	O	F	A	N	S	T	I	M	I	N	G	S	O	L	I	D
A	X	I	L	L	A	█	T	O	A	S	T	E	E	█	S	T	P	E	T	E
B	I	D	D	E	R	█	B	R	Y	A	N	S	█	A	E	D	E	S

2

D	I	M	█	S	E	A	L	█	S	T	D	S	█	I	R	O	N	Y
E	V	E	S	█	C	A	L	E	B	█	C	R	E	W	█	N	O	V	A	E
B	A	N	K	█	A	S	I	D	O	█	H	O	P	E	█	A	B	E	T	S
A	N	T	I	Q	U	E	T	A	X	C	O	L	L	E	C	T	O	R	█
C	H	I	N	U	P	S	█	O	S	O	L	E	█	O	U	T	A	G	E
L	O	O	S	E	█	B	U	F	F	A	L	O	T	A	X	B	I	L	L	S
E	E	N	█	S	T	Y	L	E	█	S	P	E	C	█	C	L	O	T
█	S	T	R	█	M	E	M	O	█	M	C	I	█
J	A	M	E	S	E	S	█	T	A	X	F	R	E	E	A	T	L	A	S	T
A	M	A	T	█	E	K	E	█	R	I	L	E	D	█	R	E	A	D	E	R
K	I	T	S	█	L	A	T	A	X	D	O	D	G	E	R	█	T	O	G	A
E	N	S	U	R	E	█	A	N	E	A	R	█	E	L	I	█	O	B	E	Y
S	O	U	P	Y	S	A	L	E	S	T	A	X	█	S	A	W	Y	E	R	S
█	E	S	L	█	E	L	O	I	█	G	I	A	█
M	B	A	S	█	T	E	A	T	█	U	N	P	E	N	█	H	I	C
G	I	M	M	E	T	A	X	S	H	E	L	T	E	R	█	G	U	A	R	E
S	T	E	E	L	E	█	P	E	E	L	E	█	E	D	I	T	I	O	N
█	M	A	N	Y	H	A	P	P	Y	T	A	X	R	E	T	U	R	N	S
M	A	O	R	I	█	A	N	T	I	█	U	R	K	E	L	█	R	I	M	E
A	L	I	E	N	█	A	S	I	T	█	S	C	E	N	E	█	N	E	A	R
P	A	R	D	O	█	S	E	C	S	█	S	S	T	S	█	R	N	S

3

```
C I T R I C   F O S S     L A M P P O S T
O N E I D A   I B E T   C A F E T E R I A
K I E V I N C L I N E   A C C R A B A T S
E T S     T O M   S P A R E     B L O T
  H O P I N   B U S I E S T   A L E N E
B E I J I N G B E A U T Y   A R T Y
L A R O S A   Y E L P S   F R O M   M O B
O T T     M E T     L A M   T O N E
W A S O N T O   S E P I A   A V E N U E
  R O O S T   P R A G U E N O S E S
  T A I P E I P E R S O N A L I T Y
  M I N S K S T O L E S   T R A C E
B E R G E N   T I L D E   T W E E D L E
A L E E   O W E     B R O   E E N
A D D   S T I R   C O C O A   H A S P E D
  A U S T   C A I R O P R O C T O R S
P O S S E   H O O D L U M   O L E A N
I N N S   B L E S S   O L D   E R A
S E O U L F O O D   K A B U L S T O N E S
A N O M A L I E S   I D O S   T I P T O E
N O T E P A D S   N E X T   O D E S S A
```

4

```
F R A S   T R E S S   L O L A   H I S T
R E N T   R U R A L   I D I O T   I N T O
O T T O   U N I T E   F O U R B A G G E R
G R O U N D S K E E P E R   T I N H O R N
S O N T A G   S P A   S T A R D A T E
  S T E L A   I L S   A L D E N
W H O   T R I P L E P L A Y   A D D U P
H U B B Y   A P E R   A I L S   N O I S E
A S I A   C R A G   E N R O L L   U R S A
T H E L M A   L A C E D   R O O S T E R S
  L O N G   L O R E S   B O A S
S N A P P E R S   W I R E D   S L I P O N
I O L A   D I E P P E   W I D E   D U K E
B A I R D   N A T O   R U N E   B E R R A
S H A K O   M A K E U P G A M E   E A R
  F R O M E   E L F   O N E A L
  S C R E W I N G   A F L   T S E T S E
M E L A M E D   R E L I E F P I T C H E R
O P E N I N G D A Y   A D O R E   H E I R
D I R K   S E N S E   N I C E R   E R N E
S A K S   T A P S   S N I P S   R E E D
```

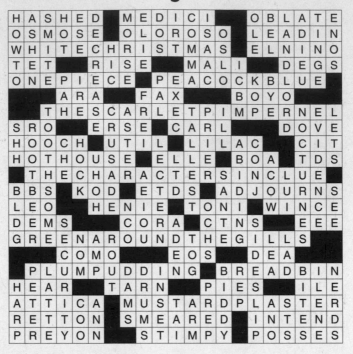

5

HASHED · MEDICI · OBLATE
OSMOSE · OLOROSO · LEADIN
WHITECHRISTMAS · ELNINO
TET · RISE · MALI · DEGS
ONEPIECE · PEACOCKBLUE
ARA · FAX · BOYO
THESCARLETPIMPERNEL
SRO · ERSE · CARL · DOVE
HOOCH · UTIL · LILAC · CIT
HOTHOUSE · ELLE · BOA · TDS
THECHARACTERSINCLUE
BBS · KOD · ETDS · ADJOURNS
LEO · HENIE · TONI · WINCE
DEMS · CORA · CTNS · EEE
GREENAROUNDTHEGILLS
COMO · EOS · DEA
PLUMPUDDING · BREADBIN
HEAR · TARN · PIES · ILE
ATTICA · MUSTARDPLASTER
RETTON · SMEARED · INTEND
PREYON · STIMPY · POSSES

6

RICHIE · SCRAPS · CREASE
EROICA · TAIPEI · SAURIAN
VENDERBENDERS · ASSERTS
ELSE · PUNTER · SAUTE · LII
LAIRD · STA · AISLE · VEAL
ENS · OCTOBERVEST · PASTE
DDT · CHER · LEAST · PAUSED
TAD · LAYS · POLL
SHADOW · VINETUNES · TREK
COLOR · GILDS · NITE · LAVA
ARID · BASIS · MIXER · IBAR
RANG · EMIT · METER · SNIDE
FLEE · VATHEADED · SWEDEN
REEL · SLID · LIE
GRAVEL · ACTIN · AONE · TBS
LEVAR · VILECABINET · EAT
OVEN · GAMER · LLD · STARR
SER · SAMSA · ENAMOR · ARNO
SNARLUP · REVERENCEBOOK
EGGNOGS · ELEVEN · MALONE
DEEDEE · DYNAST · PREMED

7

```
P R E S U M E ■ ■ C A B A L A ■ M E T H O D
R A C E G O E R ■ B A N A N A S ■ I G U A N A
I D O N O T L I K E M Y D A D S B R O T H E R
M I L D ■ ■ O K D ■ ■ M E A L ■ ■ A S E
P O I S O N E D K I N G W E D M Y M O T H E R
■ ■ ■ C A N E ■ M I L A ■ ■ A R H A T ■
T O T ■ A S S ■ ■ D E L ■ S E A N C E ■
I L E T T H E M T H I N K T H A T I A M M A D
T I M E ■ A B O U ■ T O A S T ■ E U R O
O O P S I S T A B B E D O P H E L I A S D A D
■ ■ T R I ■ A B B E ■ ■ E S T ■ I D O
A P O ■ K L U ■ T A B I T H A ■ E L O ■ N O S
D R X ■ E L S ■ ■ S H A G ■ ■ I L K ■
N O B O D Y H E L P S M E I N M Y P L I G H T
A M O I ■ E R I C H ■ T E L E ■ R A I N
N O W L A E R T E S A N D I W I L L F I G H T
■ I R I S E S ■ D O E ■ ■ P I E ■ S O S
■ S K E I N ■ ■ O W N S ■ D E L I ■
S W O R D S A R E S W I T C H E D I N A J A M
W A S ■ ■ R A M P ■ ■ U A R ■ ■ D O G E
A T H E A T R I C A L E N D I N G H A M I A M
S H E L V E ■ D E C I D E S ■ S A I L I N T O
H E R M A N ■ S E E S A W ■ ■ T S E T S E S
```

8

```
I R O N I C ■ A R T S A L E ■ E D A M E S
N E V A D A ■ B E A T S I T ■ S A V A N T
R A I S E T H E S T A K E S ■ A P A C H E
E D N A ■ L I S T E N S ■ C U P ■ H A N
D Y E ■ C I D ■ ■ D I S C O ■ E Y I N G
■ ■ M A K E A G R A N D E N T R A N C E
■ S M I L E ■ H O O T ■ I N C A ■ P E E L
C L I N E ■ F O O T ■ ■ T A X ■ P S S ■
R I N G B E L L F O R S E R V I C E ■
A M I ■ ■ R O D ■ E E R I E ■ O R D E R
V E N D O R ■ W A S P S ■ ■ E N S U R E
E D G E S ■ S N A R E ■ L O N ■ G E E
■ C H I P O F F T H E O L D B L O C K
■ C R O ■ T A N ■ ■ U R G E ■ R O U T S
S L E D ■ C R A G ■ D E M O ■ P A R T S
T A K E T H E M O N E Y A N D R U N
A R I D E ■ M E T E R ■ ■ I O N ■ O C T
M I N ■ R Y E ■ ■ S I D E A R M ■ M A R Y
E N D U R E ■ G E T D O W N T O C A S E S
N E L S O N ■ S T E E P E N ■ T U X E D O
S T E E R S ■ T E A S E R S ■ E D I S O N
```

9

Grid 9:

A	S	T	E	R	■	R	A	F	T	S	■	S	A	R	A	■	A	M	I	D
S	L	A	V	E	■	E	C	L	A	T	■	A	R	E	S	■	N	U	D	E
F	O	R	E	S	T	G	R	U	M	P	■	F	I	A	T	■	G	T	O	S
I	T	S	■	■	A	R	O	S	E	■	B	A	S	S	I	N	E	T	■	■
T	H	I	S	T	L	E	S	■	■	S	A	R	I	S	■	E	L	E	E	■
■	■	W	H	A	T	S	M	Y	W	H	I	N	E	■	W	A	R	D	S	■
A	L	G	A	E	■	■	E	O	E	■	■	G	R	A	F	■	M	I	O	■
C	A	R	P	A	T	B	A	G	G	E	R	S	■	T	E	A	B	A	L	L
T	W	I	■	■	U	R	I	A	H	■	E	C	O	■	C	L	O	Y	E	D
S	N	A	C	K	B	A	R	■	■	A	D	A	M	S	■	L	O	I	S	■
■	■	L	E	A	V	E	I	T	T	O	B	E	E	F	E	R	■	■	■	■
■	S	W	I	T	■	■	O	R	B	I	T	■	■	G	A	I	N	S	A	Y	S
S	H	I	F	T	S	■	S	E	E	■	I	R	A	T	E	■	■	N	E	O
M	A	N	T	L	E	S	■	G	R	I	P	E	S	O	F	W	R	A	T	H
E	N	D	■	E	X	E	S	■	■	E	S	E	■	■	R	A	T	I	O	■
W	A	Y	O	F	■	T	H	E	P	R	O	F	U	S	S	E	R	■	■	■
■	S	A	B	U	■	A	R	N	I	E	■	■	S	T	O	N	E	A	G	E
■	M	E	L	O	D	I	C	A	■	S	P	U	R	N	■	■	L	E	G	■
E	M	M	Y	■	L	A	V	A	■	F	E	R	R	I	S	P	U	L	E	R
G	L	E	E	■	E	T	E	S	■	T	R	I	E	D	■	U	K	A	S	E
G	I	R	D	■	G	E	R	E	■	D	E	E	R	E	■	B	E	N	E	T

10

Grid 10:

C	H	E	F	S	■	H	A	S	A	T	■	R	A	F	■	T	O	G	A
O	A	S	I	S	■	E	C	O	L	E	■	O	L	L	A	■	A	J	A	X
W	H	A	T	T	I	M	E	W	I	L	L	Y	O	U	B	E	H	O	M	E
L	A	I	T	■	N	A	T	S	■	L	U	S	T	■	A	R	I	S	E
■	■	■	E	R	A	T	O	■	A	S	A	■	■	S	L	I	T	■	■
W	H	E	R	E	W	I	L	L	Y	O	U	B	E	T	O	N	I	G	H	T
I	O	N	■	H	E	N	■	E	E	N	■	U	L	A	N	■	R	A	O
T	H	O	S	E	■	■	P	T	A	■	L	O	I	R	E	■	S	O	L	O
H	O	W	W	A	S	Y	O	U	R	D	A	Y	A	T	S	C	H	O	O	L
■	■	A	R	R	O	W	S	■	I	V	S	■	■	H	A	V	E	■	■
■	R	A	N	S	O	M	S	■	R	N	A	■	U	N	L	A	D	E	D
■	E	D	G	E	■	■	M	U	G	■	A	R	C	A	R	O	■	■	■
W	H	O	A	R	E	Y	O	U	G	O	I	N	G	O	U	T	W	I	T	H
H	A	R	T	■	N	E	R	D	S	■	H	E	E	■	E	S	T	E	E
E	S	E	■	V	L	A	D	■	H	A	M	■	T	O	R	■	T	A	C
W	H	E	N	W	I	L	L	Y	O	U	D	O	H	O	M	E	W	O	R	K
■	■	E	A	R	S	■	■	A	A	A	■	O	R	A	R	E	■	■	■
■	G	R	E	C	O	■	K	A	H	N	■	A	R	C	H	■	I	S	L	A
W	H	Y	D	O	N	T	Y	O	U	G	E	T	A	H	A	I	R	C	U	T
D	I	A	L	■	S	U	L	U	■	T	R	I	C	E	■	A	D	A	G	E
S	A	N	E	■	B	E	T	■	I	N	T	E	R	■	M	O	R	S	E

11

T	E	A	B	A	G		A	R	C	H	I	E			O	P	E	N	E	D
A	R	G	Y	L	E		B	A	A	I	N	G		E	V	I	L	E	Y	E
O	M	E	L	E	T	P	R	I	N	C	E	O	F	D	E	N	M	A	R	K
S	A	R	A			E	A	S	E			T	A	I	N	T		T	E	E
			W	H	A	T	D	I	D	J	U	I	C	E	S	A	Y			
M	A	O		E	S	S	E	N		A	P	S	E				A	C	I	D
E	T	H	E	L	S			P	S	S	T		H	O	R	M	O	N	E	
D	A	H	L	I	A	S		B	A	C	T		M	A	K	E	S	F	O	R
A	L	O	U		I	H	A	M	W	H	A	T	I	H	A	M		F	I	N
L	E	W	D		L	E	V	O		A	R	I	D		Y	O	D	E	L	S
		W	E	T		L	E	V	I		T	E	D	S		P	O	E		
S	C	A	R	E	D		R	I	N	D		U	L	E	E		G	A	E	L
O	A	F		H	O	U	S	E	K	I	P	P	E	R	S		O	N	L	Y
U	N	F	R	E	E	Z	E		I	L	E	S		A	P	H	O	N	I	C
S	A	L	I	E	R	I		L	E	A	P				I	O	D	A	T	E
A	L	E	C			L	A	S	T		S	T	R	A	W		N	E	E	
		E	G	G	S	I	S	T	E	N	T	I	A	L	L	Y				
S	T	L		O	W	E	T	O			E	A	R	N			U	V	E	A
T	H	E	Y	N	E	V	E	R	S	A	U	S	A	G	E	A	M	E	S	S
A	R	G	O	N	N	E		D	A	R	R	I	N		I	N	M	A	T	E
B	U	S	M	A	N			A	P	P	O	S	E		S	T	Y	L	E	T

12

H	A	S	E	K				R	I	F	L	E		L	I	B	E	R	A	L
E	L	O	P	E	R		T	A	N	D	E	M		E	L	E	V	A	T	E
R	E	T	I	R	E	M	E	N	T	A	G	E		C	O	H	E	R	E	S
			C	R	E	O	L	E			E	R	S	T		I	R	E	N	E
A	S	W	E		F	R	E	E	Z	I	N	G	P	O	I	N	T			
S	O	A	N	D	S	O		E	N	D	E	A	R	E	D		P	O	E	
T	U	T	E	E		C	H	A	R				A	T	H	E	N	A		
E	N	T		G	U	N	C	A	L	I	B	E	R		T	I	E	R	E	D
R	D	S		A	T	O	L	L	S		O	L	E	G		M	U	F	T	I
		I	L	S	A	S			S	N	E	E	R		E	R	E	W	E	
	A	N	E		H	O	U	R	S	I	N	A	D	A	Y		E	C	O	
S	N	A	G	S		A	R	E	A	R		H	U	R	S	T				
A	T	B	A	T		P	E	A	T		A	S	M	A	R	A		S	I	L
C	H	U	T	E	S		S	P	E	E	D	L	I	M	I	T		C	L	E
H	E	L	E	N	A			S	O	O	T			E	B	O	L	A		
A	R	B		T	H	E	S	E	A	T	S		A	B	S	O	R	B	S	
		R	O	L	L	O	F	T	H	E	D	I	C	E		N	E	E	T	
P	A	L	E	R		I	N	F	O		E	R	R	A	N	D				
O	C	U	L	I	S	T		U	N	L	U	C	K	Y	N	U	M	B	E	R
L	I	N	E	A	T	E		S	E	I	K	O	S		S	T	A	R	R	Y
A	D	D	E	N	D	S		E	S	T	E	R			S	N	O	R	E	

13

```
CHAIR ■ LAMB ■ CARB ■ PAOLO
CALLA ■ ALAR ■ AREA ■ REDUB
SHOOFLYPIE ■ MINUTERICE
■ AUNTIE ■ DABA ■ MITOSIS
■ ■ ASTRO ■ DERAT ■ TESTEE ■
AUK ■ HERD ■ LOBO ■ ANT ■ ■
CHIPPEDBEEF ■ BEANSALAD
TOWER ■ ENTREATS ■ ETUDE
SHINOLA ■ SAYS ■ OPTS ■ REL
■ MOONSET ■ ESTEE ■ TILE
HOMEFRIES ■ CORNBREAD
EVAN ■ AMATI ■ TRESTLE ■
MUD ■ CLAM ■ SHOE ■ ESOBESO
ALAMO ■ TITTERED ■ OLDER
LEMONSOLE ■ CODDLEDEGGS
■ TVA ■ EAST ■ SAID ■ YOO
BUSIER ■ SLOOP ■ YESNO
ENCORES ■ BRET ■ SEESAW
SPONGECAKE ■ SHELLSTEAK
TEPEE ■ OVER ■ TACO ■ TERRA
SNERD ■ WAYS ■ STOW ■ SOOTY
```

14

```
CRAG ■ TAMP ■ RYAN ■ ECLAT
ZOLA ■ SUSIE ■ IAMB ■ NAOMI
ELLS ■ CRIST ■ GREATBRAIN
CLASHOFTHETANS ■ BEATTY
HEYYOU ■ IRA ■ WORTHY ■
■ CREATIVEWRING
RCA ■ KERN ■ ISOLDE ■ SKEW
ALL ■ EDGING ■ NOSE ■ SHIVA
PULPY ■ MOATED ■ EARNED
■ BAA ■ OPIATE ■ VALSIGNS
■ BRIDESHEADREVISED ■
WORKPERM ■ RAINES ■ KAL
ODESSA ■ WHYNOT ■ RSVPS
MOVIE ■ DOHA ■ STRODE ■ IGO
BRET ■ MORITZ ■ AWED ■ DAY
■ BINGTHEBULLET ■
■ ALGORE ■ SEP ■ PACKET
CLEAVE ■ CENTERSOFGRAVY
PETLARCENY ■ FILAR ■ UTEP
AUGER ■ OLDS ■ USURY ■ MINE
STONY ■ ELSE ■ PEGS ■ BETA
```

```
S L I M   B I C   A T E L E S S   B L A H
K O N A   U M A   C A M I L L A   E A S E
I F I H A D A N I C K E L F O R   R U N E
P A G E R S   O R R E R Y   W A V E R E D
S T O R E   W E E U N S   S E N A T O R S
        D O H   E T O   T R A I T
  B O Z   C O S M   O N C E   C L A M P S
T E H A C H A P I     O R B     I L K
B A N T U S   I S M   E V E R Y T I M E I
A R O O M   D E C E I V E   A E O L I A
    P U T A D O L L A R I N T H E
  G A E L I C   N E E D I N G   O F O L D
B A N K I D H A V E   E N T   A L T M A N
U N A     A D E     G R A N D M A M A
S G T M A J   D Y C K   S O W N   Y R S
      U S U A L   S A N   O A K
S O R B O N N E   L I O N E L   I S A A C
C L E A N E D   L E S T E R   D E L R I O
A L A R   1 / 2 O W H A T I H A V E N O W
L I M A   S O O T I E R   C E L   D E L E
D E S K   T R O T S K Y   A X E   S L I D
```

```
C A P L E T   S A F E T Y   P L A N E T S
A S L O P E   A C A D I A   I G N O R E D
S K A T I N G S H R I N K   L E G A T E S
T I N   G N U   A T E S T S   S H E D
S N E E R   P A R D O   U N I T S
      M A R P L E   R A D N E R   S C A T
L E N D M E Y O U R S H E A R S   H A L O
A T E A S E   U N E   A R F   C A N D Y
C H I S   F A D I N G   N I A   O R E O S
T I G H T E R   O A R S   S T O R K
I C E   O R I E N T A L S H R U G   S U B
    H O S E S   A P A L   E T I E N N E
I D E A L   S T L   E M O T E R   T A D A
D A V I S   O O H   O V I   U S E R I D
E M E R   C I N C I N N A T I S H R E D S
S P R Y   A R I O S O   K U C H E N
    S A N K A   T A S S O   P E R C H
  A S H Y   S N A P O N   N O H   E L A
P I C A S S O   S A N T A S S H E L V E S
T R O P I S M   I N C O D E   T R A U M A
A S P E R S E   A G E N D A   O D D E S T
```

```
C A R   A D E L A   R A S P   A D A G I O
A D O   G E N U S   E N T O   R E M O R A
T A M T A M O S H A N T E R   S P I G O T
S M A R T E S T   M E L E E S   A N O N
      A H A     R A G E D   T H R O B
C A N C A N O P E N E R   F O O T R A C E
A L E E   S T U B S   S A L O M E   N O L
S T A R S   O L E     L O G   D R A M A
T O T   C H O P C H O P S U E Y   A N A T
      C O A L S   E R R O R   E S T A T E
D E T E R G E   M O E   V A L I S E S
E V O N N E   A L I N E   M A R I O
F E M S   N O N O N O N S E N S E   L A M
I N T E R   U N O     C D I   R A I S E
E L O   E S T O P S   M O I S T   F L I T
S Y M M E T R Y   C H O W C H O W L I N E
      T A N G O   D R E S S     R E O
    C H I T   W I R E R S   B A R N A C L E
S O U S E D   B Y E B Y E E L E C T I O N
E L M I R A   L E N I   S T O N E   A L I
A T B E S T   E R S E   S H U T S   O L D
```

```
S I D E B A R   B A B A S   B A T M A N
I R O N A G E   A R D O R S   A T O N C E
B E A T L E S   M O U N T R U S H M O R E
      R E N T   O I L E D   L I E   P O D
L O C U S T   E U L A   E S S E N
E R A S     N A N   T A C I T   A S C A P
S I L T   L I T T L E W O M E N   A L S O
S O L S T I C E   A D S   P R O   T O S S
E L I   A R E N A S     L S D   I V E S
R E N A M E S   L E G A T O   S U R E T E
      G I P   T O P R A T I N G   K I R
S A B R A S   B O S T O N   O R A C L E S
C R I B   H A S     N A C H O S   E L O
H E R A   A R C   A R E   L O V E L A N D
W A D S   D O U B L E S G A M E   A V I D
A S S E S   U R A L S   R U E   R E N E
      U P S E T   O D E S   L O G S O N
A R P   R E A   I O N I A   P O N E
S E I N F E L D S T A R S   S E A S O N S
P A P I E R   S T I N G Y   S W I S H E D
S P E N D S   C A S T E   T E R E S A S
```

19

T	E	L	S	T	A	R		E	D	G	A	R		A	N	A	G	R	A	M
I	N	A	H	O	L	E		K	O	R	D	A		S	E	Q	U	E	L	A
L	I	K	E	N	E	W		G	E	O	R	G	E	K	A	U	F	M	A	N
E	D	E	L		X	I	I		W	I	L	D		A	F	O	R	E		
		F	R	A	N	K	L	I	N	P	A	D	A	M	S					
P	T	A		A	N	D	E	A	N		N	A	R	C		H	U	R	T	
R	E	M	E	N	D	S		U	S	S	R		E	Q	U	A	T	O	R	
O	N	E	D	G	E		A	T	T	H	E	A	L		U	N	R	I	P	E
B	O	R	N	F	R	E	E		S	O	B	I	G		E	C	O	L	E	S
	R	E	A	O		A	L	F		E	U	R	O	P	E		L	E	S	S
		F	R	I	S	B	E	E		T	E	N	O	N	E	D				
C	O	D	E		S	E	A	L	U	P		S	Q	R		G	R	I	P	
H	A	I	R	D	O		T	O	R	I	I		U	N	W	O	O	D	E	D
I	S	A	B	E	L		D	N	U	O	R	N	I		O	I	S	E	A	U
L	I	N	E	M	A	N		S	N	E	E		C	O	S	S	A	C	K	
I	S	A	R		T	O	R	O		N	O	S	A	L	T		S	H	E	
			R	O	B	E	R	T	B	E	N	C	H	L	E	Y				
A	M	A	Z	E		A	G	H	A		I	O	C		A	F	R	O		
D	O	R	O	T	H	Y	P	A	R	K	E	R		K	O	O	K	I	E	R
A	N	G	O	R	A	S		N	U	K	E	S		I	T	S	O	N	M	E
H	O	O	T	O	W	L		S	M	E	L	T		A	T	A	V	I	S	M

20

I	P	E	C	A	C		E	D	I	T	S			D	O	E	S	I	N	
L	I	L	A	C	S		M	E	T	E	O	R		P	O	S	T	U	R	E
S	K	I	R	T	T	H	E	I	S	S	U	E		I	L	L	E	G	A	L
	E	S	A	I		A	R	G	O	T		P	O	L	L	O		A	T	L
		F	I	B	R	I	N		C	H	O	K	E	S		P	R	E	Y	
A	C	H	E		L	E	T		N	A	M		A	S	H	A	R	P		
T	H	O		T	O	M	A	T	O	S	O	U	P		O	M	E	L	E	T
T	I	N	C	A	N	S		O	N	E		L	I	T	U	P		U	V	A
U	S	E	R	I	D		G	M	S		P	E	S	O	S		A	M	I	R
	Y	I	P	E		N	E	E	D	Y		D	E	E	P	F	A	T		
	K	N	E	E		S	P	I	N	D	R	I	E	D		L	E	A	N	
M	A	U	R	I	C	E		S	E	A	T	S		J	I	M	I			
O	P	T	S		H	E	S	S	E		M	E	T		E	D	E	R	L	E
L	U	C		M	I	N	U	S		T	I	M		T	E	E	N	I	E	R
E	T	H	N	I	C		B	R	O	A	D	S	W	O	R	D		E	N	S
	E	R	I	K	A	S		U	S	S		E	D	E		O	S	T	E	
A	R	E	A		C	R	E	D	I	T		G	L	A	D	Y	S			
L	E	R		N	O	C	T	I		E	J	E	C	T		A	M	F	M	
L	E	I	S	U	R	E		B	A	B	E	T	H	E	B	L	U	E	O	X
A	V	O	I	D	E	D		S	L	U	D	G	E		M	I	N	U	T	E
N	E	S	T	E	A			A	D	I	O	S		W	E	D	D	E	D	

21

22

23

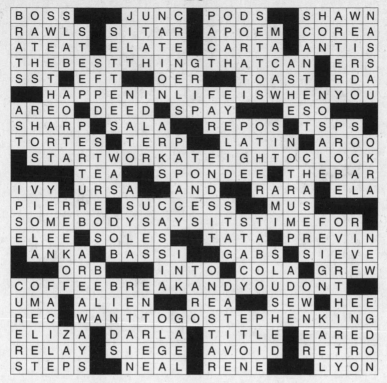

B	O	S	S			J	U	N	C		P	O	D	S		S	H	A	W	N
R	A	W	L	S		S	I	T	A	R		A	P	O	E	M		C	O	R	E	A
A	T	E	A	T		E	L	A	T	E		C	A	R	T	A		A	N	T	I	S
T	H	E	B	E	S	T	T	H	I	N	G	T	H	A	T	C	A	N		E	R	S
S	S	T		E	F	T		O	E	R		T	O	A	S	T		R	D	A
	H	A	P	P	E	N	I	N	L	I	F	E	I	S	W	H	E	N	Y	O	U
A	R	E	O		D	E	E	D		S	P	A	Y			E	S	O
S	H	A	R	P		S	A	L	A		R	E	P	O	S		T	S	P	S
T	O	R	T	E	S		T	E	R	P		L	A	T	I	N		A	R	O	O
	S	T	A	R	T	W	O	R	K	A	T	E	I	G	H	T	O	C	L	O	C	K
		T	E	A		S	P	O	N	D	E	E		T	H	E	B	A	R
I	V	Y		U	R	S	A		A	N	D		R	A	R	A		E	L	A
P	I	E	R	R	E		S	U	C	C	E	S	S		M	U	S
S	O	M	E	B	O	D	Y	S	A	Y	S	I	T	S	T	I	M	E	F	O	R
E	L	E	E		S	O	L	E	S		T	A	T	A		P	R	E	V	I	N
	A	N	K	A		B	A	S	S	I		G	A	B	S		S	I	E	V	E
		O	R	B			I	N	T	O		C	O	L	A		G	R	E	W
C	O	F	F	E	E	B	R	E	A	K	A	N	D	Y	O	U	D	O	N	T
U	M	A		A	L	I	E	N		R	E	A		S	E	W		H	E	E
R	E	C		W	A	N	T	T	O	G	O	S	T	E	P	H	E	N	K	I	N	G
E	L	I	Z	A		D	A	R	L	A		T	I	T	L	E		E	A	R	E	D
R	E	L	A	Y		S	I	E	G	E		A	V	O	I	D		R	E	T	R	O
S	T	E	P	S		N	E	A	L		R	E	N	E			L	Y	O	N

24

C	O	L	D			A	S	A	P		L	A	I	D		A	B	C	S
O	T	E	R	I		S	M	O	T	E		E	R	N	O		D	E	A	N
B	R	A	I	N	M	U	F	F	I	N		S	O	S	O		H	E	R	A
	A	S	F	L	A	T		A	C	H	E	S	M	U	R	D	E	R	E	R
			T	A	R	T			L	E	A	R		A	R	O	S	E
L	A	C	E	Y	C	O	M	E	H	O	M	E		A	D	M	E	N
O	D	O	R			N	O	L	A	N		S	N	I	P		T	A	R
G	A	S	S	E	D		B	L	U	E	G	R	A	C	E	S	T	A	T	E
O	P	T		T	E	A	S	E	S		O	A	T	E	S		A	P	O	D
S	T	A	S	H	E	D			E	T	T	U			S	T	E	M	S
		W	O	M	A	N	W	I	T	H	A	P	A	S	T	E
I	N	G	A	S		O	H	T	O			W	H	E	R	E	O	F
P	E	R	M		R	A	D	I	I		E	L	I	N	O	R		D	L	I
S	T	A	I	N	E	D	U	P	C	O	M	I	C		R	E	G	I	M	E
A	S	I		I	D	O	S			B	I	Z	E	T		O	N	A	N
		N	O	S	I	R		B	A	I	T	A	T	H	O	U	S	A	N	D
A	L	Y	C	E		A	P	E	S			I	M	P	S
B	A	K	E	I	N	T	H	E	U	S	S	R		G	R	E	A	S	E
O	N	N	A		A	I	N	T		T	H	E	T	H	I	N	M	A	N	E
I	C	O	N		T	O	O	L		L	I	A	R	S		D	E	N	I	M
L	E	T	S		O	N	M	E		O	N	L	Y			R	E	D	O

25

```
A L L A H   R O C   I T A L   R A S P S
M U L T I   U S O   L U N A   B O C C I E
A M A L 5 S S E L   I R K S   I D E A T E
S E M A N A S   O S A K A   G O T M A D
S T A N D E E   N I C E   F A T L Y
    T O N T I N E   Y E A R O 4 L O R D
T A P I R S   C A V S   U S T E N   V I R
E R I C S   M O D E M   D C I   S P O D E
A N T   S I N E   O B O I S T   R I G A
R E T A K E N   M O O R S   I B I D E M
    G O L D S M I 3 X A M I N E D
R A T I N E   H E N N Y   G E N E S I S
A W O L   S T R A I T   A D O S   O R A
K A R E N   R I G   R E L I T   C R O O N
E S S   O P I N E   Y A L E   G L E N N S
S H I F 2 R K E R S   S O M A L I S
    E R I E S   C H E W   D I N E T T E
C A V E R N   S H U L A   E N T R E E S
A R A B I C   D O O M   B O S T 1 V E N T
P O L L E E   D R O P   L A T   R E N E E
T W E E D   E E L S   E R E   A S S T S
```

26

```
M A R S H A   S A H A R A   C A B A N A S
A C E T O L   I C E M E N   E L E M E N T
J O N A T H A N S W I F T   L A V E R N E
S P O R T I N G   O I D   B E N D E R
    T E R N   N O E L C O W A R D
A D J U S T   D O M E D   G A M A   L O S
L E A P T   T I T A N   F L A G P O L E
T I M S   T R A I N   E G A D   E A U D E
A G E   F R A N C I S B A C O N   R I I S
R N S   A I M E E   A B L E   O U T S E T
    H I L T S   I T S   S I B Y L
S T I N K O   P U M A   C L O S E   A A A
H I L L   N O R M A N M A I L E R   M I G
O A T E R   T E A M   A N D E S   P O R N
P R O T E S T S   S C A D S   R O U T E
S A N   F L E A   E M O R Y   T O P R O W
    G E O R G E S A N D   L O O S
I M P A R T   E N S   P A R T I C L E
M A O I S T S   J E F F R E Y A R C H E R
P L O T T E R   O N L O A N   H O L I E R
S A L S O D A   Y E A R N S   S T E A K S
```

```
G E M I N I S ▮ U L E E ▮ W E B S ▮ D S M
R I O T A C T ▮ P A T C H E D U P ▮ R A E
E S R E V E R P S Y C H O L O G Y ▮ A I S
E N E M Y ▮ I R A ▮ H I N T ▮ S C O W L S
T E A ▮ ▮ O V A L ▮ ▮ D D E ▮ Y A P P E R
▮ R U B T H E Y A W G N O R W ▮ M A U D S
▮ ▮ L Y O N S ▮ R N A ▮ ▮ W H E L M ▮
A W F U L ▮ ▮ P E A ▮ P O W E R ▮ O H S
T H R E E F A C E S T S E W ▮ T A L B O T
T I E ▮ R O B U S T ▮ H O N I ▮ S E I N E
E N D E ▮ E A S E L ▮ O R I N G ▮ S L A W
N E E D S ▮ S A T E ▮ W I N G I T ▮ I L A
D R R U T H ▮ C A R R I A G E N R U T E R
S S I ▮ O I N K S ▮ Y E N ▮ ▮ I S Y E T
▮ ▮ C O R D E ▮ ▮ M A S ▮ M A I N E ▮
K U K L A ▮ O U T I N T F E L F I E L D ▮
O N H I G H ▮ S I N ▮ R A T S ▮ A O L
W I T N E Y ▮ E M I L ▮ A N E ▮ S W I N E
T A R ▮ B E N D O V E R S D R A W K C A B
O T O ▮ I N A T R A N C E ▮ E M I R A T E
W E N ▮ N A T O ▮ C Z A R ▮ D I M P L E D
```

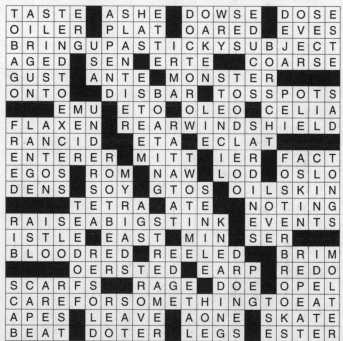

```
T A S T E ▮ A S H E ▮ D O W S E ▮ D O S E
O I L E R ▮ P L A T ▮ O A R E D ▮ E V E S
B R I N G U P A S T I C K Y S U B J E C T
A G E D ▮ S E N ▮ E R T E ▮ ▮ C O A R S E
G U S T ▮ A N T E ▮ M O N S T E R ▮ ▮
O N T O ▮ D I S B A R ▮ T O S S P O T S
▮ ▮ E M U ▮ E T O ▮ O L E O ▮ C E L I A
F L A X E N ▮ R E A R W I N D S H I E L D
R A N C I D ▮ E T A ▮ E C L A T ▮ ▮
E N T E R E R ▮ M I T T ▮ I E R ▮ F A C T
E G O S ▮ R O M ▮ N A W ▮ L O D ▮ O S L O
D E N S ▮ S O Y ▮ G T O S ▮ O I L S K I N
▮ ▮ T E T R A ▮ A T E ▮ ▮ N O T I N G
R A I S E A B I G S T I N K ▮ E V E N T S
I S T L E ▮ E A S T ▮ M I N ▮ S E R ▮
B L O O D R E D ▮ R E E L E D ▮ B R I M
▮ ▮ O E R S T E D ▮ E A R P ▮ R E D O
S C A R F S ▮ R A G E ▮ D O E ▮ O P E L
C A R E F O R S O M E T H I N G T O E A T
A P E S ▮ L E A V E ▮ A O N E ▮ S K A T E
B E A T ▮ D O T E R ▮ L E G S ▮ E S T E R
```

29

Grid 29:
```
M A S O N   · T R A D E S · P E A S A N T
E D I F Y · S E A T E R S · R E N E W E R
R O L F E · T H E B E S T D E L I V E R Y
C R A B T R E E · A R T S Y · · E D D A
· E S E · E L E C T · · E R V I N ·
· A R M A D A · B A D R E A C T I O N
· A C T I O · M E U S E · P L A I N T S
A T O · O P E N I N G A C T · M E S T A
W O R L D · D U S E · R I P E S T
A N N I E · S T O M A · P I N G · I A M
R E Y S · B E L L Y L A U G H S · S T L O
D R J · E L E E · B U L G E · M E C C A
· O D D E S T · N L E R · I N H O T
F A K I R · S H O R T B R E A K · E T S
E M E R A L D · A R E S O · P A B S T
N O S E N S A T I O N · A R M A N I
· C O U G H · A T E A R · G S A
B E E T · E D I T S · A R T C L A S S
R A S H O F O N E L I N E R S · P I N T O
A S P I R I N · N I N E V E H · A F T E R
C E N T E R S · S E E R E D · S T A R E
```

30

Grid 30:
```
H A V A N A · D A M A S K · B R A V O S
A M O R O S O · O L I V I A · V I R A G O
H A U N T I N G M E L O D Y · D A M M E D
A S S E S · E R E · T I L E · T Y P E A
· O T R A · M O D E S T · A M I
W I T C H E S B R E W S · A S S U R E S
A V A L O N · Y O N · B A R T · L E V I
C A B O T · I S A W · P E W · A M E B A E
O N U S · M O N S T E R S A L E · A D S
· E D S E L · I C E · B L T · T E T
E G G R O L L · B L A S T · N E R I S S A
D O H · D U D · E A R · M E D O C
D I O · G R A V E M A T T E R · O H M S
I N S T E P · I F S · H E N S · K N E E L
E T T E · E L M S · S R A · W E I R D O
D O W R I E S · S K E L E T O N C R E W
· R I S · D O T T I E · P E E K
S L I G O · S E A M · D I A · E U R O S
N A T A L E · C R Y P T I C M E S S A G E
O V E R D O · A R I O S E · S T E E P L E
B A R R E N · R E N N E S · S Y S T E M
```

31

```
H A I G H T   S A B R A S   Q U E S T E D
I N D O O R   S T E A M Y   U N B O R N E
E G Y P T I A N W A R P S V I S A D A T A
D E L   W A Y   O N E S T E P   N A G E L
        A G L A R E       L P S     I R S
M A N D R E A D S R I G I D E T H I C
O R E O S     E T Y M O N   R O O F
C A A N   P A L     N A S H   A R N O L D
  B R I E F R E D H O T P A S T A I R E D
      T A C T   O U T     L A S     B A A
L I S Z T   F I N D   C A L L   H U S S Y
A W E   G U M     M A X   A V O N
D I E T H E L P S C O M E R M A N A G E
E N S O U L   S A A R   O I L   G U M P
      T E A S   F R E S C A     E E R I E
    H O S T E V E R S H A L L E N D U R E
O L E     I C E       A D D E N D
B O R E R   L A S C A L A   A R P   R P I
E G O R E P U L S E S A V I D A L L I E S
L I E A B E D   S T O L E N   P A T T O N
I N S T A T E   S A F A R I   T Y R A N T
```

32

```
C R A B   S L A G   S T A B   A S M A R A
R O M A   H O U R   C R U E   B E A N E D
O D I N   A B L E   R I D E   O N L A N D
C A S T T H E D E C I D I N G V O L T
E N S U E D     K O B E     E E R   U P I
      M O S H   R E N E G E     E R I N
  T H E A M P E R E S T R I K E S B A C K
C I O N   S E M I     S I D   R E A L T Y
O M N I S   D A N Z A   K E E N E N
R E D A C T   S E L A   O R E S   A N E
P L A C E A S H E S O N O N E S F A R A D
S Y S   N I K E   T E N S     T I L I N G
    B I C A R B   S A T A N     T O O N E
S P E E C H   B O P   E L A M   A S I S
W A T T S I T A L L A B O U T A L F I E
A G H A   A L T A I R   M O R O
P E I   I R S   T R I S   A L T H E A
  O H M I M P R O V E M E N T L O A N S
S E P I A S   T U N E   O P A H   R U T S
T W I N G E   A D I N   T I N O   A T E E
L E A D E N   S E C T   E C O N   H E R S
```

33

Across/down grid answers:

REMAP · GAZA · JEB · SMITH
EARNS · OWED · AXE · BOOHOO
DR.KILDARE · NUI · INVAIN
ILSA · ADIOS · ERROR · IDLE
DEAR · MATS · REBURDEN
NAMERS · SAYITISN'TSO
ELD · AND · MICRA · DORIS
GAMBIT · BATHES · LIONIZE
AVAILS · RUSE · MISRULES
DANTE · CIVIL · ROBE · PLS
REUBEN,REUBEN
MRI · IRES · REPLY · UPTON
TEACARTS · APED · ATEASE
INVADES · CICELY · DRILLS
ELENA · AGHAS · LEI · KOS
DON'TBECRUEL · SALAMI
TEETOTAL · SIMP · ENDS
GLOW · SARIN · ALEPH · AGUT
REDANT · REO · DERRING-DO
EDDIES · ARI · DERE · BETEL
WASTE · LSD · STAY · AROSE

34

JOREL · GAUGE · THROE · BBS
APEAR · EATIT · HAING · IRA
PATSONTHESHOULDER · LIL
EQUINES · STAID · SELLTO
RUNE · IFA · SNL · JETTISON
SEER · MAN · OSOLE · STNS
MARKSOFFTHEPATH
ENSIGN · LENA · ANC · DIES
ROUTS · BEATNIKS · CONCH
RTES · BAT · TOE · GARGLES
EHS · BOBSUPANDDOWN · IBE
DEFRAYS · PES · ORS · FEAR
ROUND · FRUITFLY · SUNNI
ERST · TAO · ZEAL · DONTGO
CHUCKSOVERBOARD
SPUD · LOTTE · PLY · MAJA
NOSINESS · GAL · SER · ALES
ESTEEM · TADAS · ROSSINI
ATO · PETERSOUTATTHEEND
KID · ANIME · PRYCE · ARNIE
STY · LSATS · TAXED · MUSES

35

```
N E H I   O V E R D O   S T A S   S H E L
E X E C   H E R E O F   E R L E   H A R I
W A S H I N G T O N F O R A L L   E R I N
E C O   M O S E S   S A I D   F L E E C E
S T U M P       J E F F E R S O N M A N
T A T A   B E I R U T     O A K S
    S M E L T E D   S A L A M I   S O C
L I N C O L N A L A R M F I R E   J A N A
A D O   R O I L   S E O U L   B A R E R
C E R T A I N   N O L L   A N G I E
H A M I L T O N L I T T L E I N D I A N S
E L A T E   Y O D S   M O L E S T S
S I L L S   A C E T O   S H O O   S E E
I S L E   J A C K S O N Q U E S T I O N S
S T Y   B U C K E T   E V E R E S T
    G U M M   S A C R E D   C R A T
G R A N T P E R C E N T   S H U T E
R E S E T S   I O L E   A B B E Y   N E T
A N T I   F R A N K L I N Y E A R S W A R
S E I S   O I N K   L A T T E R   H A S A
P E N S   R O T S   S N E E R S   E Y E D
```

36

```
K N O B   P E A L   D A N C E R   S P A T
L I N A   A C R E   S L O A N E   Y A R E
I T I S   S L I T   O F M I C E A N D M E
E R O S   T A C I T   R E D B A R O N
G O N E W I T H T H E W I N   A P E R Y
    T I C   G R E E R   S S S
A D S   T H E S O U N D A N D T H E F U R
D E P O S E R S   S N A R E   A S A
A L E C   A N I L S   C E L L A R E D
M I D E A S T   L A T I S H   L I N E R S
    A C L O C K W O R K O R A N G
S H I N T O   A S S U M E   A R T E M I S
C A S S A V A S   T A W N Y   L O N E
A T L   A R E C A   N E B R A S K A
T H E N A K E D A N D T H E D E A   S Y R
    O D S   L O U I E   D I T
I M A G E   I M N O T R E A L L Y H E R
N O S I N E S S   O M A N I   C O T E
C I S F O R C O R P S   I T I N   O N U S
A R A T   S A N E S T   T A T E   B O D E
N A Y S   T R E A T Y   S T A N   B R E T
```

37

38

39

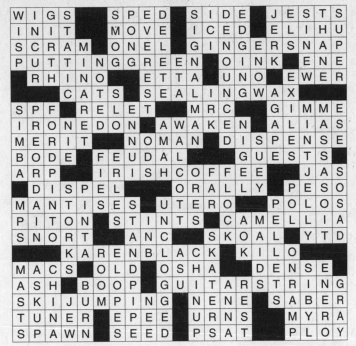

Across: WIGS, SPED, SIDE, JESTS, INIT, MOVE, ICED, ELIHU, SCRAM, ONEL, GINGERSNAP, PUTTINGGREEN, OINK, ENE, RHINO, ETTA, UNO, EWER, CATS, SEALINGWAX, SPF, RELET, MRC, GIMME, IRONEDON, AWAKEN, ALIAS, MERIT, NOMAN, DISPENSE, BODE, FEUDAL, GUESTS, ARP, IRISHCOFFEE, JAS, DISPEL, ORALLY, PESO, MANTISES, UTERO, POLOS, PITON, STINTS, CAMELLIA, SNORT, ANC, SKOAL, YTD, KARENBLACK, KILO, MACS, OLD, OSHA, DENSE, ASH, BOOP, GUITARSTRING, SKIJUMPING, NENE, SABER, TUNER, EPEE, URNS, MYRA, SPAWN, SEED, PSAT, PLOY

40

Across: TEARS, ISLA, TRAIT, MAY, AMIES, CLASP, YALTA, AMO, TURNTHEOTHERCHEEK, JAY, ASST, ABBE, ROOS, REBOZO, ARIA, STUB, SATIRES, THEBIGGERTHEBETTER, WALLA, SLOE, REINDEER, ALIENS, FLED, SLAV, MTA, IVE, THEMORETHEMERRIER, NELL, UVA, RIA, HORSE, SILENCEISGOLDEN, AURAS, LED, NEE, ARCH, CLOTHESMAKETHEMAN, EAT, LAO, LOIN, DIEM, RACINE, UNMODERN, FLAT, CONES, NICEGUYSFINISHLAST, ACCEPTS, SOWS, NOTE, CURSOR, SARI, ARTS, SAMS, IRE, LOOKBEFOREYOULEAP, NIP, EDSEL, TRAMP, PARKA, GOT, SEEDY, ELSE, SWOON

41

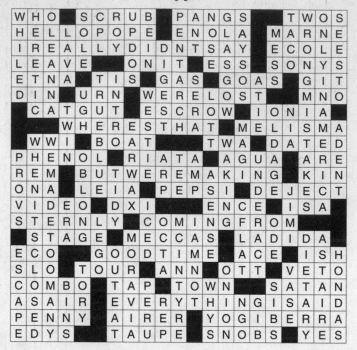

W	H	O		S	C	R	U	B		P	A	N	G	S			T	W	O	S
H	E	L	L	O	P	O	P	E		E	N	O	L	A		M	A	R	N	E
I	R	E	A	L	L	Y	D	I	D	N	T	S	A	Y		E	C	O	L	E
L	E	A	V	E		O	N	I	T		E	S	S		S	O	N	Y	S	
E	T	N	A		T	I	S		G	A	S		G	O	A	S		G	I	T
D	I	N		U	R	N		W	E	R	E	L	O	S	T		M	N	O	
	C	A	T	G	U	T		E	S	C	R	O	W		I	O	N	I	A	
	W	H	E	R	E	S	T	H	A	T		M	E	L	I	S	M	A		
	W	W	I		B	O	A	T		T	W	A		D	A	T	E	D		
P	H	E	N	O	L		R	I	A	T	A		A	G	U	A		A	R	E
R	E	M		B	U	T	W	E	R	E	M	A	K	I	N	G		K	I	N
O	N	A		L	E	I	A		P	E	P	S	I		D	E	J	E	C	T
V	I	D	E	O		D	X	I			E	N	C	E		I	S	A		
S	T	E	R	N	L	Y		C	O	M	I	N	G	F	R	O	M			
	S	T	A	G	E		M	E	C	C	A	S		L	A	D	I	D	A	
E	C	O		G	O	O	D	T	I	M	E		A	C	E		I	S	H	
S	L	O		T	O	U	R		A	N	N		O	T	T		V	E	T	O
C	O	M	B	O		T	A	P		T	O	W	N		S	A	T	A	N	
A	S	A	I	R		E	V	E	R	Y	T	H	I	N	G	I	S	A	I	D
P	E	N	N	Y		A	I	R	E	R		Y	O	G	I	B	E	R	R	A
E	D	Y	S		T	A	U	P	E		S	N	O	B	S		Y	E	S	

42

S	A	L	E	M		E	L	A	N			B	A	T	S		R	O	D	S
A	F	I	R	E		S	O	L	E	A		E	S	A	U		E	V	I	L
K	I	S	S	M	E	Q	U	I	C	K		G	I	M	M	E	F	I	V	E
S	T	A	T	O	R		V	I	K	I	N	G	S		A	L	I	N	E	D
			R	O	L	E		T	I	E		I	C	I	N	E	S	S		
M	I	N	D	Y	O	U	R	P	S	A	N	D	Q	S		T	E	S	T	
A	S	E	A		C	E	R	I	S	E		U	N	D	I	D				
S	T	A	B		F	I	D	E	L		P	I	O	U	S		S	T	S	
H	O	T	S	E	A	T		S	O	C	K	I	T	T	O	M	E	N	O	W
			G	R	E	W		R	E	N	T			S	O	F	A			
C	H	A	R	G	E		I	N	C	E	N	S	E		F	L	E	W	U	P
A	A	R	E			C	O	A	T		R	I	L	E						
S	T	E	P	T	O	T	H	E	R	E	A	R		N	E	V	A	D	A	N
T	E	A		A	B	O	I	L		C	O	P	S	E		L	U	N	A	
		A	L	E	R	T		F	A	T	A	L	E		O	M	I	T		
	H	A	L	O		M	A	K	E	M	I	N	E	A	D	O	U	B	L	E
R	E	T	I	N	A	E		A	T	E		I	M	I	T					
E	S	T	E	E	M		T	R	A	C	H	E	A		S	T	A	G	E	R
S	T	A	N	D	B	Y	M	E		H	O	L	D	T	H	E	M	A	Y	O
T	I	R	E		L	O	A	N		E	U	L	E	R		R	A	Z	E	S
S	A	S	E		E	O	N	S		R	O	S	Y		S	T	A	S	H	

43

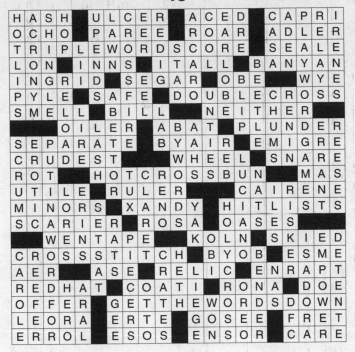

H	A	S	H		U	L	C	E	R		A	C	E	D			C	A	P	R	I
O	C	H	O		P	A	R	E	E		R	O	A	R		A	D	L	E	R
T	R	I	P	L	E	W	O	R	D	S	C	O	R	E		S	E	A	L	E
L	O	N		I	N	N	S		I	T	A	L	L		B	A	N	Y	A	N
I	N	G	R	I	D		S	E	G	A	R		O	B	E			W	Y	E
P	Y	L	E		S	A	F	E		D	O	U	B	L	E	C	R	O	S	S
S	M	E	L	L		B	I	L	L			N	E	I	T	H	E	R		
		O	I	L	E	R		A	B	A	T		P	L	U	N	D	E	R	
S	E	P	A	R	A	T	E		B	Y	A	I	R		E	M	I	G	R	E
C	R	U	D	E	S	T		W	H	E	E	L		S	N	A	R	E		
R	O	T		H	O	T	C	R	O	S	S	B	U	N		M	A	S		
U	T	I	L	E		R	U	L	E	R			C	A	I	R	E	N	E	
M	I	N	O	R	S		X	A	N	D	Y		H	I	T	L	I	S	T	S
S	C	A	R	I	E	R		R	O	S	A		O	A	S	E	S			
	W	E	N	T	A	P	E		K	O	L	N		S	K	I	E	D	
C	R	O	S	S	S	T	I	T	C	H		B	Y	O	B		E	S	M	E
A	E	R		A	S	E		R	E	L	I	C		E	N	R	A	P	T	
R	E	D	H	A	T		C	O	A	T	I		R	O	N	A		D	O	E
O	F	F	E	R		G	E	T	T	H	E	W	O	R	D	S	D	O	W	N
L	E	O	R	A		E	R	T	E		G	O	S	E	E		F	R	E	T
E	R	R	O	L		E	S	O	S		E	N	S	O	R		C	A	R	E

44

K	A	R	A	T	S		L	A	T	I	M	E	S		G	L	A	S	S
O	N	E	I	N	C	H		I	N	A	R	A	G	E		R	A	S	T	A
W	A	L	K	T	H	E	P	L	A	N	K	T	O	N		A	N	G	E	L
T	R	A	M		O	L	E		I	G	E	T		E	A	S	E	O	U	T
O	C	T	A		L	E	S		R	Y	D	E	R	C	U	P		O	B	I
W	H	E	N		A	N	T	S			R	O	A	D		A	D	E	N	
			T	R	A	S	H	C	A	N	T	O	N		C	R	A	N	E
O	S	C	A	R	S		O	H	L	O	O	K		P	A	Y	S		
K	A	R	M	A		L	A	P	E	L	S			O	R	A	N	G	E
B	L	O	B		O	I	L	S		A	E	R	O		L	O	N	E	R	S
Y	A	W		T	H	E	F	A	I	R	S	E	X	T	O	N		W	E	T
M	A	N	A	N	A		A	T	N	O		C	E	O	S		U	T	A	H
E	M	P	T	O	R			F	U	S	I	N	G		P	R	O	S	E	
		R	I	T	A		I	D	U	N	I	T		G	U	N	N	E	R
A	G	I	L	E		S	T	A	N	D	P	A	T	T	O	N			
B	U	N	T		B	L	E	U			L	E	A	P		A	B	C	S
S	E	C		D	R	A	M	B	U	I	E		N	I	L		F	L	A	Y
O	V	E	R	A	R	M		I	R	M	A		O	L	A		F	O	R	D
R	A	T	E	D		M	I	N	I	A	T	U	R	E	C	A	R	T	O	N
B	R	O	A	D		E	N	G	A	G	E	S		D	E	B	A	C	L	E
S	A	N	D	Y		R	A	S	H	E	R	S		S	A	Y	H	E	Y

45

G	R	E	C	O		S	L	O	M	O			C	L	E	M	E	N	T	E
L	I	V	E	R		H	O	N	O	R			C	O	L	O	N	I	A	L
U	P	A	N	D	A	R	O	U	N	D		E	S	C	A	P	E	K	E	Y
T	E	N	S	I	L	E		S	I	E	V	E		O	N	E	R			
		E	N	I	D			T	R	I	E	S		R	O	S	H			
O	P	E	R	A	S		S	T	O	L	E		O	U	R			W	I	T
N	A	T		L	O	T	T	E	R	Y	W	I	N	N	E	R		I	R	E
A	S	H	E		N	O	R	A			M	I	D	S	U	M	M	E	R	
I	T	E	M	S		T	O	R	I	C		A	C	E		D	E	M	O	S
R	E	L	A	T	E		D	U	B	A	I		R	E	D	L	I	N	E	
	K	I	A	S		E	P	I	G	R	A	M		D	I	O	N			
S	P	E	L	L	E	D		D	E	M	M	E		W	E	D	G	I	E	
A	R	N	E	L		E	R	S		S	A	U	T	E		R	I	N	D	S
G	E	N	D	E	R	G	A	P			L	A	T	E		C	U	L	T	
A	V	E		D	I	A	N	A	V	R	E	E	L	A	N	D		D	E	E
S	I	D		M	S	G		E	A	S	T	S		D	I	V	E	R	S	
	N	Y	S	E		E	R	E	C	T		G	I	V	E					
		T	E	T	S		U	S	E	R	S		A	V	E	R	A	G	E	
D	E	T	E	R	M	I	N	E		C	A	T	C	H	E	R	S	B	O	X
I	N	I	T	I	A	T	E		A	D	E	L	A		G	U	A	R	E	
N	O	N	S	E	N	S	E		R	A	N	I	N		E	S	S	E	S	

46

	C	U	L	T	S		R	O	S	A		M	E	S	S	A	G	E	
C	A	M	E	O	N		S	E	D	A	N		P	L	I	O	C	E	N	E
A	B	B	E	Y	L	I	N	C	O	L	N		H	I	G	H	C	O	S	T
M	A	R	K	S		H	E	A	R	T	E	N		O	N	O		R	U	N
E	R	A	S		J	E	E	P	S		R	A	N	T	S		A	G	R	A
L	E	G		O	A	R	S		M	I	N	E	S		F	L	E	E	S	
S	T	E	A	L	E	R	S		B	O	C	C	E		E	S	C			
		M	A	J		J	I	V	E	Y		A	B	S	O	L	U	T	
	A	M	A	N	A		F	A	Z	E		W	E	A	R	S		I	N	E
S	T	A	T	I	C		A	M	E	R		I	L	A	Y		G	N	M	A
A	T	R	I	S	K		D	E	T		E	L	I		A	V	A	T	A	R
M	A	I	S		S	T	E	S		R	A	S	A		N	O	B	O	D	Y
M	C	L		T	O	A	S	T		A	M	O	S		A	T	O	N	E	
S	K	Y	L	I	N	E		A	L	I	E	N		D	E	R				
	N	Y	C		L	Y	O	N	S		C	L	A	S	S	A	C	T	
D	A	M	N	S		D	E	L	I	S		A	H	E	M		B	R	A	
E	B	O	N		D	O	N	O	T		E	V	A	N	S		B	R	A	N
I	O	N		P	O	T		R	E	P	A	I	N	T		A	L	I	G	N
S	A	R	D	I	N	E	S		R	I	T	A	C	O	O	L	I	D	G	E
T	R	O	O	P	E	R	S		E	L	I	T	E		H	A	N	G	E	D
	D	E	N	S	E	S	T		R	E	N	E		M	I	K	E	D		

47

48

```
G R E G G   H A S T   A R A B S   N A D A
L A G E R   U G L I   N O N E T   E R A S
A G A T E   G O O D Y G O O D Y   S I G N
D E N G   S O G G I E S T   R E S T A G E
  O A T S   G N A T   H A S T E N E R
A R G O S Y   B E G S   R I G   A G E R S
L O A D S   H O R S   P E G G I N G
K A N G A R O O S   G I G G L E D   N O G
A N G R I E S T   B A G G I E R   W O V E
  L A L A S   N O G G I N S   R A B I N
A B I D E   B A G G I E S   E G A D S
G R E E D   J U G G L E S   F L A G G
T A S S   W I G G L E S   G I L L I G A N
S G T   B I G G I E S   G O L D E N A G E
  L O G G I N S   G O R E   A G G I E
I S S E I   L E G   N A V Y   O S T E N D
M E L A N G E S   S A G E   B A Y H
G L A S G O W   I T S G R E E K   E G A L
A L T E   D I N G A L I N G S   A D A G E
M E E R   I T I O N   N O G O   D O G E S
E R R S   S H A R K   G R O S   O G E E S
```

```
R A S H A D   A L B   L A H T I   U S P S
E D W O O D   L E E   I D A H O   N O L O
G R E E K S A L A D   N E W E D I T I O N
R E D S   R U P E E   A C I D I T Y
I N I   H E B R E W N A T I O N A L
P O S S E S S E D   D R A I N E R   F H A
  H O N K   D U B   F L A G   E R R O R
O S M O S I S   P I K   M N O P   H E M I
I C E T   M E G   G R O U P   E V E N E D
S E A S H O R E   H I N D U   R E A C T
E N T   O P E R   E S A   N E S S   H E F
  A B A C I   M O A T S   C R I T I C A L
T R A C H E   A U D I S   H E A   R O M E
H I L T   S E N T   N I P   I N T E N S E
R O L E N   A M F M   S R A   R O A N
U S S   A U R E O L E   O P I U M D E N S
  M A N D A R I N O R A N G E   C I A
  B R A C E R S   S M A R T   A T E N
J O H N P A U L I I   I T A L I A N I C E
U Z I S   S M E L T   T E D   U N D O E S
T O N E   E S S E S   S S E   M A I N S T
```

51

52

53

```
F A T S O   P A U L A   S P A T   A F R O
C H E E P   A R S O N   P O L E   T E A R
C H E R U B S C O U T   R U I N   T A I L
      G L U T     S E W E R   F L A T L Y
M O L I E R E   G E N R E   T O U C H
C R O O N S   P R U N E   S O U G H E D
C A R   C A P R I P A N T H E R S   R E B
I N D I E   R A P     A I R     B O N E
    G O N   K E Y   N E T H E R P R O F I T
    F S T O P S   O L I O S   E A T S A T
M U T T E R S   P R I M E   B R I T T L E
I N H A L E   L A T T E   S O O N E R
S M E L L A R A T H E R   I O N   G E L
D A H L     O P T     B L T   P A N I C
O D E   V A M P I R E B A T H E R   G T O
    E R M I N E S   E A R L Y   L O A T H E
    R O N D O   E N R O L   B E R T H E D
S H I N E R   C R E S C   A M A T
H O N K   E U R O   H A L F W I T H E R S
U R G E   S P U D   O D E L L   E A S E L
E A S Y   S I D E   T E X A S   S T O N Y
```

54

```
R I T U A L   I N T E L   E T H   U N C A
O N E E Y E   M A R C O   P E A G R E E N
M P A C E S T A T I O N   I N P R I S O N
P U C K S   A S O F   N O S A L E   T S E
    T H E H A J   E C O N O M I C S
    R A T   C I C H L I D   T O U G H S
E L F   W A R M T O   T E N T   N E A T
P O T   C A R A P A C E   S E E   S T U D
O F F   D R O V E   O N S   O R P H A N S
S T A R R   C A R T L O A D   S H I F T
    M O O   K T I E A L L E Y   O N A
    F I L M S   S A N T A A N A   N E H R U
F A L L S O N   L E E   R U S S E   A O L
E L I E   U N D   T E P I D I T Y   K A N
U S E D   V E E S   C H E E R Y   E R A
D E S I R E   B A L L A D S   L T D
    N O N L I N E A R   B E H A V E
I C E   S T A L A G   I A M A   E R I N S
N A G A S A K I   U P S T A D O W N S T A
C L A R I N E T   M E E T S   T H E I R S
H I D E   D R Y   E D E N S   T O R T E S
```

55

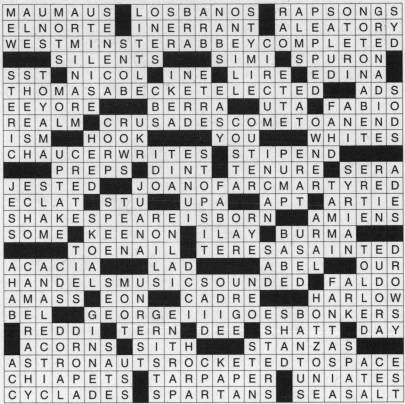

```
M A U M A U S   L O S B A N O S   R A P S O N G S
E L N O R T E   I N E R R A N T   A L E A T O R Y
W E S T M I N S T E R A B B E Y C O M P L E T E D
    S I L E N T S     S I M I   S P U R O N
S S T   N I C O L   I N E   L I R E   E D I N A
T H O M A S A B E C K E T E L E C T E D     A D S
E E Y O R E     B E R R A   U T A   F A B I O
R E A L M   C R U S A D E S C O M E T O A N E N D
I S M   H O O K     Y O U     W H I T E S
C H A U C E R W R I T E S   S T I P E N D
    P R E P S   D I N T   T E N U R E   S E R A
J E S T E D   J O A N O F A R C M A R T Y R E D
E C L A T   S T U   U P A   A P T   A R T I E
S H A K E S P E A R E I S B O R N   A M I E N S
S O M E   K E E N O N   I L A Y   B U R M A
    T O E N A I L   T E R E S A S A I N T E D
A C A C I A   L A D   A B E L   O U R
H A N D E L S M U S I C S O U N D E D   F A L D O
A M A S S   E O N   C A D R E   H A R L O W
B E L   G E O R G E I I I G O E S B O N K E R S
  R E D D I   T E R N   D E E   S H A T T   D A Y
  A C O R N S   S I T H   S T A N Z A S
A S T R O N A U T S R O C K E T E D T O S P A C E
C H I A P E T S   T A R P A P E R   U N I A T E S
C Y C L A D E S   S P A R T A N S   S E A S A L T
```

56

```
A L G   B I L O X I   A C D C   A D A M
G O U P   E R O I C A   C L I O   T R O Y
O K R A   C A L L I N G C A R D   T A R S
G I U L I A N I   I E S T   S A W T O
    A D M I T T I N G P H Y S I C I A N
G R A Z I E   A R T I S T   H A H N
M A T Z O   I C K   L O A M   G B S
S P L I T T I N G H E A D A C H E   B O P
    S U M O   G E L T   S P O O L
B O W S   B A N   A T A L L   P E L A G E
E R A T   A C T I N G M A Y O R   E R I E
A N N A L S   R O S I E   G T O   A D E N
M A D R E   A U T O   A T O P
U T E   C O M M A N D I N G O F F I C E R
P E R   T R A P   I T O   I N U S E
    I S E E   M A N U T E   A Z T E C S
C O N T R O L L I N G P A R T N E R
O R G A N   O A S T   R E G R O W T H
H A J I   F I S H I N G P O L E   I O W A
A T E N   A R E A   C A R R O L   T O O L
N E W S   T E R P   O D E S S A   D D T
```

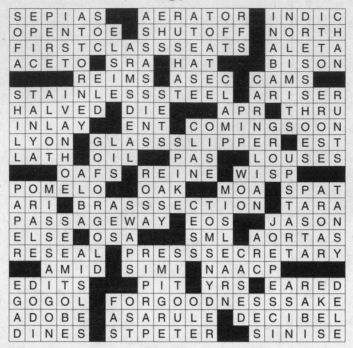

```
S E P I A S   ■ A E R A T O R ■ I N D I C
O P E N T O E ■ S H U T O F F ■ N O R T H
F I R S T C L A S S S E A T S ■ A L E T A
A C E T O ■ S R A ■ H A T ■ ■ B I S O N
■ ■ ■ R E I M S ■ A S E C ■ C A M S ■
S T A I N L E S S S T E E L ■ A R I S E R
H A L V E D ■ D I E ■ ■ A P R ■ T H R U
I N L A Y ■ ■ E N T ■ C O M I N G S O O N
L Y O N ■ G L A S S S L I P P E R ■ E S T
L A T H ■ O I L ■ P A S ■ L O U S E S
■ ■ O A F S ■ R E I N E ■ W I S P ■ ■
P O M E L O ■ O A K ■ M O A ■ S P A T
A R I ■ B R A S S S E C T I O N ■ T A R A
P A S S A G E W A Y ■ E O S ■ J A S O N
E L S E ■ O S A ■ S M L ■ A O R T A S
R E S E A L ■ P R E S S S E C R E T A R Y
■ ■ A M I D ■ S I M I ■ N A A C P ■ ■
E D I T S ■ P I T ■ Y R S ■ E A R E D
G O G O L ■ F O R G O O D N E S S S A K E
A D O B E ■ A S A R U L E ■ D E C I B E L
D I N E S ■ S T P E T E R ■ S I N I S E
```

```
S P Y N O V E L ■ P U B L I S H ■ B S A
A L O E V E R A ■ O R I E N T E ■ D U E L
Y O U R E G A I N I N G A S O N ■ I T S A
■ ■ D N A ■ O R S ■ D U D S ■ S W A M
C A N S ■ R A D O ■ B E R G ■ S C H M O
A G O ■ A R E W E T H E R E Y E T ■ Y E S
M A W ■ N E A L S ■ I N S ■ M A R C ■
E T E R N A L ■ E G G ■ G E N O A S ■
L E V E E ■ M I N E H A S S A N D O N I T
■ ■ E H S ■ D A N ■ L I P I D ■ S T L O
P A R E ■ A M A S ■ ■ T E N S ■ T I L T
I L Y A ■ C O H A B ■ B A R ■ M E W
N O B R O C C O L I F O R M E ■ E R E C T
■ T O S S E S ■ T O P ■ M A R S A L A
■ D E R N ■ O E R ■ B E I N G ■ R E M
A M Y ■ I T S A N O T H E R T I E ■ I A M
B A S I C ■ E T O N ■ O L E S ■ I T T Y
A R M S ■ L A H R ■ Z O E ■ Z E N ■
S K I M ■ I M A D E I T M Y S E L F M O M
E E L S ■ N A N E T T E ■ M A S E R A T I
D R E ■ A N D R O I D ■ A N T E A T E R
```

59

A	G	I	T	A	T	E	S		C	L	A	M	O	R		C	O	I	F		N	I	B	S
V	I	N	E	G	A	R	Y		H	E	G	I	R	A		H	A	R	I		A	S	A	P
E	V	A	P	E	R	O	N		I	S	A	K	D	I	N	E	S	E	N		P	A	S	A
R	E	N	E		S	O	D	A	S		E	N	D	O	R		D	E	C	O	D	E	R
S	N	E	E	R	S		D	I	N	E	R		A	S	T	I	R		S	A	L	O	M	E
			C	O	M		S	T	R	E	W	N		I	S	E		S	P	I	R	E	S
E	L	I	Z	A	B	E	T	H	I		C	O	C	O	C	H	A	N	E	L		A	N	T
P	E	D	I		E	A	R			R	E	E	V	E		R	E	S	E	N	D	
I	R	O	N	S	I	D	E		S	L	O		E	S	S	E	S		T	O	U	R	S
C	O	L	G	A	T	E	S		A	L	O	M	A	R		E	N	T		O	N	A	N
S	I	S	S	Y		S	A	L	A	M	I	S		A	D	E	S		D	C	I	I
			E	P	I		D	O	M		N	O	M	A	N		G	A	L	L	A	N	T
	E	D	I	S	O	N		J	O	A	N	O	F	A	R	C		G	R	E	E	N	S
A	B	O	R	T	E	D		U	N	S	E	R		N	N	E		S	A	T	
C	O	R	E		M	A	W	S		I	C	I	N	E	S	S		S	P	A	T	E
E	L	O	N		N	E	T		P	L	A	N	E	S		A	R	M	O	I	R	E	S
D	A	T	E	D		G	A	S	P	E		B	R	S		B	O	U	N	C	E	R	S
	H	E	A	T	E	R		A	R	D	O	R		R	A	F		T	A	R	A
C	A	Y		M	A	R	I	E	C	U	R	I	E		D	I	A	N	F	O	S	S	E	Y
A	S	P	E	N	S		E	L	K		E	L	E	V	E	N		S	E	W	
S	T	A	R	E	S		D	O	R	M	S		D	I	C	K	S		D	I	S	C	O	S
P	A	R	A	D	E	D		P	A	E	S	E		E	A	S	E	L		H	A	L	T
I	R	K	S		L	O	R	E	T	T	A	L	Y	N	N		V	I	C	T	O	R	I	A
A	T	E	E		E	V	E	R		A	G	L	I	N	T		E	N	D	E	A	V	O	R
N	E	R	D		D	E	B	S		L	E	O	N	A	S		R	E	S	T	L	E	S	S

60

C	H	A	S	E		F	C	C		U	S	E	D		S	C	R	E	W
H	A	S	T	A		G	U	A	R	A	N	T	E	E		H	O	O	C	H
I	N	P	U	T		A	L	M	A	N	D	I	N	E		A	M	P	L	E
C	O	I	N	C	O	L	L	E	C	T	O	R		R	E	D	M	E	A	T
K	I	N		R	U	E		K	E	N			J	O	U	S	T	S
		C	O	T		L	A	P	S	E	S		S	E	W	N
E	L	B	O	W		B	O	N	O		C	H	I	C		I	S	T
P	E	A	L		C	O	U	N	T	Y	C	O	U	R	T		T	O	M	E
I	N	D	O	L	E	N	T		E	A	R	N	S		T	Y	L	E	R
C	O	M	R	A	D	E		B	A	S	I	N	S		F	A	C	I	N	G
	I	C	I	E	R		O	Z	O	N	E		A	L	L	O	T
M	A	N	O	R	S		H	A	T	R	E	D		V	I	L	L	A	I	N
A	L	T	O	S		S	I	R	E	N		B	E	R	Y	L	I	N	E
O	D	O	R		C	O	L	D	C	O	M	F	O	R	T		E	R	O	S
	A	N	D		A	B	L	E		O	U	S	T		A	G	E	N	T
	I	M	P	S		D	E	M	U	R	S		A	P	E
B	E	A	N	I	E		V	A	R		H	E	R		A	B	E
A	T	L	A	N	T	A		C	O	U	N	T	R	Y	C	O	U	S	I	N
S	U	I	T	E		S	M	O	L	D	E	R	E	D		P	R	I	N	T
E	D	G	E	R		W	O	L	V	E	R	I	N	E		O	S	A	G	E
S	E	N	D	S		E	T	T	E		S	G	T		S	A	N	E	R

61

```
A F L █ G A T O R █ A D E E █ █ O K R A
T R Y █ R O M E R O █ C O M F Y █ R O A R
H O C K E Y P L A Y E R ' S F A C E O F F
O N E I D A S █ T A X E S █ U N B O L T S
S T E A L █ █ W E L T █ █ A S K S █
█ █ E T T E █ R O O M I E █ O R D O
█ S I N G E R ' S B O W L O V E R T E E N
S O M E █ M A R I A █ E I R E █ E R A S E
C R E A M █ N E L L █ R O I █ I T A L I A
A T A L O S S █ O E D █ █ T E T E █ █
M A N S H O O T S R I O T E R ' S D O W N
█ █ A L M A █ █ S K Y █ A S T O R I A
M A S H I E █ C C C █ A S P S █ S U D S Y
O S I E R █ S T A R █ P O E M S █ S E P S
D O C ' S S L I P U P I N S U R G E R Y
I N K S █ H A L T E R █ █ T S A R █
█ █ N A V E █ E S A S █ █ A L I S T
A S T A I R E █ E A G E R █ D I S O B E Y
F I R M H I R E S W O R K E R ' S B A C K
A D A M █ F E T A L █ F I N E L Y █ R T E
R E P O █ D A I S █ S N A I L █ S S S
```

62

```
T A P E R S O F F █ H A S █ S A F E █ T R E P I D
A L L B E T T E R █ A G L I T T E R █ H U M A N E
S E A B R E E Z E █ R E U S A B L E █ E M E R G E
T R Y █ E E L E D █ D I G I T A L C O M P U T E R
E T E █ A L L S O U L S █ █ T I T H A L █
█ R A D I O █ T I T L E █ N O N L E V E L █
D E P O S E █ T E N S E U P █ G R O T █ E M I T
E M I R █ S P A R S E █ O R A L █ █ E S T A T E
A M A T I █ I D A █ S A N E L Y █ R O S Y █ C T A
L E N I N S T O M B █ T A K E S L I B E R T I E S
S T O C K T I P █ A S T R A █ A S I F █ H A R E
█ P I E T █ S A I D █ T A L K █ A G A T E S
█ B E H O L D █ M A R C O P O L O █ A L L I E D
P E Y O T L █ S A L K █ D O T O █ A R C O
L E E K █ L X I I █ M A S O N █ C R O S S B O W
U L T E R I O R M O T I V E █ G E T I N S H A P E
T I E █ U F O S █ R E T I R E █ R I B █ Y E N T A
O N E O N E █ B A R N █ M A N I A C █ A G I N
N E T S █ P A S S █ R E C I P E S █ H A V O C S
█ S H U T A W A Y █ D I T T O █ F I N E R █
█ S I E N N A █ S I N G S O N G █ M E R
L I S T E N S T O R E A S O N █ A T W A R █ A X E
A L C O T T █ I D E A T I V E █ F A L S I F I E S
B L O U S E █ N I T R A T E S █ F R E E L A N C E
S E T T E R █ I C E S █ E R S █ E S S A Y T E S T
```

63

64

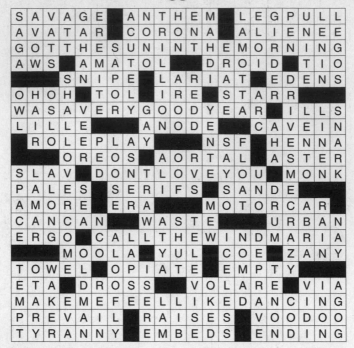

```
S A V A G E   ■ A N T H E M ■ L E G P U L L
A V A T A R   ■ C O R O N A ■ A L I E N E E
G O T T H E S U N I N T H E M O R N I N G
A W S ■ A M A T O L ■   D R O I D ■ T I O
■   S N I P E ■ L A R I A T ■ E D E N S
O H O H ■ T O L ■ I R E ■ S T A R R ■
W A S A V E R Y G O O D Y E A R ■ I L L S
L I L L E ■   A N O D E ■   C A V E I N
■ R O L E P L A Y ■   N S F ■ H E N N A
■ O R E O S ■ A O R T A L ■ A S T E R
S L A V ■ D O N T L O V E Y O U ■ M O N K
P A L E S ■ S E R I F S ■ S A N D E ■
A M O R E ■ E R A ■   M O T O R C A R
C A N C A N ■   W A S T E ■   U R B A N
E R G O ■ C A L L T H E W I N D M A R I A
■ M O O L A ■ Y U L ■ C O E ■ Z A N Y
T O W E L ■ O P I A T E ■ E M P T Y ■
E T A ■ D R O S S ■ V O L A R E ■ V I A
M A K E M E F E E L L I K E D A N C I N G
P R E V A I L ■ R A I S E S ■ V O O D O O
T Y R A N N Y ■ E M B E D S ■ E N D I N G
```

```
D A L I ■ A N G E L ■ H I R E D ■ S H E A
E T O N ■ W O R R Y ■ I N U R E ■ T E N S
M O N S T E R E O S ■ T O B A C C O R D S
S M I T H ■ M E D I C I N E S ■ I M B U E
■ A E R ■ D E N O T E S ■ C L A S P S
S C E N T E D ■ D E N ■ L A I C ■
C A N T A T A S ■ T E A ■ I D A H O A N
O M A R ■ T O P L E S S O N S ■ I D L E
P E T U L A ■ B R U N E T T E ■ S N O B S
E L E M E N T ■ A G T ■ E T C E T E R A S
■ T O R I C ■ R O U T E ■
P R O M I N E N T ■ S R I ■ T U N E S U P
L E M O N ■ S K I R M I S H ■ I O D I N E
O D I N ■ P S Y C H I C K E N ■ I N C A
P O T A B L E ■ E E L ■ N E R F B A L L
■ R O O S ■ E G O ■ G O A L I E S
H E P C A T ■ C A R R A R A ■ E K E ■
A M A H S ■ S A V E S T I M E ■ I S L A M
D I G I T A L I A N ■ H O O V E R S I O N
S L A V ■ C U R I A ■ E L V I S ■ E R N O
T Y N E ■ T R O L L ■ R E E L S ■ D E E P
```

```
P E A C E ■ S C A R ■ S A A R ■ C O N C H
A T H O S ■ O L G A ■ O G R E ■ O M A H A
S T A N S ■ T E R I ■ R E E L ■ T A P I R
S U B C A P T A I N ■ T R A I N T R A C K
■ ■ ■ E Y E O N ■ G E O ■ ■ G O O S ■ ■
S N I D E R ■ C O N F U S I O N ■ M I T
W I N E D ■ T R A D E ■ N E O N ■ R A M A
A M T S ■ D I O S ■ ■ P R E S S C O R P S
M B E ■ D U T C H C H E E S E ■ L O X E S
P I L L A G E S ■ R O O S T ■ G A M B L E
■ L U N A R ■ T A U N T ■ S L I E R ■
M A I L I N ■ C E N S E ■ S P A R R O W S
A N G L E ■ S H A K E S P E A R E ■ T O O
S T E E L G L A S S ■ L A K E ■ C H O U
S E N D ■ E A S E ■ C H U T E ■ S L E E P
E S T ■ A N T E L O P E S ■ G O U R D S
■ ■ A B E T ■ G A R ■ A N T I C ■ ■
E M P H A S I Z E D ■ S C H O O L K I D S
T Y R O S ■ N O T E ■ E L E V ■ A E R I E
A N I M E ■ G L E N ■ L U A U ■ G R A N T
T A X E D ■ S A S S ■ F E D S ■ E S S E S
```

```
■ J O K E R S ■ S A L T S ■ S C A L P E D
A U R A L E E ■ U B O A T ■ H A V A R T I
P L A Y I N G A R O U N D ■ O V A T I O N
E E C ■ ■ ■ H E R D ■ M O A T ■ N I N
S P L I T A P A R T ■ A C U T E A N G L E
■ S E D O N A ■ ■ T H A R P ■ R U L E R
■ L E A D I N G A S T R A Y ■ B E S S
A B B E S S ■ R E E K ■ E R O S ■ ■
L Y E S ■ H I T L I S T S ■ U R B A N E
I R R ■ L A O S ■ N C O ■ A N T I G E N
N O T W O R T H F I G H T I N G A B O U T
E T H I C A L ■ A D A ■ R O S S ■ U R I
S E A L A B ■ P R O B A T E D ■ S T A T
■ ■ L I S I ■ A X O N ■ F A M I L Y
G L E E ■ A W A R D C E R E M O N Y ■
R E N T A ■ A N O U K ■ M E N T H E
A C R O S S T O W N ■ M O V E S A H E A D
V O A ■ H A T S ■ N O W I ■ ■ C S A
E N G R A V E ■ A G A I N A N D A G A I N
S T E A M E R ■ M E T R E ■ B E R A T E S
T E S T E R S ■ A R O A R ■ A N T L E R
```

71

A	M	A	S	S	E	S			P	A	S	T	A			C	R	A	T	E
L	I	B	E	R	I	A			K	E	E	P	A	T		E	R	O	D	E	D
A	L	E	X	A	N	D	R	A	S	R	A	G	T	I	M	E	B	A	N	D
D	O	L	T			S	O	S	O	O	N		I	C	B	M		P	T	A
		O	F	L	A	T	E				F	R	E	R	E		T	A	S
J	O	A	N	I	E	C	O	M	E	L	A	T	E	L	Y		S	A	T
A	P	T		D	A	K		N	E	R	D			O	U	T	B	I	D
W	E	T	M	O	P		S	T	D	E	N	I	S		S	A	L	V	E
E	R	E	S		S	H	A	R	I		E	X	P	I	R	E		E	E	E
D	A	N	D	D		A	T	O	N	E			A	Z	U	R	E
		D	O	U	B	T	I	N	G	T	H	O	M	A	S	I	N	A
	S	T	E	E	R			D	O	G	M	A		D	A	L	A	I
D	A	B		I	N	D	I	C	T		G	E	E	K	S		T	K	T	S
O	S	A	G	E		C	H	A	N	T	E	D		I	D	E	A	T	E
A	T	T	E	S	T		A	T	O	I		E	D	E		L	E	R
	R	T	E		A	V	E	R	A	G	E	J	O	S	E	P	H	I	N	E
S	O	L		C	B	E	R	S			O	N	T	A	P	E
A	L	E		O	L	I	O		S	W	A	N	E	E		C	A	B	S
J	A	C	Q	U	E	L	I	N	E	O	F	A	L	L	T	R	A	D	E	S
A	B	R	U	P	T		C	A	N	V	A	S		L	A	O	T	I	A	N
K	E	Y	E	S		A	S	T	E	R			E	X	T	E	N	D	S

72

G	A	P	E	R	S		A	T	M	O	S	T		B	U	S	I	E	R
O	C	U	L	A	R		S	H	O	O	T	E	E		O	T	E	L	L	O
F	U	L	L	H	O	U	S	E	C	H	E	E	R	S	D	A	L	L	A	S
A	R	P		N	O	S	H		O	H	S		D	U	N	E
R	E	F	E	R		D	R	E	A	D		A	D	O		S	O	S
	I	V	E	G	O	T	A	S	E	C	R	E	T	F	A	M	I	L	Y
D	A	C	A	P	O			W	A	Y		D	I	N		O	S	U
I	T	T		O	L	E	I	C		S	A	T	O	R	I		N	A	P
C	H	I	P	S	F	A	T	H	E	R	K	N	O	W	S	B	E	S	T
K	O	O	L		U	S	A	G	E		E	N	T	E	R
	S	N	A	P	S		P	O	L	A	R		S	L	A	P	S
	T	U	T	T	I		I	B	I	Z	A		T	R	O	T
	S	I	S	T	E	R	S	G	E	T	S	M	A	R	T	C	O	A	C	H
J	O	N		S	N	O	R	E	D		S	P	I	E	L		C	L	U
O	P	T		O	O	P		N	T	H		S	E	A	T	E	D
T	H	E	F	U	G	I	T	I	V	E	C	O	P	S	T	A	X	I
	R	I	T		C	E	E		S	U	P	R	A		T	E	C	H	S
A	T	V	S		S	A	N		R	I	O	T		E	A	T
H	E	E	H	A	W	L	A	U	G	H	I	N	J	E	O	P	A	R	D	Y
S	E	N	E	C	A		M	A	N	A	T	E	E		M	A	N	U	A	L
O	N	E	S	E	T		R	U	P	E	R	T		B	R	O	N	T	E

```
DEGAS ■ ANITA ■ ALAN ■ THOR
ARECA ■ LOCAL ■ LYRE ■ HOME
WITHHOLDINGTACKS ■ UVEA
GESTURES ■ KEENEST ■ MELL
■ ■ AIL ■ ■ ARNIE ■ EMBLEM
REVERSE ■ TRIOS ■ EGOISTS
OVOLO ■ CEDAR ■ ARGON ■ ■
MICKSWELL ■ SONG ■ ■ DOOR
ALE ■ ARAL ■ VAST ■ EMERGE
■ ■ TRIAD ■ FICHE ■ RECALL
LABRATS ■ POLKA ■ BERKLEY
ARRIVE ■ HURLS ■ TONES ■ ■
SLICER ■ ALTA ■ SHOO ■ SSE
HOOK ■ ■ BILK ■ EARWHACKS
■ ■ SAFER ■ NAOMI ■ ■ AWAIT
BISCUIT ■ TOQUE ■ DETENTE
ORTEGA ■ RECUT ■ ETC ■ ■
DOUR ■ STARKER ■ PACHINKO
INCE ■ COKESOUTOFHIDING
COCA ■ ODES ■ USEME ■ NOPAR
ENOL ■ SODA ■ SHEEN ■ GLARE
```

```
ACTS ■ AREEL ■ GLEE ■ SPRAY
WARP ■ ROLLO ■ LUGS ■ CRIME
ELIA ■ GOLAN ■ OLIO ■ AUDEN
■ LARRYKINGSSUSPENDERS
■ ALKALIS ■ SASS ■ HATE ■ ■
■ ■ ISLE ■ LILY ■ CAGY ■ CPR
ASSNS ■ ■ SINS ■ SAGE ■ SHOE
DOUGLASMACARTHURSPIPE
ALI ■ ENTIRE ■ EONS ■ WIPED
MEND ■ GAL ■ ■ SIP ■ LIN ■ ■
■ GEORGEBURNSSCIGAR
■ ROY ■ ORO ■ OHO ■ LEEK
EMAIL ■ CANS ■ DEMONS ■ ACE
SALVADORDALISMUSTACHE
MULE ■ OWNS ■ ESSE ■ ANTON
ELY ■ LUBE ■ ATMO ■ UCLA ■ ■
■ ■ LEGO ■ ARGO ■ OPHELIA
DOROTHYLAMOURSSARONG
ABOUT ■ HORA ■ NISAN ■ GANG
MOOSE ■ ANON ■ TOILE ■ ULEE
PETER ■ TEND ■ STEAL ■ ELSE
```

```
L A B R A T   A N N E A L   F R I S K E D
A N Y O N E   L O A T H E   L I N E A G E
C I T I E S   A R C H E D   O C T A V A L
E T E   W H E N T H E M A N W H O M A D E
S A S S   A B H O R   O I L
    O H A R A     E B O N Y   D I A L
T H E F I R S T D R A W I N G   M E C C A
S E P T E T   E R O D E D   E M E R Y
A R O O   I N S O L E   E T A   L O D E S
R E D N O S E   N A S A   A N T O N
S S E   S T E V E N   W R I G H T   B R A
    M I S D O   D A N A   L I T H I U M
M E L E E   S A T   B I D D E R   A N N O
B L E A R     B E A N I E   S A I G O N
A B E T S   B O A R D G O T I T W R O N G
S A K S   H O U R S     R A Y E D
    A R C   T A T A S   O I N K
W H A T D I D H E G O B A C K T O   M O M
A U R E O L E   R A R E S T   A R M A D A
S L E N D E R   A V I A T E   M E A G E R
P A S T O R S   T E S T E D   S L Y E S T
```

The New York Times

Crossword Puzzles

The #1 name in crosswords

Available at your local bookstore or online at nytimes.com/nytstore

Coming Soon!

Brainbuilder Crossword	0-312-35276-X	$6.95/$9.95 Can.
Crosswords for a Weekend Getaway	0-312-35198-4	$11.95/$15.95 Can.
Easy Crossword Puzzles Vol. 7	0-312-35261-1	$9.95/$14.95 Can.
Fitness for the Mind Vol. 2	0-312-35278-6	$10.95/$14.95 Can.
Lazy Sunday Crossword Puzzle Omnibus	0-312-35279-4	$11.95/$15.95 Can.
Supersized Book of Easy Crosswords	0-312-35277-8	$15.95/$21.95 Can.
Vocabulary Power Crosswords	0-312-35199-2	$6.95/$9.95 Can.
Will Shortz's Xtreme Xwords	0-312-35203-4	$8.95/$12.95 Can.

Special Editions

Will Shortz's Greatest Hits	0-312-34242-X	$8.95/$12.95 Can.
Super Sunday Crosswords	0-312-33115-0	$10.95/$15.95 Can.
Will Shortz's Funniest Crosswords Vol. 2	0-312-33960-7	$9.95/$14.95 Can.
Will Shortz's Funniest Crosswords	0-312-32489-8	$9.95/$14.95 Can.
Will Shortz's Favorite Sunday Crosswords	0-312-32488-X	$9.95/$14.95 Can.
Crosswords for a Brain Workout	0-312-32610-6	$6.95/$9.95 Can.
Crosswords to Boost Your Brainpower	0-312-32033-7	$6.95/$9.95 Can.
Crossword All-Stars	0-312-31004-8	$9.95/$14.95 Can.
Will Shortz's Favorites	0-312-30613-X	$9.95/$14.95 Can.
Ultimate Omnibus	0-312-31622-4	$17.95/$25.95 Can.

Daily Crosswords

Fitness for the Mind Vol. 1	0-312-34955-6	$10.95/$14.95 Can.
Crosswords for the Weekend	0-312-34332-9	$9.95/$14.95 Can.
Monday Through Friday Vol. 2	0-312-31459-0	$9.95/$14.95 Can.
Monday Through Friday	0-312-30058-1	$9.95/$14.95 Can.
Daily Crosswords Vol. 71	0-312-34858-4	$9.95/$14.95 Can.
Daily Crosswords Vol. 70	0-312-34239-X	$9.95/$14.95 Can.
Daily Crosswords Vol. 69	0-312-33956-9	$9.95/$14.95 Can.
Daily Crosswords Vol. 68	0-312-33434-6	$9.95/$14.95 Can.
Daily Crosswords Vol. 67	0-312-32437-5	$9.95/$14.95 Can.
Daily Crosswords Vol. 66	0-312-32436-7	$9.95/$14.95 Can.
Daily Crosswords Vol. 65	0-312-32034-5	$9.95/$14.95 Can.
Daily Crosswords Vol. 64	0-312-31458-2	$9.95/$14.95 Can.
Volumes 57-63 also available		

Easy Crosswords

Easy Crosswords Vol. 6	0-312-33957-7	$10.95/$15.95 Can.
Easy Crosswords Vol. 5	0-312-32438-3	$9.95/$14.95 Can.
Volumes 2-4 also available		

Tough Crosswords

Tough Crosswords Vol. 13	0-312-34240-3	$10.95/$14.95 Can.
Tough Crosswords Vol. 12	0-312-32442-1	$10.95/$15.95 Can.
Tough Crosswords Vol. 11	0-312-31456-6	$10.95/$15.95 Can.
Volumes 9-10 also available		

Sunday Crosswords

Sunday Crosswords Vol. 30	0-312-33538-5	$9.95/$14.95 Can.
Sunday Crosswords Vol. 29	0-312-32038-8	$9.95/$14.95 Can.
Sunday Crosswords Vol. 28	0-312-30515-X	$9.95/$14.95 Can.
Sunday Crosswords Vol. 27	0-312-20414-4	$9.95/$14.95 Can.

Large-Print Crosswords

Large-Print Crosswords for Your Bedside	0-312-34245-4	$10.95/$14.95 Can.
Large-Print Will Shortz's Favorite Crosswords	0-312-33959-3	$10.95/$15.95 Can.
Large-Print Big Book of Easy Crosswords	0-312-33958-5	$12.95/$18.95 Can.
Large-Print Big Book of Holiday Crosswords	0-312-33092-8	$12.95/$18.95 Can.

Large-Print Crosswords for Your Coffeebreak	0-312-33109-6	$10.95/$15.95 Can.
Large Print Crosswords to Boost Your Brainpower	0-312-32037-X	$11.95/$17.95 Can.
Large-Print Crosswords for a Brain Workout	0-312-32612-2	$10.95/$15.95 Can.
Large-Print Easy Omnibus	0-312-32439-1	$12.95/$18.95 Can.
Large-Print Daily Crosswords Vol. 2	0-312-33111-8	$10.95/$15.95 Can.
Large-Print Daily Crosswords	0-312-31457-4	$10.95/$15.95 Can.
Large-Print Omnibus Vol. 6	0-312-34861-4	$12.95/$18.95 Can.
Large-Print Omnibus Vol. 5	0-312-32036-1	$12.95/$18.95 Can.
Previous volumes also available		

Omnibus

Crossword Challenge	0-312-33951-8	$12.95/$18.95 Can.
Giant Book of Holiday Crosswords	0-312-34927-0	$11.95/$15.95 Can.
Big Book of Holiday Crosswords	0-312-33533-4	$11.95/$16.95 Can.
Lazy Weekend Crosswords	0-312-34247-0	$11.95/$15.95 Can.
Crosswords for a Lazy Afternoon	0-312-33108-8	$11.95/$17.95 Can.
Tough Omnibus Vol. 1	0-312-32441-3	$11.95/$17.95 Can.
Easy Omnibus Vol. 4	0-312-34859-2	$11.95/$17.95 Can.
Easy Omnibus Vol. 3	0-312-33537-7	$11.95/$17.95 Can.
Easy Omnibus Vol. 2	0-312-32035-3	$11.95/$17.95 Can.
Easy Omnibus Vol. 1	0-312-30513-3	$11.95/$17.95 Can.
Daily Omnibus Vol. 15	0-312-34856-8	$11.95/$17.95 Can.
Daily Omnibus Vol. 14	0-312-33534-2	$11.95/$17.95 Can.
Daily Omnibus Vol. 13	0-312-32031-0	$11.95/$17.95 Can.
Sunday Omnibus Vol. 8	0-312-32440-5	$11.95/$17.95 Can.
Sunday Omnibus Vol. 7	0-312-30950-3	$11.95/$17.95 Can.
Sunday Omnibus Vol. 6	0-312-28913-8	$11.95/$17.95 Can.

Variety Puzzles

Acrostic Puzzles Vol. 10	0-312-34853-3	$9.95/$14.95 Can.
Acrostic Puzzles Vol. 9	0-312-30949-X	$9.95/$14.95 Can.
Sunday Variety Puzzles	0-312-30059-X	$9.95/$14.95 Can.
Previous volumes also available		

Portable Size Format

Crosswords for Your Lunch Hour	0-312-34857-6	$6.95/$9.95 Can.
Café Crosswords	0-312-34854-1	$6.95/$9.95 Can.
Easy as Pie Crosswords	0-312-34331-0	$6.95/$9.95 Can.
More Quick Crosswords	0-312-34246-2	$6.95/$9.95 Can.
Crosswords to Soothe Your Soul	0-312-34244-6	$6.95/$9.95 Can.
Beach Blanket Crosswords	0-312-34250-0	$6.95/$9.95 Can.
Simply Sunday Crosswords	0-312-34243-8	$6.95/$9.95 Can.
Crosswords for a Rainy Day	0-312-33952-6	$6.95/$9.95 Can.
Crosswords for Stress Relief	0-312-33953-4	$6.95/$9.95 Can.
Crosswords to Beat the Clock	0-312-33954-2	$6.95/$9.95 Can.
Quick Crosswords	0-312-33114-2	$6.95/$9.95 Can.
More Sun, Sand and Crosswords	0-312-33112-6	$6.95/$9.95 Can.
Planes, Trains and Crosswords	0-312-33113-4	$6.95/$9.95 Can.
A Cup of Tea and Crosswords	0-312-32435-9	$6.95/$9.95 Can.
Crosswords for Your Bedside	0-312-32032-9	$6.95/$9.95 Can.
Beach Bag Crosswords	0-312-31455-8	$6.95/$9.95 Can.
T.G.I.F. Crosswords	0-312-33116-9	$6.95/$9.95 Can.
Super Saturday	0-312-30604-0	$6.95/$9.95 Can.
Other volumes also available		

For Young Solvers

New York Times on the Web Crosswords for Teens	0-312-28911-1	$6.95/$9.95 Can.
Outrageous Crossword Puzzles and Word Games for Kids	0-312-28915-1	$6.95/$9.95 Can.
More Outrageous Crossword Puzzles for Kids	0-312-30062-X	$6.95/$9.95 Can.

St. Martin's Griffin